"Susan B. Smith offers a compelling study of women's leadership and influence in Khyber Pakhtunkhwa, Pakistan, engaging participants from diverse social and religious backgrounds. Notably, she has not positioned these practices against Western models, instead situating Pakistani women's influence on its own terms. Influence in the Global South does not necessarily mirror Western paradigms; rather, the women Smith discusses employ the very strategies such as honor and hard work often used to constrain them, to reclaim agency and exert leadership and influence. A must read!

—MUTALE MULENGA KAUNDA, Research Tutor, Oxford Centre for Mission Studies

"This book is a groundbreaking exploration of the exercise of influence and leadership among a cohort often ignored in Western scholarship—women in a religiously conservative, patriarchal society. Smith explores beyond women from the majority Muslim population who exercise influence by including women from minority groups. Smith pays careful attention to the role the cultural context plays. Anyone interested in leadership, Islamic, cultural, or women's studies will find Smith's careful research illuminating."

—NIGEL D. PEGRAM, Senior Lecturer in Practical Theology, Alphacrucis University College, Australia

"Having herself worked as an executive director in Pakistan, Dr. Susan Smith is ideally qualified to write about influence exercised by working women in Khyber Pakhtunkhwa. Comparative sociological studies, a series of interviews, and some well-placed metaphors come together in a scholarly approach that is also very human, engaging with respondents' realities, hopes, and frustrations. These women are shaping their world, as they interact with male colleagues and pass on new opportunities to their daughters and sons."

—ANDY WARREN-ROTHLIN, Global Translation Consultant, United Bible Societies

"Having known Susan Smith (and her husband Geoffrey) for over twenty years, there is a sense that the research in this book, and the careful description of the people and situations represented are a positive reflection of Susan herself. That is, how she understands and is able to document what makes her local friends, colleagues, and acquaintances so significant, and through that process, to encourage these women while pointing outsiders to the transformation she has observed over many years."

—KEVIN HOVEY, Senior Lecturer in Cross Cultural Ministry, Alphacrucis University College, Australia

Voices of Change

Voices of Change

Women's Influence in Northwest Pakistan

SUSAN B. SMITH

Foreword by Jacqueline Grey

WIPF & STOCK · Eugene, Oregon

VOICES OF CHANGE
Women's Influence in Northwest Pakistan

Wipf & Stock
An Imprint of Wipf and Stock Publishers
199 W. 8th Ave., Suite 3
Eugene, OR 97401

www.wipfandstock.com

PAPERBACK ISBN: 979-8-3852-6330-1
HARDCOVER ISBN: 979-8-3852-6331-8
EBOOK ISBN: 979-8-3852-6332-5

VERSION NUMBER 03/04/26

Permission was gained from Professor David Krackhardt to reproduce his kite structure in the text of this thesis.

Dedicated to
The strong, capable, and gracious women
of Khyber Pakhtunkhwa, Pakistan who work with honor,
dignity, courage, and confidence in the public sphere.

Contents

SECTION III. ANALYZING THE VOICES

Figures and Tables

Foreword

Female leadership is a contested space in our globalized world. While women's experiences in leadership are increasingly well documented in Western locations, there is very little research on female leadership and influence in places such as Khyber Pakhtunkhwa (KP), located in northwest Pakistan. Yet, it is essential for scholars of leadership to engage intercultural spaces and experiences. Cities across the globe are increasingly multicultural. Navigating leadership for and within collectivist communities is not just a novel sideline, but an essential commitment for contemporary leaders in Western contexts. Greater understanding of how leaders exert influence across cultural contexts is needed for global leaders. Importantly and less known is how female leaders exert influence within religiously conservative, hierarchical and patriarchal communities. Susan Smith's research breaks new ground in this area as she engages women leaders across multiple religious and social groups within the context of KP. These women are not always leaders in the sense that they have senior roles in organizations or movements. Smith's research includes those who lead because they are trailblazers, such as the first woman in a family to go out to work or attend university; and the first woman to be doing what was previously a male job.

One of the strengths of Smith's works is that she explores the experiences of women across diverse religious backgrounds. While Smith's research is conducted in the culturally conservative Muslim-majority society of KP, she listens carefully to both Muslim and non-Muslim women's voices, including Christian, Sikh and Baha'i. Smith highlights the similarities and differences of how religious identity impacts the experiences of women leaders. Yet, Smith also sees the bigger picture of the cultural landscape in which women of all religious backgrounds operate. From this, she highlights some central strategies successfully utilized by women in their experience of exerting leadership in public contexts not normally open to women. There is much to learn from women in collectivist cultures, particularly how they navigate public position through the cultural value of honor.

Of the many valuable insights into female leadership explored by Smith, many readers from the Christian tradition will be interested in her study of honor and shame. The cultural context of KP reflects the honor-shame culture of many parts of the world today. It may also arguably reflect somewhat the culture of many ancient societies, including the ancient Near Eastern context of the Bible. Reading the cultures of KP and the Bible through the lens of cultural anthropology, particularly the cultural values of honor and shame within the hierarchical and patriarchal environment, there appears to be much resonance.

Most studies on the honor-shame culture of the Bible highlight key concepts such as the power of public opinion, and the process of gaining honor through competition. They emphasize the honor of men and sometimes note that women are associated with shame. They describe the experience of men and give very little consideration to the experience of women. However, Smith provides a rich exploration of women's honor that is used as a mechanism to influence others in the public space.

The cultures of the biblical world are generally identified as an honor-shame culture. In such cultures, including many today, there are clear boundaries between the public and private spheres as well as expectations regarding gender roles in those spaces. Mostly, women could not participate in the public sphere, although there were some exceptions for wealthy and socially elite women.[1] That churches met in homes, which were considered a private space, meant that women could exercise leadership in the Christian community. Generally, though, women had to adhere to a strict code of moral behavior and maintain their reputation as virtuous to ensure their family's honor.[2] The challenge was for women to exert influence as community leaders without compromising their honor.

To demonstrate how women in KP and other conservative contexts have navigated this, Smith demonstrates the links between women's influence, and the place of honor intertwined with hard work. Despite the social restrictions of their culture, Smith notes that the single mechanism of a good reputation plus hard work gives women a voice, and the

---

1. See Hylen, *Women in the New Testament World*.
2. Pizzuto-Pomaco, *From Shame to Honor*, 99.

opportunity to work in public roles. When women fulfill social expectations by maintaining their honor, they are respected even as they work in public roles alongside men who are not family members, which otherwise would be seen as breaking the social code.

We see these same values reflected in a number of biblical texts. For example, in the Old Testament/Hebrew Bible, we see dignity and worth ascribed to the industrious woman of Proverbs 31:10–31. Her influence within the community is derived from her reputation as a woman of honor. Paul publicly honored his female co-workers as model leaders. Paul's promotion of Phoebe in Romans 16 is founded on her active help to the Christian community (16:1–2). Similarly, another female co-worker, Mary, is described as one "who labored much for us" (16:6). This is reflected in the admonition in 1 Timothy 3:7 that church leaders "have a good reputation with outsiders." Therefore, in many contexts of an honor-shame culture, a key mechanism for women to be effective in leadership is having a reputation for hard work in the community.

However, hard work is not enough. It is unlikely that Paul would have endorsed the ministry of Phoebe and Mary unless they were known as honorable women. Honor is a many splendored term and concept, particularly in KP society. This is also reflected in the research of Louise Simon, who reports on a global project exploring the concept of honor among Muslim women.[3] Simon highlights that for women, honor is either ascribed or acquired. While women may have honor for who they are in terms of their family relationship (ascribed), they can achieve honor through their actions and behavior.[4] Yet, a woman's honor must be maintained through modesty and sexual propriety. Simon demonstrates this through an Arab proverb: "A man's honor [*sic*] lies between the legs of a woman."[5] Therefore a woman must preserve the honor of the family through her modest behavior and avoid bringing shame upon the family. Again, this is reflected in the culture of the biblical world through the expectation that women be sexually pure, modest, and industrious. In fact, many of these virtues also align with the ideal Christian woman (and man), including generosity, integrity, diligence, and self-sacrifice.

For women leaders today, this strategy of emphasizing a woman's honor and good reputation can turn a cultural obstacle into an opportunity. In essence, it provides a way to empower women in cultural contexts

3. Simon, "Muslim Women's Perspectives on Honor," 297–308.

4. Simon, "Muslim Women's Perspectives," 299.

5. Simon, "Muslim Women's Perspectives," 301.

that may otherwise restrict or even reject their participation. It would benefit women leaders in multicultural contexts to promote their honor, good reputation and industriousness as a mechanism for influence. These same methods have been used by women in the biblical text and continue to prove successful by women in conservative cultures today. There is much that contemporary leadership studies and leadership ethics can discover from the women leaders of KP. Smith opens the door for us to observe and learn.

REV PROF JACQUELINE GREY
BA, BTh(hons), PhD
Professor of Biblical Studies
Alphacrucis University College

Acknowledgments

In my research, I was assisted by Mariya and Idris, a married couple from Pakistan with fluency in Urdu, Pukhto, and English. Mariya provided wonderful help during the interview process, and Idris worked with me as a language consultant and cultural adviser. He helped fill the gaps of socio-religious and linguistic capital that I lacked. A third Pakistani research assistant, Mysha, helped me with the Urdu to English transcription process. Mysha and I worked together over many days to ensure that the final English transcriptions were an accurate representation of the Urdu interviews. Mysha also helped me to unpack some of the cultural norms that lay behind women's comments. Idris, and other friends and colleagues, assisted me in the Pukhto to English translations of the interviews. They also took time to help me understand the meanings behind the many idioms that formed part of the transcribed interviews.

Alisdair Smith is responsible for the excellence of the graphics. He took my simple sketches and turned them into something worthy of presenting in a book.

My thanks are extended to Dr. Jacqueline Grey and Dr. Nigel Pegram, my supervisors, who supported me in the labor of producing a PhD. thesis. That thesis, entitled *Sitting with Melons*, is the research framework for this book. My thanks also go to my husband, Geoffrey Smith, for his support in so many areas, and to the friends who listened to my ideas and read through the manuscript.

Conventions

A modified form of the International Phonetic Alphabet (IPA) is used for the transcription of non-English words.[1] The IPA phonetics follow, as far as possible, the inflection of the Urdu and Pukhto spoken in the interviews. All non-English words are italicized except where they have become standardized in English, such as hijab. An exception is the word *Pukhto*. Italics are used to distinguish *Pukhto*, as culture and identity, from any reference to the Pukhto language.

Italics are also used to capture the respondents' use of language-mixing—the conscious and unconscious use of words from another language dropped into one's speech. This is a common feature of conversations in Pakistan. Usually these are English words dropped into a conversation in another Pakistani language, but non-English words can also be brought into English-language conversations. In this book, italics have been used to distinguish the English words that have been dropped into interviews conducted in Urdu and Pukhto. For example, English language-mixing in the transcription of this observation, made in Urdu by one of the respondents, appears as: "her *character* has to be *strong* [enough] that she can cross all these *barriers* and *hurdles* by herself."

A number of the interviews were given in English by women for whom this is their second or third language. In the verbatim quotes from these interviews, I have used square brackets [ ] where needed to fill in the gaps of grammar so that their conversations flow in print, just as they did when they were talking to me.

In all of the interviews, where some point of explanation is needed, I have used standard brackets ( ). They are also used to provide context where it may not be clear who or what is being referred to. Also, to

1. International Phonetic Association, *Handbook of the International Phonetic Association.*

facilitate clear communication in print, I have removed the hesitations, repetitions, and vagaries of speech that appear in the interviews and replaced them with an ellipsis (. . .). This includes the "okay," "you know," "I mean" and other mannerisms that came into the women's conversations. I have also used three dots to cover those places where the interviewee digressed from her main point only to return to it a few moments later.

All the names of the women from Khyber Pakhtunkhwa who participated in my research have been changed to protect their identities. In the same way, I have changed the names of the three research assistants.

Abbreviations

(I)NGO	(International) Non-Governmental Organization
IPA	International Phonetic Alphabet
IRLE	Institute for Research on Labor and Employment
ISPR	Inter-Services Public Relations
ISTR	International Society for Third Sector Research
IVP	InterVarsity Press
JI	Jamaat-e-Islami
KP	also KPK: Khyber Pakhtunkhwa
PLOS	Public Library of Science
RA	Research Assistant
SI	Social Influence
SIP	Social Information Processing
TA	Thematic Analysis

Glossary

əbā'yə	a robe-like outer covering worn together with the hijab
Alhamdulillah	praise God
asr	influence; effect
asr o rasukh	influence (in Urdu); (literally) effect and influence
aurat	woman, women
badāl	revenge, exchange, reciprocity
bakhshish	(eternal) reward
beta	son
betak	(male) guest room used for entertaining
bɪrādari	(literally) brotherhood; a network of patrilineal kinship
burka	in KP, this is often the shuttlecock burka that covers the wearer from head to toe
bura	evil, very bad
chador	shawl, veil. The traditional Pukhtun *chador* is white, although women from certain tribes can be identified by the patterns on their *chadors*.
chowkɪdār	male security guard
dai	female hospital attendant; (literally) midwife
ḍanḍa	club (as used by security guards)
dars	home-based Qur'anic study group
da'wa	formal religious instruction

dekhna	to see, to watch, to look at
dhımmi	protected person status
dupatta	small scarf often worn around the shoulders rather than over the head
ekhtıārāt, ekhtıār	authority, power, influence
ekhtıār yā asr	influence (in Pukhto); (literally) influence or effect
gham-khādi	grief-celebration events such as funerals and weddings
ghe'rət	honor, pride in autonomy, zeal, bravery
hijab	a headscarf used to cover the hair, neck, and ears. The term hijab is also used to reference a system of pious female veiling.
huǰra	a room, or series of rooms, set aside for male use
ıǰtıhād	interpretation of religious texts
ı'zət	(also *izzat*) honor, respect, worth, dignity, prestige, reputation, esteem, and status
ı'zət-e nafs	self-respect, dignity, honor
jır'ga	council of elders
kamāl	(literally) excellence, superiority; (idiomatically) as if by magic!
karo-kari	honor violence
Khan	a general term for feudal landlord; as a collective term, it refers to the whole land-owning family.
kharbuza	yellow muskmelon
kuffar	non-Muslim, infidel
lāt'hi	stick; police baton (used for crowd control)
maghreb-zada	tainted by the West; used as an insult
melmastiā	hospitality
Mohajir	Muslims from India who emigrated to Pakistan at Partition
mutāsir	affected or impressed by
nənawāti	refuge

na mahrām	the men a woman must do *parda* before
nang	reputation, to be defended for the sake of honor
nikokyrio	a Greek economic structure in which men and women share responsibility
nɪqāb	a type of veil that covers the whole face apart from the eyes
pāk	clean, holy; used as an honorific
parda	a system of female seclusion
plārwāki	patriarchy (*padārāna nazām* in Urdu)
Pukhto, Paxto	Pukhtun identity and culture, as distinct from the Pukhto language. *Pukhto* is also the name given to the Pukhtun tribal code. This code is also known as *Pukhtunwali* or *Pashtunwali*, the way of Pukhtuns. As a code, and as an identity, *Pukhto* dictates religio-social practice for Pukhtuns.
Shari'a	Islamic law based on the teachings of the Qur'an and collected traditions of the Prophet of Islam
sharm	shame
Salafi	one who adheres to the beliefs and practices of the first three generations of Muslims (*salaf al-salih*)
sɪfārish	a recommendation in order to obtain preferential treatment
sɪnf-e-nāzuk	the weaker sex
shokh	difficult and obstructive; (literally) naughty
tang	obstructionism
tāqat	power, authority
taqlid	the Islamic doctrine of conformity
tāsir	effect
ta'sub	bigotry, discrimination
tərburwali	agnatic rivalry
tor	blame, accusation; extended to include the safeguarding of female honor

ummə	community of believers, the Muslim community
ziādti	abuse, misbehavior
zina	adultery, fornication, prostitution

Introduction

Over the past decades, women have held high public office in Pakistan, including the positions of prime minister, speaker of the national assembly, and federal and provincial ministers. Throughout the country, women are active in science, engineering, technology, and the media. They serve in the armed forces, they exercise influence as lawyers, judges, and scholars, and they occupy leadership roles in national and international organizations. They also quietly assist as nurses, teachers, and support workers. Observably, women have obtained and maintained positions of influence in the public realm. Yet, in this space, female influence remains an awkward concept.

This is captured in a popular local proverb that says, "A melon gains its color by sitting with melons."[1] The reference is to the yellow musk melons (*kharbuza*) that change color from green to yellow as they ripen alongside each other in small, dusty fields, as seen in figure 1. The proverb implies that a person is influenced by the company *he* keeps. Yet herein lies a problem. In Urdu, *kharbuza* is masculine, giving the whole metaphor a cultural inappropriateness when applied to female influence. The issue is more complex in Pukhto, the language of the Pukhtuns of Khyber Pakhtunkhwa (KP) in Pakistan's northwest. Although *kharbuza* is grammatically female, and linguistically the proverb can be used of anyone, it *feels* wrong when talking of female influence. In effect, the proverb is saying that there is little expectation in Pakistani society that women can influence. They can be powerful, yes! But influential, no!

---

1. The proverb in Urdu is *kharbuza kharbuzey ko dekh rang pa tā tā* and in Pukhto *kharbuza da kharbuzey na rang ākhley.*

Figure 1. Melons Ripening in a Field, Khyber Pakhtunkhwa.
Source: **Photograph by Idris.**

Yet, influence is exactly what women in KP's religiously conservative Muslim-majority society are exercising. In October 2020, Aafiya, a feudal Pukhtun landlord[2] and retired politician, suddenly proclaimed in the middle of our conversation, "All my life I have been influencing people, but I never thought about it. It is this limited, myopic thinking that I want to help [change]." It took a conversation with an outsider for her to realize that she has been doing what women were not supposed to do: influencing others for change. Her comment was also an affirmation of the importance of my study to women in KP. She had unwittingly underscored the reasons why I had deliberately chosen to study influence in preference to power. I trust that many more women in Pakistan and elsewhere will stop and consider their own lives; and then begin to view them through a new lens—that of influence.

In *Voices of Change*, I go behind the scenes to explore the ways in which women are influencing in the public arena in KP. This book enables the voices of ordinary Muslim and non-Muslim women to be

---

2. The term landlord encompasses the power and influence of large landowning families. As such, women in these families can be referred to as landlords, even if the property is not in their own names.

heard as they talk of the realities of working and studying alongside men; some of whom can be resistant to female intrusion into traditionally male spaces. I use the terms Muslim, non-Muslim, Islam, Christian, Hindu, Sikh, and Baha'i as a useful means of identifying general categories of society and religious identity. At the same time, I recognize that within each of these categories lie multiple and sometimes disparate sub-groups. However, when writing of Islam or the majority Muslim community in KP-Pakistan, the reference is primarily to Pakistan's Sunni Muslim population. The term "KP-Pakistan" indicates factors that are found within the wider country, not simply within the province of Khyber Pakhtunkhwa.

I am a British-born Australian who has observed the changes to KP's public sphere over the course of my 40-year interaction with Pakistan: 30-years spent living in KP. For 20 of those years, I was the executive director of an organization staffed primarily by men. As the director, I occupied a similar place to a number of the women I spoke to as part of my research: a female in a place of public sphere authority. Working in KP, I joined the ranks of women who were using their influence, consciously and unconsciously, within a religiously conservative, hierarchical and patriarchal society. As a non-Pukhtun, non-Muslim, I also experienced the challenges, and joys, of living and working in KP society from an ethno-religious minority position.

I approached the subject of female influence as an informed and yet enculturated outsider. That is, I stood outside the familial and ethnic networks of indigenous culture, but my years of experience gave me some insights into what was happening at a deeper, latent level. While my experience was a strength, I was also aware of the bias implicit in my non-indigenous identity, and its potential to impact my understanding of what was going on. That is, I might hold attitudes or beliefs about people and issues in KP-Pakistan formed by my inadequate understanding of what was really going on, or simply because I was unfamiliar with a cultural practice or value. When analyzing the data, I therefore employed an analytical method that acknowledged this bias and allowed it to be used positively.

When I first started working in KP in 1984, there were very few women in public spaces. This situation has radically changed over the past twenty or so years. This growing number of women in a strongly patriarchal setting is evidence of women's ability to negotiate the religio-societal norms that traditionally confine them to the domestic realm. It also points to the use of strategies that empower women to successfully occupy positions of responsibility and leadership outside of the home. This book is thus an exploration of the concrete, yet formerly unanalyzed, techniques and tactics, strategies and devices—the mechanisms—that women consciously or unconsciously use to exercise influence.[3] My research adds to the discussion about societal change in Pakistan and the wider Middle East by demonstrating *how* female influence is a catalyst for change as well as a response to changes happening locally and globally. The geographic location of Khyber Pakhtunkhwa, Pakistan provides the frame for the discussion.

Voices of Change originated from a place of simple curiosity: my desire to know *how* women from KP's diverse ethno-religious communities and social groups are exercising seemingly counter-cultural influence on different levels in the public sphere. I expected that the tactics they were using would not necessarily be the same as those used by women in the West. Curiosity, however, soon changed to urgency. The current political and economic climate in Pakistan, and neighboring Afghanistan, has given a new importance to the findings that emerged from my research, especially as a wide variety of organizations seek to help women living in this region. I learned that honor coupled with hard work, societal status, and effective persuasion are foundational to female influence. Are these strategies enough to enable women to retain—or in the Afghan context, regain—their presence and their influence in a male-dominated public sphere? *Voices of Change* suggests that they might.

3. Foucault, as cited in Rabinow, *The Foucault Reader*, 58.

SECTION I

Setting the Context

1

Ordinary Female Influence

IN A COUNTRY WHERE influence is culturally male, women in the public spaces of education and employment may occupy *positions* of influence, but such places may not automatically provide them with the *right* to influence. This is illustrated by a popular proverb, found in Urdu and Pukhto, that says, "A person is influenced by the company *he* keeps." Literally, "A melon gains its color by sitting with melons." Culturally, this proverb is never used of women, implying that they do not influence. Yet, over the past twenty-five years, women in Khyber Pakhtunkhwa are observably holding positions of public responsibility that have positioned them as influencers. The *how* of tangible and dynamic female influence lies at the heart of this book.

Setting aside the importance of female activism in Pakistan—some of which has been extremely influential—I propose that everyday female influence in KP's public sphere is happening on three levels. Firstly, influence is linked to *honor* (*ı'zət*) coupled with hard work. The term *ı'zət* includes the concepts of honor, worth, respect, dignity, prestige, reputation, esteem, and status.[1] In KP society, *ı'zət* takes several forms, all of which run concurrently. In the first form, *ı'zət* is the respect or honor ascribed to you. It is a state of being based on who you are, for example, through ancestry, age, gender, or social status. In the second form, *ı'zət* can be achieved because it is behavioral. It is the reputation you hold that

---

1. Shah, *Honour Unmasked*, 57.

is established by your observed performance.[2] In its third form, *i'zət* is an ethic, a code. It speaks of morality. This is especially true for the Pukhtuns of KP, as *i'zət* is central to *Pukhto*, Pukhtun culture and identity. It is something they have and do.[3] In addition, as I argue in this book, *i'zət* has a fourth form or role. Reinforced by hard work, *i'zət* is an *influence mechanism* that women are using to change societal norms.

My second proposal is that, in the hierarchical and patriarchal environment of KP where people are ranked according to societal norms, public sphere influence is linked to societal *status*. That is, a woman's social rank or her position within an organization will advance or detract from her ability to influence. Influence, however, is not synonymous with power, although the two things can be closely linked. For example, the leadership scholar Bass proposed that people are better influencers when they perceive themselves as having the power that others attribute to them.[4] Power and status go hand-in-hand. Status based power is "the ability to get things done" despite resistance, the "ability to mobilize resources," and the ability to control.[5] Such power can be bureaucratic, manipulating, authoritarian, dominating, and coercive.[6] It encompasses command and the expectation of obedience. It does not, necessarily, require admiration or respect. Yet, status-based power can also be exercised by those one respects, who have referent power, personal charisma, or expertise.[7] As will be seen later in this book, these definitions of power also function as descriptions of influence in the minds of some of the women in my sample group. There was also the acknowledgement that, while influence and power are actions requiring compliance, those upon whom the influence/power is being acted may not choose to submit.[8]

Thirdly, I propose that influence is *persuasive*. A relational transaction takes place in which a person or people are persuaded to do what the influencer wants, or they are influenced to move her ideas forward.[9] Such persuasive influence is described by Klein in her study of power. She proposes that influence is diplomatic; used in a framework of social

2. Loewen, *Towards True Honor*, chap. 1.

3. Grima, *Performance of Emotion*, 1, 4.

4. Bass, *Handbook of Leadership*, 230.

5. Krackhardt, "Assessing the Political Landscape," 343.

6. Weber, "Domination"; Boulding, *Three Faces of Power*.

7. Krackhardt, "Assessing the Political Landscape," 344.

8. Foucault, "The Subject and Power," 790.

9. Banks and Ledbetter, *Reviewing Leadership*, 21.

networks that operate "behind the scenes, where people with no public authority but with social connections to those who do use these powerful allies to obtain their own ends."[10] In such a scenario the influencer does not need to be a decision maker. The goal is simply to change the ideas of the "opinion leader," the key person who has the ability to change the minds of others.[11]

To function as influence mechanisms, especially for *i'zət* and status, legitimization is required. This is the same for men and women. That is, the place of influence and the right to influence in that place, must be recognized and endorsed by followers, peers, and superiors.[12] The psychologist Cialdini argued that legitimacy is connected to "social proof."[13] The power of social proof is its ability to produce compliance in others. Namely, if people are seen to endorse a value or behavior as correct, others are more likely to follow their example and accept it as legitimate. The weakness of such compliance is that any dependency on the opinions of others can be short-lived. People can change their minds and believe in and follow another proof.

In KP, in the arena of social proof, unlike men, women do not automatically carry the social right to influence. As illustrated by the opening *melon proverb*, where influence is concerned men do not need any social proof beyond that of their gender. However, a woman must provide a social proof that validates her status and/or *i'zət* if she is to have any influence in the public sphere. It is only when some in society recognize this proof, and thereby legitimize it, that others also come to accept a woman's right to public sphere status/*i'zət*, and allow themselves to be influenced by her. Obversely, a woman's failure to influence in the traditional public sphere may be due to a lack of legitimacy in the face of social, ethnic, and religious norms that marginalize women. Therefore, among all of the strategies used to influence others, the ability to provide recognized social proof of one's status and *i'zət* is perhaps the most vital for women in KP's public sphere.

Honor, status, and persuasion, in addition to being influence mechanisms in their own right, also operate as broad or meta- themes or categories containing other related influence mechanisms. The meta-category of *honor* groups together the tactics of personal integrity, dedication to

10. Klein, *Women and Men*, 192.

11. Contractor and DeChurch, "Integrating Social Networks," 1.

12. Bass, *Handbook of Leadership*, 308.

13. Cialdini, *Influence*, 88–90.

duty, and positivity, as well as *i'zət* coupled with hard work. *Status* brings together the mechanisms of status-based compliance and patronage. In KP's hierarchical society, seniors require automatic compliance from everyone deemed to be junior to them; and juniors understand their need to comply. The meta-theme of *persuasion* includes the strategies of persuasive argument, role model exemplar, celebrity endorser, mentor, networking, and *sifārish* (recommendation).

The reasons why women are now to be found in KP's public spaces, where formerly they were not, are as varied as the women themselves. Referencing the Middle East, the sociologist Moghadam observed that women's presence in the public sphere could be the result of political conflict, war and revolution, and also the societal changes caused by "economic development and state expansion."[14] The emergence of women into spaces that were formerly male-only has led scholars to address the complexities of gender, identity and patriarchy. They have explored women's presence within uprisings, as well as women's part in social change in the Middle East. They have also investigated the quieter voice of women's influence that is changing the shape of sacred spaces, including within Islam.[15]

Research, such as Mahmood's study of religious difference in a secular age,[16] helpfully brings together Muslim majority and ethno-religious minority voices within a shared space. However, Mahmood's research, and that of others who focus on majoritarianism and religious identity, continue the discussion of issues that separate communities. *Voices of Change* takes a different approach. It moves away from socio-religious differences to focus on a shared action—influence—exercised by both Muslim and non-Muslim women within the same geographic setting.

In Pakistan, studies have tended to focus on Muslim women located in the Punjab and Sindh provinces. The changes to women's status as a consequence of decisions made by successive provincial and national governments have prompted studies of Muslim identity, and the women's movement, with case studies often coming from the Punjab and Sindh because of reasons of access.[17] In contrast, studies of the lives of women

14. Moghadam, *Modernizing Women*, 22.

15. For example, Hasso and Salime have brought together studies that look at the impact of Arab women's voices in times of revolution and uprising. The scholars Abu-Lughod, Leila Ahmed and Mernissi have addressed the complexities of gender, identity, patriarchy and social change in the Middle East. Aghaie and Shanneik explored female influence within sacred spaces.

16. Mahmood, *Religious Difference*.

17. Studies of Pakistani Muslim women's identity in response to societal change

in KP have been anthropological in nature, centered on the Pukhtuns.[18] Research into the situation for ethno-religious minorities in Pakistan has tended to focus on the consequences of nationalism and Muslim majoritarianism for ethno-religious minority communities.[19] However, these studies of the nation's minority communities contain little of the female voice. *Voices of Change* works to fill this gap because of its focus on non-Muslim and Muslim minority women, as well as those coming from the Muslim majority community. Using KP as the geographical setting spotlights the situation for women living and working in that province. In addition, my focus on influence enables the female voice to come through loud and clear.

In this book, I explore women's public visibility and the influence they exercise not only as a result of societal change, but as a catalyst for that change. To aid this level of exploration, I have used social influence theories. My focus is the *everyday* influence as obtained, exercised, and maintained by women in KP's public sphere. Therefore, as lenses through which to understand how such influence works, I have used aspects of social network theory, and social information processing (SIP) within a non-Western setting. I looked at different minority and majority influence theories, and the theory of self-categorization.[20] In addition, I used Foucault's analyses of power as lenses by which female influence in KP might be understood.[21]

However, the aim of this book is not simply to identify specific influence mechanisms, but to understand the *who* (person), *where* (place), and *how* (pace and scope) of female influence. That is, who uses what mechanisms in what contexts and how effective they are. Yet, I am not seeking to determine the relative importance of different mechanisms

---

have been made by Mumtaz and Shaheed, and Weiss, and more recently in the articles collected by Sherry Rehman in *Womansplaining*.

18. Two key explorations into Pukhtun women's performance of *Pukhto* were conducted by Amineh Ahmed and Grima.

19. Sookhdeo studied the effects of Islamization on the Christian minority in Pakistan. Recent studies by Simon Fuchs, Ispahani, and Schaflechner move the discussion of the situation for Pakistan's minority communities into the twenty-first century.

20. For networking I looked at theories developed by Krackhardt, and by Contractor & DeChurch. For minority and majority influence theories, including societal legitimization, I turned to Asch's studies on conformity, Moscovici's theory of conversion behavior, and Turner's book on Social Influence. For the theory of self-categorization, I looked at the study of self and the collective by Turner et. al.

21. Foucault, *The History of Sexuality*, vol. 1; "The Subject and Power"; *Discipline and Punish*.

based on usage, although such numerical information can be used to highlight emphasis. My aim is to understand the ways in which influence mechanisms function as tools or strategies that women can use to achieve goals that include societal change. To do this, I have correlated influence mechanisms with the underlying external factors of religion, culture, and some of the many other societal factors into which they are entwined. This provides a depth of insight into their use and effectiveness—for Muslim and non-Muslim women in KP.

To aid this investigation, I asked two questions. The first was, "What are some of the mechanisms by which Muslim and non-Muslim women obtain, exercise and maintain influence in KP's public sphere?" Secondly, I asked, "How does the ethno-religious background and/or societal status of the women affect influence mechanisms?" Together these questions enabled me to explore actual influence tactics as used in the complex *melon field* that is KP's public sphere. Understanding the proverbial melon field helped me determine what socio-religious factors enable or obstruct women's successful influence. I was also aware that understanding how influence works in the KP context could identify mechanisms that best support female influence in other settings, including other Muslim-majority and/or religiously patriarchal contexts.

FORTY-EIGHT EXTRAORDINARY ORDINARY WOMEN

Many of the women who exercise influence and power in KP's public sphere are leaders. However, I only indirectly explore female leadership. The goal of this book is to increase understanding regarding the tactics used by ordinary Muslim and non-Muslim women as they work and study in a strongly patriarchal, hierarchical, and religiously conservative Muslim-majority setting. As a part of my research, I interviewed forty-eight women who were resident in or recently resident in Khyber Pakhtunkhwa. The interviews were both online, using social media platforms, and in person. These forty-eight women formed my sample group. They ranged in age from under twenty-five to over seventy. Just one woman was circumspect about her age. Educationally, the group included women with no or little formal education, those with vocational qualifications, and those who held undergraduate and postgraduate degrees. The group was comprised of thirty-five Muslims and thirteen non-Muslims. Thirty of the women were Sunni Muslim Pukhtuns; and five identified as non-Pukhtun Muslims. Unexpectedly, three of the non-Muslim women called themselves Pukhtun for reasons of ancestry. The remainder were Christians, Baha'is, and Sikhs.

Sadly, the sample group did not include anyone from the Hindu community. The invitation for Hindu women to participate in my research was made through their male gatekeepers, but no one came forward. It is not possible to accurately determine the reasons why some of those who received an invitation to contribute to the project declined to be involved. It may have been perceptions of my non-indigenous identity. At the same time, an unwillingness to publicly express personal opinions may also have been in play.

Although the size and makeup of the group was limited, it was representative of the broad category of Muslim and non-Muslim women exercising influence in KP's public sphere. The number of non-Muslim voices was deliberately disproportionate to their demographic representation in KP society: just 0.56 percent of the total population.[22] I allowed this disproportion firstly, because the non-Muslim voice often goes unheard in studies of women in KP-Pakistan. Secondly, the non-Muslim respondents were talking about women's experience in general, not just their own experiences, therefore the results were not skewed by this demographic imbalance. Instead, the contribution made by these non-Muslim respondents provided insights into a part of Pakistani culture that require further exploration.

Every respondent in the sample group gave an interview centered on ten predetermined, open-ended questions. These questions were designed to provide the opportunity for the women to give their opinions and beliefs regarding influence as a concept, and as something they and other women were engaged in. As we conversed, these ladies recounted the beneficial changes they had seen as a direct result of their/female influence, and the support they had received from their families. They also were clear about the obstacles they and others had encountered in the exercise of their influence.

As we collected data about the women in the sample group that would enable me to position them in KP society, Mariya, my research assistant (RA), and I had to negotiate the cultural inappropriateness of directly asking them about their class or social status. Therefore, when I designed the interview template, I used two questions that indirectly

22. Pakistan Bureau of Statistics, *Population Census 2023*.

approached the topic of class. The first question asked what their father's profession was. The second enquired how they, as a working woman, contributed to their family's economic situation. Their replies, together with the indicators of education and professional status, helped me to determine social ranking within the general terms of elite, upper, middle, and lower class. I was, therefore, able to identify three of the Muslim respondents as holding elite social status. Eighteen of the respondents, including three non-Muslims, I ranked as belonging to the upper class. Twenty others, fourteen Muslims and six non-Muslims, I classified as middle class. The remaining seven women, three Muslims and four non-Muslims, I categorized as lower class.

Among these women, with their varied social status and ethno-religious backgrounds, were some working in the traditional fields of education and medicine. This included women who worked as lowest echelon public servants, including one hospital attendant (*dai*). The voices of women from this slice of Pakistani society can often go unheard in research—except when talking about marginalization—so their contribution to this study was invaluable. I also interviewed women moving into what had been male-orientated fields of employment such as banking, engineering, technology, and politics. Although women have been involved in politics from Pakistan's foundation, in KP conservative social practices still mitigate against their involvement in this traditional male sphere. In addition, I spoke to women forging a place for themselves in areas that are still resistant to their presence, such as journalism and entrepreneurial business. The voices of all of the forty-eight women in my sample group resound through this book.

APPROACHING THE STUDY OF INFLUENCE

The task I had set myself sounded so easy. I simply needed to talk to my sample group about influence. That would enable me to identify and analyze the ways in which they and other women are exercising influence in their settings. Reality soon set in. The multiple levels of society in Khyber Pakhtunkhwa, and the interconnected environments of socio-religious practice that permeate the spaces in which women study and work, soon revealed the complexity of the task before me. Understanding the melon field that is KP's public sphere, and then articulating the ways in which proverbial color is transferred to others, was analogous to unravelling a ball of fine wool—one intertwined thread at a time (see figure 2). Each thread represented a facet of society into which the strategies for influence were interwoven. I was required to investigate each individual thread if I was to truly understand how influence mechanisms operate and explore the contexts in which they were exercised.

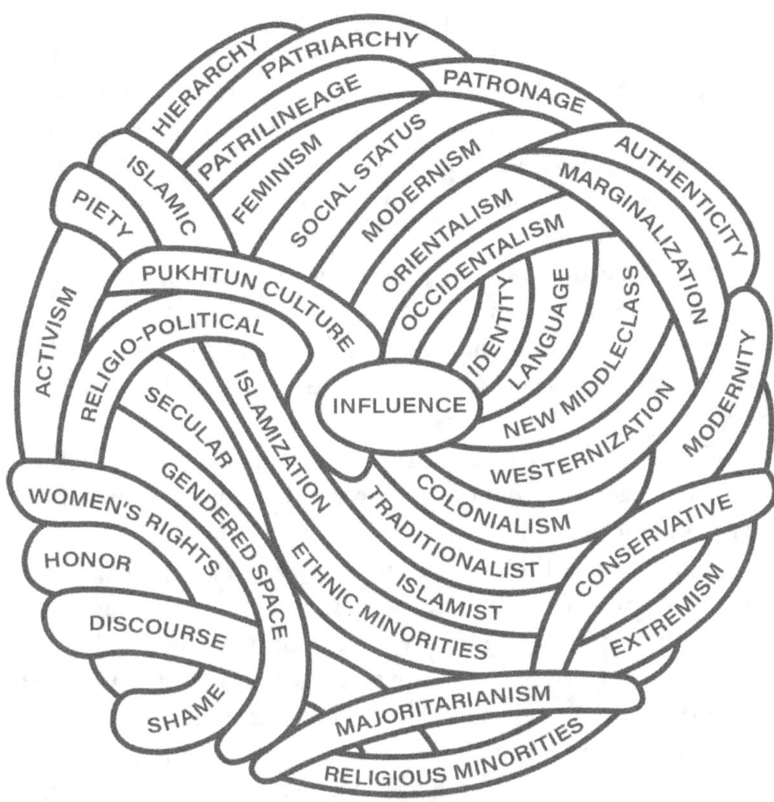

Figure 2. The Ball of Entangled Religio-Cultural Norms.

I chose a qualitative, inductive (non-positivist) interpretive methodology as the design for the research that underpins this book. I selected this approach because it was not my intent to propose a hypothetical influence-reality shared by all women that could be empirically confirmed or adjusted. Rather, I wanted to gain insights into the ways in which influence works for women within the micro and macro contexts of the complex public sphere environments in which they were located. An inductive approach thus best enabled my investigation into the unique context in which women live and work in Khyber Pakhtunkhwa. An inductive approach allowed all voices to be treated equally without reference to ethnicity, religion, professional or social status, or other demographic considerations. It also facilitated the discovery of unknown factors, including social constructs that underpin the issues being analyzed. Lastly, it allowed value to be attributed to the language: the actual words and phrases the women used to describe concepts and experiences.

I was aware that I shared some understandings of female influence in KP's public spaces with the women I was interviewing. The same was true of Mariya who helped me with a number of the interviews. Mariya is a well-educated, middle class Pakistani Christian who has lived in KP. An Urdu speaker, she conducted interviews when I could not be physically present, or if the respondent wanted to give an interview in Urdu, or, as in one case, did not want to be in direct contact with a Westerner. To mitigate against our influencing the interviewees in their responses, I designed a simple questionnaire that used ten set, yet open-ended questions. The open-ended nature of the questions meant that each respondent was free to develop her answer in her own way.

When it came to analysis, again I looked for a method that would lessen the danger of fitting the data into any of my or my research assistants' preconceived frames. I therefore selected thematic analysis (TA) as an appropriate method for data analysis, using a critical realist framework. The method of inductive TA recognizes that everyone engaged with the data brings epistemological preconceptions to translation and to the analysis of the interviews.[23] That approach gave space for the translation and analysis of the women's interviews to be mediated through my and the RAs' interpretations of phenomena, language, culture, religion, and society. This inductive, interpretative approach to analysis gave a positive space for the subjectivity we brought to the topic of female influence.

The interview data captured by this qualitative, thematic approach presented the respondents' reported understandings of influence as a lived reality. Themes were understood to be the mechanisms by which the women of my study exercised influence. Behind each of these themes/mechanisms lay the processes that led to the exercise of that particular type of influence. These processes gave insight into the phenomena: women's lived experiences. These experiences were present in the interviews but also present in the literature I reviewed as part of my

23. Terry, "Doing Thematic Analysis," 149.

research. I wanted to identify and explore the ideas, ideologies, conceptualizations and beliefs that underpin the many influences at work in the public sphere. I also wanted to explore the religio-cultural assumptions that were not explicitly stated by the sample group but were key to understanding the realities they described. Thus, thematic analysis provided a flexible tool by which to plumb the depths of the respondents' experiences as meaning-filled lived realities occurring within the frame of KP.

Thematic analysis also provided the methodology by which I could analyze the functional linguistic choices made by the respondents as they presented or emphasized their ideas and beliefs. It acknowledged the dynamics of collecting such data from women who related to me as an enculturated outsider. It also recognized that I carried with me my own understandings and values that could not be separated from the research process.[24] Thus, the themes—the influence mechanisms—that were identified from analyzing the transcribed interviews were the outcomes of my interaction with and understanding of the raw data *plus* the socio-religious context of the environments in which the women lived and worked.

Mariya and I conducted the forty-eight interviews between 2019 to 2021. My original plan had been to be based in Pakistan through 2020 and be present at every interview. This plan was badly impacted by Covid-19 travel restrictions that curtailed the amount of time I could spend in the country. As a result, I held a number of interviews on digital platforms, with and without video depending on the quality of the connection. I also enabled Mariya to conduct face-to-face interviews on her own when I could not be physically present.

In the interviews Mariya conducted, her social status or rank may have played a part in determining what was said, and how it was communicated. As a Pakistani Christian, Mariya belongs to an ethno-religious minority community. Although used to interacting professionally with Muslims, Mariya's non-Muslim status may have ranked her as lower or other in the minds of some of the women she interviewed. In the same way, responses to questions in the interviews I conducted were almost certainly determined in part by the respondents' perceptions of who I am: someone who belongs to a different religion whose aims were in some way linked to the West.

---

24. Alessandrini, "Non-Positivist Approaches," 3–5.

In her analysis of Lahore's new emerging middle class, the Pakistani researcher Maqsood had recorded a sense of embarrassment or shame related to Pakistan's shortcomings when compared to a perception of the West where life was understood to be easier.[25] She argued that there exists in culture "aspects of identity which are a source of embarrassment but, at the same time, form a sign of commonality."[26] In some of the interviews I conducted there was a sense that socio-religious beliefs were being defended by women who were, to some degree, embarrassed at speaking openly about these issues. Yet at the same time, these beliefs were also being promoted by women who did not want me to record their views as a complaint against culture and tradition. To lessen any need for the women to protect, even subconsciously, aspects of their identity and beliefs, Mariya and I worked to establish a positive interaction between interviewee and interviewer. However, I was aware that what the respondents chose to speak about and how they framed their thoughts, including language choices, were in part negotiated by their perceptions of those conducting the interviews and their interpretations of the purpose behind the questions.[27] Yet, such perceptions, attitudes or prejudices were never overtly expressed in the interview process.

LANGUAGE

The ways in which the women negotiated language in their interviews was key to my understanding of how influence works within culture. As noted by the psychology academics Braun and Clarke, language enables reflection upon and the articulation of experiences and their meanings.[28] All the interviews were offered in Urdu, Pukhto or English to ensure that each participant could express her thoughts in a language she was comfortable with. Of the forty-eight interviews, sixteen were in Urdu, one in Pukhto and the remainder in English. At one level, the choice of interview language was linked to education. The language of instruction in most schools in KP is Urdu or English. University education is in English, although this can be heavily mixed with Urdu. It was not surprising, therefore, that eight well-educated women, fluent in Urdu, chose to give their

25. Maqsood, *Pakistani Middle Class*, 35.

26. Maqsood, *Pakistani Middle Class*, 35.

27. Thompson, *Introducing Functional Grammar*, 10.

28. Braun and Clarke, "Using Thematic Analysis," 14.

interviews in English even when speaking with Mariya, a mother-tongue Urdu speaker. Yet more than this, issues of perception—conscious and unconscious—impacted the language choices made by each participant. It meant that understanding language/word choice became a fundamental part of my analysis of the women's stories.

In Pakistan language-mixing is common. This is the unconscious insertion into one language of words that come from another.[29] This is most commonly the insertion of an English word into a narrative being conducted in another language. In this study, over half of the respondents who gave their interviews in Urdu inserted English words into their conversations. These words were often used to explain key concepts, coming alongside the equivalent Urdu words they used elsewhere in their conversations. For example, speaking in Urdu in June 2019, Khadijah, an administrator in a school, used English language-mixing to emphasize her point. She said, "In the *public sectors*, those females who want to put influence, should put it! But my one *suggestion* is that, *please*, they must take care of their dignity, their *dignity*." (The *italics* indicate the English words she dropped into her conversation.) The insertion of words like "please" and "suggestion" reflects Khadijah's easy familiarity with English as someone with high social status and a good education who unconsciously mixed her languages. At the same time, her use of the word "dignity," repeating in English what she had already said in Urdu, suggests a deliberate choice designed to ensure that I, as a Western researcher, understood the emphasis she was making.

Khadijah was not alone in choosing specific words alongside or instead of other available, synonymous ones to express personal beliefs and understandings. For example, in the interviews, the respondents used the English phrase "male domination" to talk of patriarchy despite the existence of adequate terms in Urdu and Pukhto.[30] The choice of the English term suggests that women in KP-Pakistan have learned to view patriarchy—male domination—with an external lens; that is, from a Western viewpoint. Thus, male domination required expression in English no matter what the ethnicity, religion or social status of the respondent.

Shahid Siddiqui, in his book *Language, Gender, and Power*, argued that language not only reflects "what is happening in life," but also is used

---

29. Akhtar et al., "Language-Mixing"; Siddiqui, *Language*, 21.

30. *plārwāki* (Pukhto) and *padārāna nazām* (Urdu) are available terms, although they put an emphasis on the domination of women by their fathers rather than by all men.

politically, socially and culturally "in the construction of social reality."[31] In the interviews for my research, women's use of the term male domination, therefore, can be viewed as a conscious language choice made by those seeking to emphasize their/female marginalization on a global as well as a local stage. This borrowed phrase was not used simply to help me, a non-Pakistani, understand culture, or as a wry reference to my personal understanding of the plight of women in KP-Pakistan. Rather, for some of the women in the sample group, setting the term male domination in English was a deliberate language tool used "to shift the advantage in their favour."[32] These respondents were well aware that English is a global language much used on the political stage.

The Language of Research

Seventeen of the forty-eight interviews Mariya and I conducted were in Urdu or Pukhto. Consequently, the process of translating these interviews into English for data analysis was extremely important. The RAs and I took care to select English words and phrases that communicated clearly, whose usage was natural, but that also helped to protect the context and referential meanings associated with the original language. It meant that, at every level of translation, I was drawing on my own familiarity with language and culture, as well as the expertise of the research assistants. The aim was to ensure, as far as possible, that the intent and meaning of what was being communicated was preserved in the English renderings. This required me to understand the "context-embeddedness of [the] real language" the respondents were using.[33] In analytical terms, I was dealing with functional grammar, where the context gives sense and meaning to what is being said. Real language is the way in which people express themselves through word choice, expression, emphasis, and other nuances of language set within the specific context in which they live. The functional language choices made by the respondents in their interviews were, therefore, an important part of their stories.

There was also another level of intricacy in representing Urdu and Pukhto words in English for analysis, because "categories encoded in one language do not always stand in a one-to-one correspondence with the

31. Siddiqui, *Language*, 5, 6.

32. Siddiqui, *Language*, 7.

33. Thompson, *Introducing Functional Grammar*, 11.

categories of another language."[34] To use an SIL Global senior translation consultant's illustration: a native speaker of English knows when the word "snake" means a reptile, a treacherous person, or a cable to clean blocked drains. The context provides the right meaning, applied subconsciously to the word by those who are speaking or hearing. However, the matter becomes complicated when moving into other languages, because these languages may have assigned different semantic meanings to the same words. Therefore, not every language will have assigned the meaning "drain un-blocker" to the word snake, but they may, for example, use the word snake to refer to both snakes and lizards. It comes down to what each individual, within their micro and macro contexts, understands a word to mean (Richard Brown, unpublished data, June 22, 2020).

In the interviews a potential point of misunderstanding due solely to different semantic meanings was illustrated by the English word "grooming." In Pakistan, grooming does not carry the same lexical meaning as is common in the West, where it can have a negative connotation. Instead, grooming is widely and positively used to mean mentoring. Terms like grooming underscored for me the importance of using context to determine meaning if I was to fully understand what the respondents were communicating. In practical terms, it meant that when I was analyzing responses from the sample group, even where a woman had given her interview in English, I needed to determine whether the words the respondents' used carried the same or similar meanings or cultural values to those I might automatically assign to them. I attributed the same importance to the use of synonyms in repetition and to the expansion of ideas through the choice of overlapping relational words.[35]

Clear meaning was especially important to the way the word *influence* was translated, and to the way Mariya and I explained the term when interacting with the respondents in their interviews. After much discussion between myself and the research assistants, I rendered influence as *asr o rasukh* in Urdu and *ekhtiār yā asr* in Pukhto. Where needed, synonymous terms for influence were used during the interviews to aid understanding. I was looking for terms that would carry the idea of influence, rather than power, for women who interpret their experiences through their language choices. However, I also recognized the limitations contained in the communication of this key concept using words that were

---

34. Taylor, *Linguistic Categorization*, ix.

35. Halliday and Matthiessen, *Functional Grammar*, 644–47.

lesser known in KP as compared to the whole range of words associated with power. In addition, I understood that any of the words used to communicate influence would not carry the same cultural resonance or weight in Urdu/Pukhto as they did in English. Rather, they would carry the values attributed to them by KP society and individual experiences. I also expected that some of those interviewed would struggle with the concept of *female* influence, as distinct from *male* influence. This was because of the specific cultural resonance—the gender—attached to the idea of influence in the religiously conservative, patriarchal context of Muslim-majority KP.

The relationship of status, and thus of education, with language choice was also a consideration. The Pakistani anthropologist Sadaf Ahmad suggested that private English medium education affordable to the upper echelons of society enabled greater critical thinking than the rote learning in state-run, Urdu-medium schools.[36] However, education in all Pakistani schools and colleges is centered on textbook memorization. Therefore, rather than education, I would argue that exposure to the West through opportunities for Western training or study/travel overseas enabled some of the middle and upper-class and elite respondents to critically engage with the interview questions.

Those with less education and exposure to the West provided cultural insights not necessarily contained in the interviews given by the more travelled respondents. However, many of these middle and lower-class women used idiomatic language when talking about influence, which brought an additional challenge on an analytical level. I had to engage with the cultural logic of colloquial language expressed through the metaphors of Urdu and Pukhto idioms, sayings, and proverbs. These metaphors were used by the respondents as explanations of why things are the way they are. The challenge was to understand the meaning, including any biases contained in the proverb or idiom they chose. A full analysis of the conscious and unconscious use of language choice negotiation, the role played by language-mixing, and the reasons why idioms were chosen as the best way to describe reality lies outside the scope of this book. It would make a fascinating study. It would also provide an additional window into the lives of women in KP.

Lastly, on an analytical level, I was aware of the losses that would accompany working through multiple languages, despite all of the efforts

36. Ahmad, *Transforming Faith*, 84.

by the RAs and myself to ensure parity and clarity in translation and transcription. Not least, there was the potential loss of language fluency, meaning, and nuance in those interviews carried out in languages that were not the interviewer's or the participant's mother tongue. Such losses could not be mitigated against, but I judged their impact on the overall findings of my research to be minimal.

OTHER VOICES

Working with research assistants as translators, and cultural and linguistic advisors, and allowing their voices to speak into the project, was part of the research design; they were involved from the outset. My assistants, Mariya, Idris, and Mysha, acted as interpreters of language and culture as well as translators. Sometimes, differences of opinion occurred between them. Where possible, I worked to include all of their opinions in my analysis. For example, when handling the idiomatic term *kamāl* used in one interview, two meanings emerged: "as if by magic" and "superiority." Both were applicable to the topic of influence, and I included both meanings in my analysis.

At times, interaction with the respondents' stories could produce a positive or negative reaction in the RAs which they would explain to me, often relating it to their own experiences. With their permission, I noted their stories in the data as points of reference. I retained the final authority to define a term based on my interaction with the conversation, but I always considered the RAs' opinions and insights. If further clarification was needed, I took a specific word, idiom, or proverb to Pukhtun friends for their input. This process ensured that cultural as well as linguistic meaning was obtained. Discussion over some key terms lasted for months as we bounced ideas back and forth.

This level of interaction with the RAs resulted in a "sharing of power" that influenced my research on multiple levels.[37] Positively, the RAs were supportive of me and the aims of my research. Mariya and Idris especially understood the level of my Pakistani enculturation because of a pre-existing professional and friendship relationship that existed between us. At the same time, I had to take into account the differences in our status. On one level I was *junior* to the RAs because I did not share their cultural and linguistic expertise. On another level, I was their *senior*

37. Berman and Tyyskä, "Translators/Interpreters," 184.

because of their cultural respect for my age, my professional status, and my British-Australian nationality. However, the depth of relationship between myself and all three RAs enabled a horizontal platform upon which knowledge could be shared collectively.[38]

Negatively, there was some loss of narrative associated with the sharing of power/control. For example, there was some loss of respondents' narratives where interviews were conducted by Mariya on her own. She tended to be more structured in her approach to the interviews—sticking to the prepared questions rather than probing deeper as the interviewees engaged with the topic of influence. However, this loss of narrative was offset by the many longer interviews I conducted in which respondents shared their stories and provided a breadth and depth of information. Overall, the positives of the RAs' cultural and linguistic insights overcame any negatives associated with power sharing.

In this way, the cultural and linguistic input the RAs brought to the research was not only part of the structure of my project, but it added to the richness of the findings, which are now captured in this book. With the RAs' support, I have been able to present previously unidentified influence tactics and strategies as used by women living and working in the remarkable province of Khyber Pakhtunkhwa. These are the influence mechanisms they are using to change not just their own situations but some of KP's cultural and societal norms. The impact of these women's influence could well change KP society forever.

---

38. Kirkpatrick and Teijlingen, "Lost in Translation," 26.

2

The Place and People
of Khyber Pakhtunkhwa

SOME FACTS AND FIGURES

TO BETTER UNDERSTAND THE place that is Khyber Pakhtunkhwa—and to give context to this study of female influence—some historical and statistical information is required. Khyber Pakhtunkhwa, called the North West Frontier Province from 1901 to 2010, is situated on Pakistan's northwest border with Afghanistan. Pakistan is an Islamic Republic founded on the fourteenth of August 1947. According to the 2023 census, the total population is 241.5 million.[1] The census recorded the total population of KP as just under 41 million of whom 49 percent were female. Only 15 percent of KP's population live in urban settings.

The 2023 census does not detail language groups or ethnicity. However, Pukhto is the dominant language of KP. Some of the other languages spoken, representing other ethnic groups in the province, are Hindko, Saraiki, Khowar, and Punjabi.[2] Urdu and English are the official languages of Pakistan. Arabic is the religious language of the majority. In the census, 64.5 percent of men living in KP aged ten and above, were recorded as literate. For women, this number dropped to 37 percent. For

1. Pakistan Bureau of Statistics, *Population Census 2023*.
2. Government of Khyber Pakhtunkhwa, "Languages."

the 2017 census, literacy included the ability to read and understand a simple text found in a newspaper or magazine, write a simple letter, and be able to accurately count or subtract some simple numbers.

The writer, Shaikh, in her 2018 book *Making Sense of Pakistan*, points to a religious uncertainty that still exists in the country as it works out its identity as an Islamic republic both nationally and internationally. This uncertainty is happening within a socio-political framework that inseparably links religion to identity on every level. In statistical terms, 96.3 percent of Pakistan's population identify as Muslim. In KP, this percentage rises to 99.4 percent of the population.[3] In the province of KP, Islam is practiced by Hindko, Saraiki, Khowar, Punjabi, Urdu, and other language speakers, as well as by Pukhtuns.

In 1973, Pakistan's Constitution confirmed Islam as the state religion and also established the rights of the nation's religious minorities.[4] For example, Article 20 gives every citizen the right to profess, practice, and propagate his/her religion, and to establish and operate religious institutions. According to the 2023 census, the total non-Muslim population in Pakistan is 3.65 percent. In KP the percentage is much less; religious minorities form just 0.56 percent of the population. This number includes Christians (0.21 percent), Hindus (0.03 percent) and Ahmadi (0.24 percent). All remaining minorities, including the Sikh, Baha'i, and Parsi communities total just 0.08 percent of the population.[5] Figure 3 presents a map of Khyber Pakhtunkhwa that includes some census data.

The Pakistani American writer and former politician Farahnaz Ispahani, and the scholar Patrick Sookhdeo,[6] have argued that the strength of Pakistan's Sunni identity can result in an uneasy reality for the country's ethno-religious minorities. This broad minority grouping also includes the Shi'as who form approximately 20 percent of Pakistan's Muslim population.[7] Terms such as Islamization, Muslim majoritarianism, and Sunnification have been used to describe the impact of marginalization and loss of national identity felt by the country's minorities.[8]

3. Pakistan Bureau of Statistics, *Population Census 2023*.

4. Constitution of Pakistan.

5. Pakistan Bureau of Statistics, *Population Census 2023*.

6. Ispahani, *Purifying the Land*; Sookhdeo, *A People Betrayed*.

7. Vatanka, "Pakistan's Shia." Some *guess-timate* the total Shi'a population to be closer to 15 percent or less.

8. Nayyar and Salim, *The Subtle Subversion*, 9; Shaikh, *Making Sense of Pakistan*, 64.

The province of Khyber Pakhtunkhwa

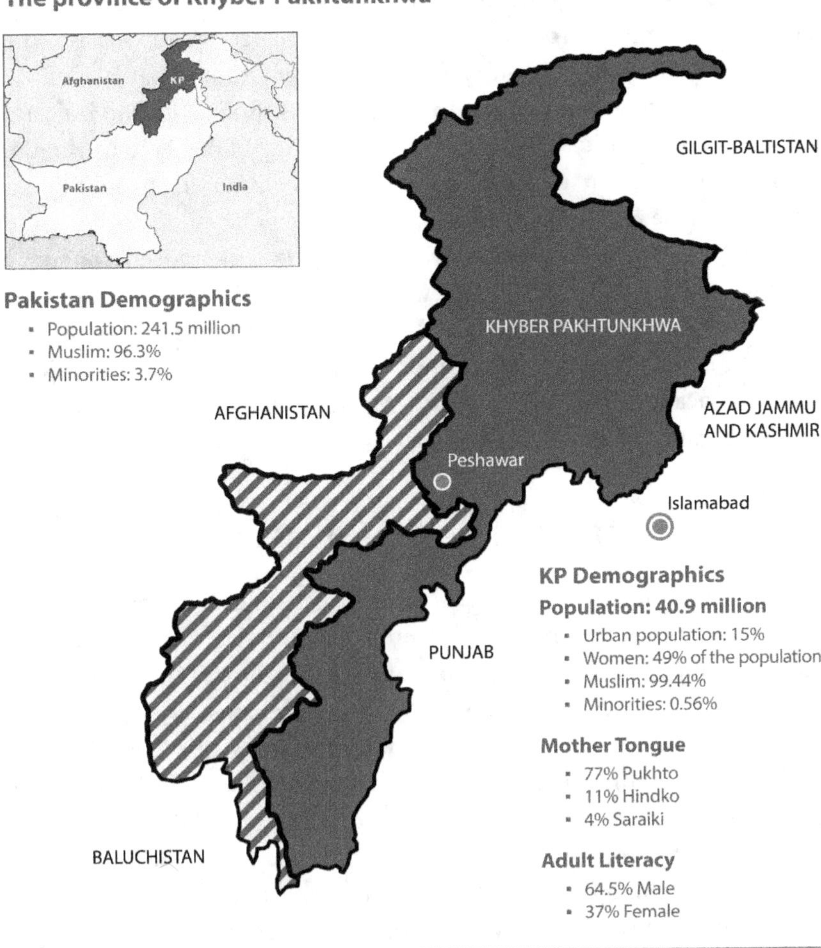

Pakistan Demographics
- Population: 241.5 million
- Muslim: 96.3%
- Minorities: 3.7%

KP Demographics
Population: 40.9 million
- Urban population: 15%
- Women: 49% of the population
- Muslim: 99.44%
- Minorities: 0.56%

Mother Tongue
- 77% Pukhto
- 11% Hindko
- 4% Saraiki

Adult Literacy
- 64.5% Male
- 37% Female

Figure 3. Map of Khyber Pakhtunkhwa, Pakistan.
Source: Map hand drawn by author. Statistics from the 2023 census.

However, despite the division into majority-minority, all of KP's Muslim and non-Muslim communities share similarities of "ethnicity, gender, linguistic and cultural belonging, regional history, caste, social class, political allegiance and occupational status."[9] The differences between them are of religious allegiance and expression. Yet, as the anthropologist Mahmood proposed from her experience within the Middle East, these differences could pose "an incipient threat to the identity of the nation that is grounded in the religious, linguistic, and cultural norms of the majority."[10] In the same vein, writing of the Arab world, the sociologist Mernissi suggested that minority communities could be an uncomfortable reality for Muslim-majority states.[11]

Against this background, in *Voices of Change* I use the term *minority* to reference the Muslim and non-Muslim communities that are not part of the majority Sunni Muslim population. In addition, to avoid confusion with, for example, women as a minority group in Pakistan, I have added the classification of "Muslim," "non-Muslim," and "ethno-religious" to the term minority as appropriate.

THE PUKHTUNS AND *PUKHTO*

As a people-group, Pukhtuns—also known as Pashtuns and Pathans—do not easily fit into the frames of Central Asian, South Asian or Middle Eastern studies. In part, this is because of the 1893 Durand Line that split the tribal grouping into those who live in Afghanistan (Central Asia) and those who remained in India, now Pakistan (South Asia).[12] In KP, the Pukhtuns comprise the majority, Sunni Muslim ethnic group. Their language is Pukhto or Pashto depending on the regional dialect.

The anthropologist Barth identified three factors that form the basis of being Pukhtun: patrilineal descent, adherence to orthodox Islam, and a strict observance of "a body of customs . . . thought of as common and distinctive to all Pathans."[13] Pukhtun tribes trace their descent to Qais (Abdur Rashid) from Ghor, Afghanistan, who was favored by the Prophet of Islam. This shared patrilineal descent provides Pukhtuns with a sense of corporate identity, equality, and autonomy that is not dependent on economic or social status.[14]

9. Fuchs and Fuchs, "Religious Minorities in Pakistan," 8.

10. Mahmood, *Religious Difference*, 32.

11. Mernissi, "Arab Women's Rights," 42.

12. Grima, *Performance of Emotion*, 2–3.

13. Barth, "Pathan Identity," 119.

14. A. S. Ahmed, *Pukhtun Economy and Society*, 128–29; Lindholm, *Generosity and Jealousy*, 212–13.

Secondly, being Pukhtun is considered as inseparable from being Muslim because of their shared ancestral heritage that is rooted in Islam.[15] Most Pukhtuns follow a conservative form of Sunni Islam, expressed socially and politically as well as religiously. This is in contrast to the majority of Sunni Muslims in Pakistan who subscribe to Barelvi Islam, an expression of belief that includes worship at shrines, and has close links with Sufiism. The conservative form of Islam practiced by many in KP has its origins in Deobandi and Saudi Arabian Wahabi Islam. These ideologies seek a return to the golden age of Islam as established in the seventh century.[16] The Deobandi worldview includes conservative attitudes to women, a regulating of citizens' morals, support of an Islamic education system, and a rejection of other forms of religious practice. It also gives strong support to religio-political movements such as the Jamaat-e-Islami (JI).[17] However, in her study of Pukhtun culture, the anthropologist Banerjee noted that adherence to culture could override the adherence to Islam in certain situations.[18] In my own conversations with Pukhtun friends and colleagues, they have told me that faced with a religious or cultural choice, they would follow culture.

The third factor in Pukhtun identity, as presented by Barth, is a strict observance of Pukhtun customs.[19] Pukhtun identity is as much about *doing Pukhto* as it is about *being* Pukhtun. Grima observed that *Pukhto* is something that every Pukhtun *has* and *does*. As an expression of identity, *Pukhto* is "equivalent to both honor and modesty in a complex system of morality."[20] *Pukhto* is also the name given to the Pukhtun tribal code, as code cannot be separated from identity. This body of customs is also known as *Pukhtunwali* or *Pashtunwali*, the way of Pukhtuns. As a code, and as an identity, *Pukhto* dictates religio-social practice for Pukhtuns.

As a system of morality, it may be possible to view *Pukhto* as a type of religious ritual containing symbols, "coded as either male or female," that both restrict and release women.[21] However, this may be over-emphasizing the religious component within *Pukhto*. Lindholm,

---

15. Glatzer, "Being Pashtun," 9.

16. Ahmad, *Transforming Faith*, 26–28; Zaidi, "The Ulema," 11; Saigol, "Decades of Disaster," 73.

17. The Middle East Institute, *Islamization of Pakistan*.

18. Banerjee, *The Pathan Unarmed*, 153.

19. Barth, "Pathan Identity," 119.

20. Grima, *Performance of Emotion*, 1, 4.

21. Aghaie, "Symbols and Rituals," 48.

who lived among the Pukhtuns of Swat in KP at the end of the twentieth century, called *Pukhto* a code of honor that operates as a "charter for public action" known to all.[22] As such, *Pukhto* could be understood as fitting within Foucault's analysis of the domains in which the mechanisms of judgement and punishment operate. In this frame, *Pukhto* could be viewed as an ethic: a system by which people and actions are judged and punished. When understood to be a body of moral principles, the hold that *Pukhto* has over individuals can be justified.[23] It is this hold on individuals and communities that is emphasized in academic definitions of *Pukhto*.

Lindholm placed the code of *Pukhto* on three pillars: *badāl* (revenge), *melmastiā* (hospitality) and *nanawāti* (refuge).[24] Based on these pillars were *ghe'rət* (honor, zeal), *parda* (female seclusion) and the preservation of *i'zət* (honor, respect). For the Pakistani American scholar A. S. Ahmed, *tərburwali* (agnatic rivalry) and *tor* (safeguarding female honor) stand at the center of *Pukhto*.[25] *Nang* (reputation) is judged against observable adherence to the codes of *Pukhto*.[26] A family's good name is inextricably linked with their women's demonstrable submission to *Pukhto*. "Without honor s/he is no longer considered a Pashtun, and is not given the rights, protection, and support of the Pashtun community."[27] Women's honor, her sexual respectability, and her purity are protected by *parda* as a system of gender segregation that includes veiling and female seclusion. Key to understanding how *parda* operates is the recognition that female separation from the public sphere is not only traditional practice but is central to *Pukhto* as an expression of identity.

In addition, women have established traditions by which they engage with *Pukhto* within the boundaries of *parda*. Thus, as the Pakistani scholar Amineh Ahmed observed, women participate in *gham-khādi* (grief-celebration events like funerals and weddings) as a "set of complex activities" that are integral to their identity as Pukhtuns.[28] At the same time, female honor is proved through the personal cost of submission to socio-religious tradition. As explained by Grima, "Both paxto and Islam

22. Lindholm, *Generosity and Jealousy*, 210.

23. Foucault, *Discipline and Punish*, 18.

24. Lindholm, *Generosity and Jealousy*, 211.

25. A. S. Ahmed, *Pukhtun Economy*, 3.

26. Lindholm, *Generosity and Jealousy*, 237.

27. Kakar, "Tribal Law," 3.

28. A. Ahmed, *Sorrow and Joy*, 3.

. . . dictate that women should bear with their hardship and not seek to escape or ameliorate it. This endurance is what earns a Paxtun woman honor and reputation among other women and makes her worthy of being called Paxtun by them."[29] Grima's comments underscore the inseparability of Islam from *Pukhto* for most Pukhtuns; women as well as men.

ISLAM: SOME DEFINITIONS

As adherence to orthodox Islam is central to Pukhtun identity, some definitions of the terminology used in this book to reference different aspects of Islam is required. I use the term *Islamic* to indicate the association of a person, practice, or idea to Islam. *Islamic modernists* are those who focus "their efforts on a reinterpretation of Islam in order to modernize its teachings and traditions."[30] I include Islamic piety movements within this grouping, although their message leans towards the traditionalist.

Islamist refers to an ideology that seeks to establish an Islamic order on a political and legal as well as a societal level. The Jamaat-e-Islami, as a religio-political movement working to redefine Islam through the merging together of the *Shari'a* (Islamic law) and political power, falls within this frame.[31] The term *Islamist modernist*, therefore, is used to describe those who work to Islamize modernity.[32] The sociologist Amina Jamal places the Women's Wing of the JI in the vanguard of a new Islamist modernity.[33]

Traditionalists are those who "revere the Islamic tradition" but are willing to explore and apply new interpretations (*ijtihād*) of the *Shari'a* to give authenticity to their reforms. *Conservatives* represent a worldview in which "Islam is an already comprehensive religious and cultural system fully articulated in the past."[34] Conservatives hold that it is the natural order for women to be segregated from men and remain in the domestic realm under male authority, just as it is the natural order for men to be in leadership, as those who have superior physical and mental capacity. Man

---

29. Grima, *Performance of Emotion*, 127.

30. Haddad, "Islam and Gender," 7; Esposito, *Islam*, 267.

31. Jamal, *Jamaat-e-Islami Women*, 6–7.

32. Haddad, "Islam and Gender," 7.

33. Jamal, *Jamaat-e-Islami Women*.

34. Esposito, *Islam*, 265.

is by nature the influencer; women are the influenced.[35] From her studies of women in Islam, Stowasser argued that, since the 1960s, the belief in "women's innate physical and mental deficiency" has been replaced by an emphasis on spiritual equality.[36] Nevertheless, it remains part of the conservative worldview in KP.

Islamism references the broad movement to bring all aspects of society into accordance with Islam. It is both "a response to modernity and Western culture" and a "product" of the West's political intervention in Muslim nations.[37] In its conservative form, Islamism allows women little access to the public sphere.[38]

Islamization is the process begun by (General) Zia-ul-Haq (President of Pakistan from 1978–1988) in the 1980s. As a movement determined to remove the inroads of secularization in Pakistan, Islamization introduced legislative, penal, economic, and educational reforms "aimed at laying the foundations for a comprehensive Islamic system."[39] Commentators from the women's movement in Pakistan have suggested that the institutionalization of female status, and that of the country's ethnoreligious minorities, were side-effects of the Islamization process. These commentators also suggest that it initiated a change in ideology that continues to impact twenty-first century KP-Pakistan, including women's ability to exercise influence in the public sphere. One outworking of Islamization has been to take the struggle for women's rights out of the secular realm and place it firmly within the framework of Islam.[40]

THE PUBLIC SPHERE OF KHYBER PAKHTUNKHWA

Khyber Pakhtunkhwa's public sphere is the setting for this book. Yet, the term *public sphere* is not simply a grouping together of everything that is not the domestic realm. The German philosopher Habermas had conceived of the public sphere as an open place of unrestricted access; a space not controlled by the state.[41] It stood in contrast to the private

35. Maududi, *Al-Hijab*, 132–35; Maududi, *Towards Understanding Islam*, 164–66.

36. Stowasser, *Women in the Qur'an*, 6.

37. Afary, "Seeking a Feminist Politics," 131.

38. Coleman, *Paradise beneath Her Feet*, ix.

39. Shaikh, *Making Sense of Pakistan*, 101.

40. Khan, *Women's Movement in Pakistan*, 54–74.

41. Habermas, *Structural Transformation*, 27.

sphere centered around a home or limited institution. The energy researcher, Overland, summarized this (Habermasian) space as a place "where citizens could engage as equals in critical discussion about the state and society and influence their development in the process."[42]

In contrast, the public sphere in its traditional form in Muslim-majority contexts is a gendered space broadly determined by religion, culture, tradition, patriarchy, politics, and to some extent by the state's assumption of a "moral agency" for the common good of its citizens.[43] This public sphere is masculine in its concept and structure as determined by the religio-cultural norms of patriarchy.[44] As described by the conservative Sayed Abul Ala Maududi in his book on *parda*, the public sphere is inhabited by men as the traditional providers, protectors, and influencers, and thus is a space associated with power, authority, and responsibility.[45] This conservative worldview is reflected in the proverb about influence that I presented in the introduction to this book: a melon gains its color by sitting with melons. It makes influence culturally male because the public spaces within which influence occurs are male. This traditional view of the nation's public space is being challenged by feminism and female activism. However, public resistance to change means that the move to create an open public space shared by men and women is slow.[46] Thus, the public sphere in KP-Pakistan remains largely male-dominated and conservative.

Khyber Pakhtunkhwa's public sphere is also a hierarchical space in which people are ranked in accordance with their power and importance, and in which juniors are expected to obey and respect their elders as a socialized cultural norm. It places power into the hands of men as those who are societally senior. It also contains spaces that are traditionally closed to female participation socially, professionally, or religiously.[47] The mosque, for example, is a space set apart by tradition for male worship. In addition, honorable female access to male spaces requires senior male permission.[48] Thus, where conservative patriarchy operates, the public

---

42. Overland, "Public Brainpower," 4.

43. Willemse and Bergh, "Struggles over Access," 300–301.

44. Mernissi, *Beyond the Veil*, 143; Weiss, "Within the Walls," 12–15; Willemse and Bergh, "Struggles over Access," 300–301.

45. Maududi, *Al-Hijab*.

46. Rehman, *Womansplaining*.

47. Mohydin, "Field Notes," 247.

48. Maududi, *Al-Hijab*, 146–47.

sphere is a place of Habermasian visibility that provides an opportunity to communicate and debate in a wider social context—*but rarely for women.*

However, opportunities to speak and be heard, to protest and resist, currently exist in the twenty-first century on a scale probably not anticipated by Habermas.[49] In the context of Arab revolution, Hasso and Salime describe the "public square" as both a physical and a "cyberspace" place of occupation, where women create new relationships, sensibilities, and communities "in a historically unprecedented manner."[50] Cyberspace, together with the new forms of communication it facilitates, are also changing the shape of the public sphere for women in KP-Pakistan. The use of social media, especially by the younger generation, is enabling the formation of digital public spaces where issues that relate to gender, sexuality and abuse can be discussed in relative anonymity. An estimated two-thirds of Pakistan's population is under 29 years of age, according to a United Nations Development report.[51] In addition, social media enables the dissemination and discussion of knowledge by global "netizens" in ways that bypass the traditional boundaries established by state and religious authorities. This includes new opportunities for women to explore religious texts and practices. Social media is thus challenging male control of the (socio-religious) public sphere.[52]

As a working definition, I therefore use the term public sphere in this book to designate the non-domestic spaces, physical and digital, where women in KP interact with men who are not part of their close or extended families. This sphere refers primarily to the place of public visibility in which women engage with men, although not with the equality that Habermas had envisioned.[53] It includes enclaves of gynesocial working environments, such as all-female schools and colleges. However, most of KP's physical public sphere is a hierarchical, religiously conservative and patriarchal space, where men automatically and naturally exercise power and influence. In contrast, women do not automatically have the same right to influence, despite their visibility.

---

49. Habermas, *Structural Transformation.*

50. Hasso and Salime, "Freedom," 5.

51. United Nations Development Programme, *A Young Pakistan,* v.

52. Shanneik, *Art of Resistance,* 2; Dad and Khan, "#MeToo"; Willemse and Bergh, "Struggles over Access," 302–4.

53. Habermas, *Structural Transformation.*

Honor and Status

To capture the sense of change occurring within KP's public sphere, as women take up positions of responsibility, I use the adjective "honorable" alongside the nouns of "identity" and "status." Honorable functions as a counterbalance to a widespread perception in KP-Pakistan that women in the public sphere have lost their *ı'zət*. The word "evil" (*bura*) was used by five of the respondents in my research to indicate the depth of shame attributed to them by many in society for having moved out of the domestic sphere. Honorable thus emphasizes an acknowledged and legitimized place of respect attributed to women at work in the public sphere.

Also, for clarity of terminology, I use the term "social status" to identify class or social rank. The term "professional status" references those who occupy a position of status because of their place within an organization, while "gendered status" refers to the placement of women in society as determined by patriarchy and religio-cultural codes. I use the term "societal status" as a heading on which to hook these, and other forms of status held by women living and working in KP-Pakistan.

THE FEMALE LABOR FORCE IN KHYBER PAKHTUNKHWA

Despite their new visibility, the female labor force in KP remains small. The government statistics for employed persons in the 2023 census identified that only 18 percent of women aged ten and above were engaged in a "major occupation."[54]These occupations range from agriculture and crafts through to science and technology.[55] Of these working women, 13.6 percent were involved in the traditional activities of agriculture and crafts, including tailoring, embroidery, and carpet weaving.[56] Just under

54. Pakistan Bureau of Statistics, *Population Census 2023*.

55. The Government of Pakistan includes in its list of major occupations agriculture; mining; manufacturing; construction; the provision of services such as electricity and water; transport and the vehicle industry; information and communication; the wholesale and retail trade; accommodation and food services; finances and insurance; real estate; science and technology; administrative services, defense; social security; health and social work; education; and the arts and recreation.

56. Definitions for the different occupational categories are taken from the 2015 *Pakistan Standard Classification of Occupations* compiled by Bajwa and Aslam. Weiss's "Within the Walls: Home-Based Work in Lahore" study of invisible, home-based work in Lahore's old city adds lived-reality to these demographics.

2 percent were employed in the lowest category of "elementary occupations" such as maids, cleaners, hospital attendants, and road sweepers, or as unskilled or semi-skilled factory workers. A very few women, only 0.2 percent, had a skilled trade, or they worked in the service industry or as clerks. Just 2.5 percent of women were listed as "professionals" or "associate professionals," terms which include the fields of medicine, education, social work and technical support. Just 0.02 percent of women were employed in arts and entertainment. (This is a 2021 figure.) The number of employed women working as "managers," a category that includes senior officials and legislators, was under 0.2 percent. No women were recorded as working in the transport or hotel industries, nor in IT or professional scientific activities. An overview of these classifications and percentages as they impact KP is presented in table 1.

TABLE 1. *The Percentages of Women Working in Khyber Pakhtunkhwa's Public Sphere*

Occupational Groups	Female %	Male %
Skilled agricultural workers	11.31	19.26
Craft (tailoring, embroidery, carpet weaving)	2.34	10.96
Elementary (house servants, cleaners, hospital attendants, road sweepers) & unskilled/semi-skilled factory workers	1.84	15.80
Service industry and clerical support	0.21	26.45
Technicians and associate professionals	0.55	3.26
Professionals involved in the education and medical fields	1.98	3.89
Managers	0.19	1.96
Totals	18.42	81.58

Source: **Adapted from the Percentage Distribution of Employed Persons 10 Years of Age and Over by Major Occupation Groups, Sex and Area 2020–21, Pakistan Bureau of Statistics,** *Population Census 2023.*
Note: **The percentage of male employment is given alongside the female percentages for reference.**

Khyber Pakhtunkhwa, Pakistan has provided the geographic location in which to seat my study of female influence in a conservative Muslim majority setting. In addition, the proverb *sitting with melons* has provided a backdrop against which I can explore the awkwardness of female influence. Another Pukhtun proverb states, "Great work requires long hands." Literally, "Long matters require long hands" or a "long reach." It means that those undertaking something of significance require access to people with power, resources, and influence.[57] In *Voices of Change*, I test the accuracy of this assertion when applied to women. Do women need the help of powerful others if they are to influence in an environment where public sphere influence is traditionally male rather than female? Or are they able to influence in their own right, as those who have the necessary power and resources at their disposal?

57. Bartlotti and Khattak, *Rohi Mataluna*, 63.

3

Perspectives on Female Influence

THERE ARE MANY BOOKS that focus on the societal changes to Middle Eastern public spheres caused by women's visible presence in those spaces. These include accounts of female resistance and negotiation in revolution in the Middle East, of women's activism in Pakistan, and the changes taking place for women in some religious spaces within Islam. These stories have enabled me to identify, in broad terms, how women were and are influencing for change in their families, communities, and nations. However, there was little in the literature that specifically explored how influence *works*. That is, there was little that explained the techniques and strategies—the influence mechanisms—those women used to achieve their goals. There was also little that took the influence being exercised by ordinary non-Muslim women, resident in the same Middle Eastern spaces, to contrast and compare it with the influence of their Muslim counterparts.

I therefore turned to two separate strands of research: women's studies and social influence theories. For the second strand, I considered specific social influence theories for the ways in which they can be applied to female influence in KP-Pakistan. This included women's negotiation of Islam and patriarchy, and also the situation for the province's ethno-religious minorities. Firstly, however, I considered the strand of women's studies.

At this point, I became aware of the vast amount of literature written about power within the broad frame of this field of study. It encompassed issues of identity, social status, and ethnicity, as well as gender and gendered roles. Needing a starting point, I looked at what has been written about women in other patriarchal societies, beyond that of Pakistan and the Middle East. This led me to consider the exercise of female power in rural Greece in the 1980s. This was a society that had significant similarities to twenty-first century Pakistan. It gave me a pathway towards understanding the influence tactics used by Muslim and non-Muslim women living in some Muslim-majority contexts that include Pakistan and KP.

FEMALE INFLUENCE IN 1980S RURAL GREECE

The essays I reviewed as the beginning point of understanding female influence in KP are found in *Gender & Power in Rural Greece* edited by the anthropologist Dubisch. These articles explore female power in a religiously conservative and highly patriarchal society. For example, Du Boulay describes a religio-cultural belief found in 1980s rural Greece regarding the nature of men and women.[1] This belief held that men are superior in nature, and in the power and authority they exercise. Their place of authority is primarily the public sphere. In contrast, "the unequivocal association of women . . . with symbolic, moral and physical" weakness had led to the societal "conclusion that all women should at all times be subordinated to male authority."[2] For this reason, their realm was limited to the domestic sphere. The symbolic aspect of female weakness, in this context, had a religious base. Women were associated with Eve as the "weak link" in creation while men were associated with Adam as the superior and stronger being.[3]

Du Boulay contrasted the concept of female subordination with what she observed to be women's real power and authority in the domestic sphere. She wrote that women held "the house together," which she asserted was a significant socio-religious position in rural Greek culture.[4] She used the term "redemption" to describe how the paradox of female inferiority and power operates. Redemption occurs when the deficit of women's moral and physical weakness is offset by the credit of their honorable socio-religious status as those who reflect "the figure of the Mother

1. Du Boulay, "Women."
2. Du Boulay, "Women," 139,140.
3. Du Boulay, "Women," 139–40, 152.
4. Du Boulay, "Women," 141, 144.

of God."[5] This did not, however, prevent men from taking advantage of their dominant position to abuse their wives verbally and physically. Such practices found societal acceptability as expressions of the cultural code or contract under which the women lived. Du Boulay significantly observed that the women of her study wished "only to modify this behavior, not reverse the order of reality on which it was symbolically based."[6]

Du Boulay's description of a prevalent belief in the presumed lesser ontology of women was echoed in the studies of women's nature that I explored within Muslim-majority contexts. For example, Mernissi had studied theories of women's "divinely decreed inferiority," "her weak constitution," and paradoxically, her power.[7] In the same way, Leila Ahmed's study of female honor and shame within Islam echoed Du Boulay's observations of the socio-religious complexity of female identity, and the paradox of inferiority and honorable status.[8] Du Boulay's study showed how, within culture, a negative ontology can be offset by a positive identity—both shaped by religious belief. She had also shown that although these Greek women might complain about the excesses of male dominance, they accepted the religio-cultural rightness of a male-female hierarchy in society even as it apparently placed them in a lesser position. Women's acceptance of the societal rightness of male superiority is similarly found in *Pukhto* and other cultural contracts in KP; themes that are explored later in this book.

It could be presumed that the acceptance of male dominance and female inferiority, enhanced by female restriction to the domestic realm, would render women powerless. However, in her introduction to *Gender & Power*, Dubisch argued that women have developed their own structures of power, authority, and status that were equal to those exercised by men.[9] Friedl's article in the same book described this reality.[10] Writing as an anthropologist, Friedl observed that although formal power and public prestige were male, yet the informal but "very real" power of women

5. Du Boulay, "Women," 165–66.

6. Du Boulay, "Women, 167.

7. Mernissi, *Beyond the Veil*, 32–33.

8. L. Ahmed, *Women and Gender*.

9. Dubisch, *Gender & Power*, 13.

10. Friedl, "The Position of Women." Friedl's paper originally appeared in *Anthropological Quarterly*, Vol. 40, No. 3, Appearance and Reality: Status and Roles of Women in Mediterranean Societies (Special Issue) (July 1967), pp. 97–108. It was the springboard for Dubisch's own research.

was felt in the home.[11] Her aim was to demonstrate that power is not exclusive to the male public sphere but also exists in the domestic realm where it is exercised by women.

Friedl's essay is a reflection on the public and domestic roles, and associated prestige, of men and women in rural Greece at that time. She had observed that the informal power women exercised domestically, in its *positive* form, was their participation in economic and social decision-making as determined by cultural norms. At the same time, these Greek women could also exercise their informal power in a *negative* manner based on the sense of obligation they created in men with regard to family honor. That is, they influenced through the cultural reality that their (female) toil and their (female) modest and chaste behavior was the basis of male honor. Bluntly, male honor was dependent on female behavior. The power of this influence mechanism was women's ability to "disrupt" the family by bringing shame to it.[12]

However, missing from Friedl's study were the consequences facing women who brought shame on their families. This separates her findings from the extensive documentation in Muslim-majority settings of private and state retribution against women accused of dishonoring their families, and thus points to the different ways in which societies deal with public shame. In the Pakistan context, the academic Ayesha Khan gives case-study examples of reprisals against women in her book on activism, Islam and democracy.[13] This suggests that the Greek culture of Friedl's study did not give the same weight to the honor-shame dynamic as it carries in some Middle Eastern and South Asian societies where issues of honor and shame are key elements in the domestic-public divide.[14] In addition, the respondents at the center of the essays in *Gender & Power* seemed to have a greater public space and domestic authority than is given to women in Pakistan's religiously conservative and patriarchal settings.

One of the central dialogues in *Gender & Power* was the issue of power exercised from a place of prestige. Prestige was understood to be the status of a formalized position, recognized by society, that carried power. Dubisch proposed that women exercise real power, equal to that of their husbands, but without the prestige or legitimacy of a publicly recognized

---

11. Friedl, "The Position of Women," 51.

12. Friedl, "The Position of Women," 51–52.

13. Khan, *The Women's Movement*, 232–43.

14. Boxberger, "Two States to One," 127; Siddiqi, "Taslima Nasreen," 214–15.

title.[15] The anthropologists Salamone and Stanton built on this assertion to argue that a household economic structure, the *nikokyrio*, within 1980s rural Greek society, provided women with "public prestige and social equality."[16] That is, women obtained some *public* prestige and equality because the *nikokyrio* was a recognized *semi-public* societal institution. The suggestion was that women's right to be influential was endorsed by society in and through this semi-public structure, and that women influenced because of the power and authority acknowledged to be implicit in the *nikokyrio* system. Salamone and Stanton also argued that female prestige did not detract from male status within the frame of the *nikokyrio*.[17]

The construct of Greek domestic and public institutions lies outside the scope of this book. However, the concept of a society's recognition of a woman's *right* to be influential in the public sphere is part of the socio-religious complexity I am seeking to unravel. The interviews contained in the Iranian anthropologist Haeri's study of the lives of professional Pakistani women at the end of the twentieth century speaks to this complexity.[18] She concluded that while the state gave Pakistani women the right to be active in the public sphere, socio-religious norms obstructed the practice of this right within a system of patriarchy that was commonly present although not equally practiced.

Haeri's study reflected the challenge of the new and different to traditional ways of thought and practice in Pakistan. This was also a theme in *Gender & Power*. Included in the essays was an exploration of the impact of the modern (Western) women's movement on Greek women's prestige. In a definition of terms, I understand modernization to be an often non-indigenous process by which, it is asserted, less-developed nations can improve economically. Modernization brings changes to traditional cultures, beliefs, values, and work ethics, and thus carries with it an underlying assumption of cultural failure within the receiving nation. Its implementation, can, albeit unintentionally, worsen as well as improve the situation for women, and also work to strengthen those ideologies that it is seeking to remove.[19]

---

15. Dubisch, *Gender & Power*, 13.

16. Salamone and Stanton, "The *Nikokyra*," 97–98.

17. Salamone and Stanton, "The *Nikokyra*," 98.

18. Haeri, *No Shame*, 407–8.

19. L. Ahmed, *Women and Gender*, 131–33; Inglehart and Baker, "Modernization"; Kendall, *Sociology*, 575.

In the Greek context of the 1980s, modernization as the result of Western influence had led to the seemingly positive removal of structures that designated one sex as inferior to another. Yet this change worked to effectively reduce women's status and power because it reshaped their role in society. In addition, the positioning of the struggle for equality within the frame of the public sphere had further marginalized women in the home by reducing their significance as contributors to society through their domestic labors.[20]

The scholars in the social sciences of architecture, Pavlides and Hesser, described the impact of modernization on rural Greece through the lens of house decoration.[21] Their study pointed to the changes that were radically altering the shape of a conservative, patriarchal society. They had observed the structural and psychological ways in which 1980's Greek society was adjusting its traditional norms to accommodate the modern—both products and ideas. This included radical changes to women's roles in the domestic and public spheres, the loss of traditional norms, and even the physical restructuring of family to accommodate higher level female education.[22]

Although the context and types of change Pavlides and Hesser reviewed did not reflect the situation in KP-Pakistan, their study pointed to change that was radically altering the shape of a conservative, patriarchal society. Pavlides and Hesser's study did not cover the religious dynamic of these changes which is a key factor in Pakistan and other Muslim-majority nations as they interact with Western modernization. Neither did they explore the impact of the women's movement on society. However, their research highlighted the manner in which a society can accommodate the intrusion of the modern, even as some object to the changes it brings to the comfortable norms of a traditional way of life. This is a major theme in Ammara Maqsood's study of a newly emerging middle class in Pakistan.[23] As a class, they are seeking to establish a modern Muslim identity that takes advantage of advances coming from the West but without the loss of Islamic values. This was also a topic that arose in some of the interviews with the women in my own sample group.

20. Dubisch, *Gender & Power.*

21. Pavlides and Hesser, "Women's Roles."

22. Pavlides and Hesser, "Women's Roles," 89–94.

23. Maqsood, *Pakistani Middle Class.*

PATRIARCHY

Patriarchy is a fundamental part of traditional life in KP-Pakistan—as it was in the rural Greek setting of *Gender & Power*.[24] The sociologist Walby defined "patriarchy as a system of social structures and practices in which men dominate, oppress and exploit women."[25] She distinguished between what she called "private" and "public" patriarchy, although she argued that the exploitation of women was found in both spheres.[26] Private patriarchy encompasses the complete control of women by husband or father, and restricts female access to the public sphere. Public patriarchy recognizes women's right of access to the public sphere but continues the practice of male subordination of women within that space. However, Walby rejected the idea that a hierarchical structure among men, where generational juniors are in submission to seniors, was a part of patriarchy in most contexts.[27]

In contrast, Moghadam, described a system of hierarchical patriarchy operating in the Middle East in which the senior man holds "authority over everyone else in the family, including younger men."[28] She used the term "classic patriarchy" first coined by Kandiyoti to describe this form of male dominance.[29] Within this system, women are regarded as a "form of property" and anything they produce, including children, belongs to the men of the family. Women are not allowed to hold formal positions within the public sphere, understood to be a place of power. Access to that sphere is through the patriarch. Female power is thus limited to any influence they can extend, informally, through their relationship with the family patriarch.[30]

Writing in 1987, the women's rights activists Mumtaz and Shaheed asserted that this type of hierarchical patriarchal system is entrenched in Pakistani society, propagating an inequality among men as well as between men and women.[31] Not least, there is a societal understanding that *every* adult male has the right to tell every female what she is or is

24. Dubisch, *Gender & Power*.

25. Walby, *Theorizing Patriarchy*, 20.

26. Walby, *Theorizing Patriarchy*, 178.

27. Walby, *Theorizing Patriarchy*, 20.

28. Moghadam, *Modernizing Women*, 118.

29. Kandiyoti, "Bargaining with Patriarchy," 276.

30. Moghadam, *Modernizing Women*, 119–20.

31. Mumtaz and Shaheed, *Women of Pakistan*, 154.

not permitted to do. Over thirty years later, the Pakistani feminist Mohydin described patriarchy in Pakistan as a system that places power in the hands of men in the home, and also in government, politics, and the legal system.[32]

Writing in the early days of modern female activism in Pakistan, Mumtaz and Shaheed argued that the patriarchal system operating in the nation pre-dates Islam.[33] This approach enabled them to criticize the system without disparaging religious belief. In contrast, the scholar Ahmed-Ghosh, from her research into Islamic feminisms, referred to systems of "Islamic patriarchy" active in Muslim contexts.[34] She did not define the term Islamic patriarchy, but her argument seems to point to a patriarchal system seemingly deeply rooted in the Qur'an and religious tradition. Within this frame, any challenge to the principles of patriarchy, including by Islamic feminism, could be viewed as an attack on religious values.

From the studies by Mumtaz and Shaheed, Ahmed-Ghosh, and others, patriarchy is seen to operate as an entrenched system that is not easily changed. Yet, as Moghadam observed, women's increasing visibility in the public sphere *is* changing the shape of patriarchy in the Middle East.[35] In Pakistan, studies by Ahmad, Jamal, and Maqsood record changes to women's place in Pakistani society that point to changing attitudes within the nation's patriarchal system.[36] There are two major forces in play. The first is the challenge to female influence coming from men and a patriarchal system. The second force is the challenge that female influence is to patriarchy.

Therefore, as a basis for understanding patriarchy in KP, I propose that Muslim women in Pakistan are part of a hierarchical patriarchal system deeply rooted in Islam and culture. This system is one of male privileging and domination that requires all women to be in submission to all adult men within the domestic and public spheres. However, Pakistan's social hierarchy, determined by class, education, and ethnicity, means that patriarchy is not uniformly expressed or experienced across society.

I also propose that non-Muslim women in KP submit to the same broad framework of patriarchal norms established in Muslim-majority

32. Mohydin, "Field Notes," 247.

33. Mumtaz and Shaheed, *Women of Pakistan*, 154.

34. Ahmed-Ghosh, "Feminists and Feminisms," 5.

35. Moghadam, *Modernizing Women*, 152.

36. Ahmad, *Transforming Faith*; Jamal, *Jamaat-e-Islami Women*; Maqsood, *Pakistani Middle Class*.

socio-religious practice, but with the additional expressions of their own religious community. This proposal is based solely on my own understanding formed from decades of observation. This led me to conclude that the small size of non-Muslim communities in KP, just 0.46 percent of the population, renders it unlikely that they operate systems that do not align in some way with the majority. The impact of patriarchal attitudes on non-Muslim women in KP's public sphere forms part of the later discussion in this book, as I record conversations held with Christian, Baha'i and other women who were interviewed as part of my research.

In addition, I also propose that through resistance and negotiation, what Kandiyoti calls "the *patriarchal bargain*," women are challenging the traditional structures of private and public patriarchy as they seek greater access to the public sphere.[37] "These patriarchal bargains exert a powerful influence on the shaping of women's gendered subjectivity and determine the nature of gender ideology in different contexts. They also influence both the potential for and specific forms of women's active or passive resistance in the face of their oppression."[38] Thus, within the space of KP's public sphere, some women are using the influence of a patriarchal bargain to obtain positions that give them the power and authority to influence in other ways. Importantly, however, in KP, the majority of Muslim and non-Muslim women are not seeking to throw off patriarchy as a social system. As with the women in 1980s Greece, they simply wish to modify and recast its application within the frames of religion and culture in the twenty-first century.

Association of Women with Weakness

A socialized belief in women's lesser ontology, one of the products of classic patriarchy, has consequences for women on multiple levels. Not least, it impacts not only how they are viewed by others but how they view themselves. The folklorist Mills, in her essay on Afghan women's agency, examined the established tradition, she called it a "stereotype," that designates women as lesser than men.[39] She wrote that, "probably the 'loudest,' most widely held negative stereotype about women, . . . in Middle Eastern Muslim cultures in general, is the idea that trickery, deviousness, is an essential

37. Kandiyoti, "Bargaining with Patriarchy," 275.
38. Kandiyoti, "Bargaining with Patriarchy," 275.
39. Mills, "Covered and Covert."

part of female nature. . . . [She is] a 'true daughter of Eve.'"[40] Mills quoted a Dari proverb that is used as a proof of women's antisocial and devious nature: "Women are seven steps ahead of the devil."[41] In 2020, the same proverb, with the same attributed meaning, was told to me by a group of Afghan Pukhtun men. Such female deviousness—held by some to be God's assessment of women—is linked to Sura 12 of the Qur'an and the story of a wife's attempt to deceive her husband. The anthropologist Lindholm recorded the belief, prevalent among conservative and largely rural Pakistani Pukhtuns, that the Qur'an taught the need for the strict seclusion of women whose "licentious nature" would otherwise lead them astray.[42] Conversely, and of interest to my study of the mechanisms of female influence, Mills's research showed that women's lack of personal agency within conservative patriarchal structures could necessitate a degree of cunning if they were to overcome obstacles in pursuit of their goals.[43]

THE LANGUAGE OF IDENTITY

The language used to identify or categorize womanhood is important to this study because it reflects beliefs and practices, which in turn can be used by those with power to exercise control. Such language expressed through idioms, proverbs, and stories are used and repeated in religious, socio-cultural, and legal contexts, as well as in mainstream and social media. They provide a narrative that contributes to the shaping of women's religio-cultural identity in the public mind. Hasso, for example, described the allegations of impropriety made on television and digital platforms by the state against female activists in Bahrain.[44] The aim was to publicly shame the activists and put pressure on their families to control the activities of their women. In the same way, in Pakistan, Shaheed spoke of the derogatory Urdu term *maghreb-zada* (literally, tainted by the West) used by those with conservative views to label activists for women's rights.[45] The activists' supposed Western-ness had allegedly tainted them with the same immorality and lack of faith attributed to Western women.

40. Mills, "Covered and Covert," 62.

41. Mills, "Covered and Covert," 62. In Pukhto the proverb says, "*khəza də šetān na u'wə qa'dəma 'makhke zi.*"

42. Lindholm, *Generosity and Jealousy*, 219.

43. Mills, "Covered and Covert," 68–70.

44. Hasso, "The Sect-Sex-Police Nexus," 126.

45. Shaheed, *Great Ancestors*, xiii.

The power to harm contained in the term *maghreb-zada* and similar labels is founded in their contrast to the socialized image of the ideal Muslim woman. This woman is presented as "passive and obedient."[46] She remains in the domestic realm and upholds the family honor through her modest dress and demonstrable purity. This view of ideal female identity has been internalized by many in Pakistan simply because it had been presented to them as reality since childhood. Allegations of impropriety attack this identity. They are designed to shame and discredit female activists, trivialize their message, and separate them from a "potential support base" among other women.[47] The resulting cumulative effect takes away from women their right to disagree because it places them outside the fold of Islam. It also works to shrink and/or remove any space for secular rather than religious argument.

The importance of socialized beliefs for women seeking to influence for change in Pakistan, and the wider Middle East, cannot be overstated. Positioned by these beliefs as a marginalized minority, women are required to find ways to tell their stories that give religious as well as societal legitimacy to, for example, their claims for justice and equality. Their message has to acknowledge and yet push through the "strong subconscious restraints" of internalized, conservative definitions of women's nature to provide another acceptable narrative for honorable female identity.[48]

One avenue for this alternative narrative is found in academic research that challenges stereotypical views of Muslim women included in popular (Western) media; what the anthropologist Abu-Lughod calls "the common Western story of the hapless Muslim woman oppressed by her culture."[49] This approach illustrates the tension felt by modern women unhappy that, historically, their stories have been presented by those from outside their cultures who have inadequately understood the complexities of the lived experiences of Muslim women.[50] At the same time, setting aside the aims of each individual text, this form of academic literature operates as a declaration of female self-confidence. The challenge to popular (Western) preconceptions points to a confidence in identity. This confidence is an essential part of overturning negative stereotypes and exercising influence in the public sphere.

46. Ahmad, *Transforming Faith*, 55.

47. Shaheed, *Great Ancestors*, xiii.

48. Shaheed, *Great Ancestor*, xiv.

49. Abu-Lughod, *Muslim Women*, 9.

50. Abu-Lughod, *Muslim Women*, 221–23.

4

Social Influence Theories

To fully comprehend issues of female self-confidence and the influence women are having in KP's public sphere, it was important for me to understand how influence works. Specifically, I wanted to know how woman A is able to influence person B or group C, and how such influence results in change, including societal change. I therefore turned to social influence theories to provide lenses through which to explore the mechanics of influence. Social influence (SI) is understood to be the ways "by which individuals adapt their opinion, revise their beliefs, or change their behavior as a result of social interactions with other people."[1] While women's studies research had provided me with perspectives of influence as a lived reality, SI theories gave me an insight into what needs to be in place relationally if a person or people are to be persuaded to do what the influencer wants. This includes the ways in which influence is linked to societal status and the power of social proof. Social proof is the visible, demonstrable evidence that causes others in society to endorse as correct a value that I/we hold.

From the vast array of social influence theories, I selected those I believed gave me the best approaches to understanding the mechanisms of female influence as they were acted out in KP-Pakistan. The theories included social networking, social information processing, minority influence, conflict, conformity, self-categorization, and societal legitimization. Although the empirical tests that underpin these theories were

1. Moussaïd et al., "Social Influence," para. 1.

conducted primarily in Western contexts where there is little difference between male-female authority and male-female spaces, the social norms they investigated included traditions, customs and public opinion that were broad enough to include the KP context.[2]

At the same time, I recognized that missing from most Western studies was the religious worldview through which social norms are processed. This is hugely important when considering female influence in KP. As has been noted in the context of female leadership, culture and religion in Jordan, "In many Muslim majority countries (MMCs), Islam is an important driver of ethical understandings and behaviors."[3] In addition, my research had made me aware that patriarchy functions as another driver of understanding and behavior that has to be considered when discussing female influence in KP. Every influence theory, therefore, had to be tested against the lived realities of religious belief and tradition, and patriarchy.

RELATIONAL SOCIAL NETWORKS

Given the strength of patriarchy and other socio-religious norms in KP-Pakistan, it could be assumed that social networks would provide marginalized women with a strategic means of relational influence. Social networks are those formal and informal connections that provide a structure by which women can be in close relationship with others to receive information and gain knowledge. Such networked connections are vital for any women wishing to align people and systems to their ideas.

Studying the use of power in relational social networks, Krackhardt explored the ways in which information is accessed and controlled through "friendship and advice networks" within an organizational structure, as well as by the more formal work-based systems.[4] He argued that power lay not only with those who occupy formal decision-making authority by reasons of appointment, personality, and expertise, but also with those who know how their organization's networks operate. As part of his argument, Krackhardt developed a kite structure by which to present the three indices of power centrality used in network analysis: degree,

2. Turner, *Social Influence*, 4.

3. Koburtay et al., "Women Leadership," para. 6.

4. Krackhardt, "Assessing the Political Landscape," 342–343.

closeness, and betweenness.[5] Krackhardt was aware that for influence to occur, some form of relationship must exist between the influencer and influenced. His model provides a visual means of understanding and thereby measuring the ways power operates within a relational network. The indices of degree, closeness, and betweenness enable the examination of how, and by whom, opinion is communicated.

Krackhardt's kite model demonstrates how power centrality operates across a minimum network structure of ten people (figure 4). The first indicator is "degree centrality." This suggests that the person with the most connections (D) within a network is well-positioned by the number of her connections to influence others as well as be influenced by them. The second indicator, "betweenness centrality," demonstrates the influence exercised by a "gatekeeper" (H). Person H is the one who operates as the link or "broker" between those members in the network who have no direct connection with each other, both receiving information and using it to influence others. The third indicator, presented by Krackhardt is "closeness centrality." This relationship enables those with close direct and indirect connections with everyone else in the network (F and G) to receive and circulate opinion and gossip, as the "pulse-takers."[6]

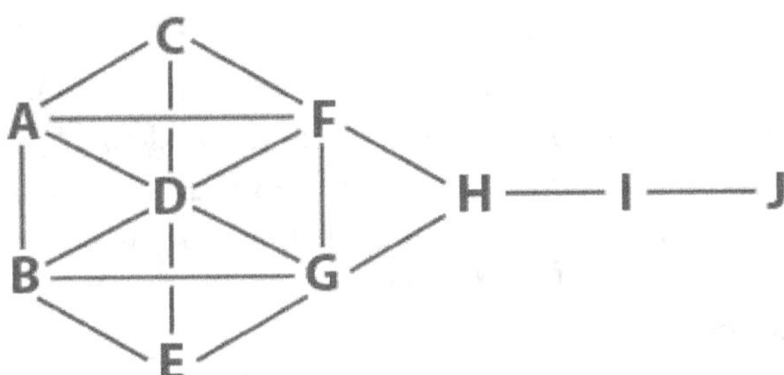

Figure 4. Centrality in Social Networks.
Source: Network exhibiting a kite structure developed by D. Krackhardt; used with permission.

The social network scientist Contractor and the psychologist DeChurch brought the kite model into the social information processing framework as part of their application of SIP to a specific medical

5. Krackhardt, "Assessing the Political Landscape," 351.

6. Krackhardt, "Assessing the Political Landscape," 351–52; Contractor and DeChurch, "Integrating Social Networks," 2.

situation in India.[7] Their research assisted my exploration of networked influence in KP because it applied a Western influence model to a non-Western context. They defined SIP as an explanation of how "social networks (i.e., the structure of social influence) and human social motives (i.e., the process of social influence wherein one person's attitudes and behaviors affect another's)" can be used to enact social influence within a community.[8]

Contractor and DeChurch added a fourth indicator, "prestige centrality," to Krackhardt's model, suggesting that the person with the highest prestige is influential because of her connections to "opinion leaders" within the network in which she is embedded.[9] Other studies, for example by the sociologists Hanneman and Riddle, argue that "prestige" is not a separate indicator, but simply one aspect of degree centrality.[10] As such, prestige reflects the prominence given to those people who gain importance from the number of ties they have, through which they can extend their views out to others. It is their "out-degree" centrality which makes them people of prestige and, therefore, people of influence.

Contractor and DeChurch, however, used prestige centrality as a separate indicator by which to measure the *quality* of strategic relationships within a network. Therefore, if in the kite model person G was an opinion leader, the nature of B, D, E, F, and H's connections with G would be examined to see whose relationship placed them in a prestigious position above the others. A favored position would improve relational quality, enabling that person, for example, to negotiate for better deals. As explained by Hanneman and Riddle, the demonstration of greater influence would then lead to "deference and attention from those in less favored positions."[11]

The ability of women to influence by being strategically placed within a social or organizational network was explored by the anthropologist Klein in her book *Women and Men in World Cultures*. In chapter 8, dealing with gender and political control, Klein examined literature focused on gender inequality. She looked at examples of female authority,

7. Contractor and DeChurch, "Integrating Social Networks," 5. Contractor and DeChurch used the abbreviation SIP as an acronym for "structured influence process." However, their research fits within the social information frame.

8. Contractor and DeChurch, "Integrating Social Networks," 1.

9. Contractor and DeChurch, "Integrating Social Networks," 2.

10. Hanneman and Riddle, "Centrality and Power," Degree Centrality, para. 2.

11. Hanneman and Riddle, "Centrality and Power," Degree Centrality, para. 2.

power, and influence exercised from positions of prestige within patriarchal public spheres that traditionally excluded women from holding high office. Against this background, Klein proposed that influence, "the weakest form of public power," was used (diplomatically) in a framework of social networks by those with "no public authority but with social connections to those who do."[12]

This argument was closely aligned with her second proposal, that even in societies where female authority is rejected, a woman can exercise influence from a position that contains the prestige attributed to it by society.[13] This is not the prestige or prominence attributed to the one who holds many connections within a network. This is a transferred prestige, with its origins in the status of the (male) influencer to whom a woman is connected. In illustration, Klein used the example of the USA's First Lady.[14] The office of First Lady is without policymaking ability but gives the officeholder the prestige of someone who has the ear of the President. Klein's argument was that a woman with high prestige could exercise influence even if she held no decision-making authority.

The SIP frame, as developed by Krackhardt, and Contractor and DeChurch, was seemingly able to accommodate Klein's proposals, because it is *centrality* in the network that enables a woman to be influential, not the status of the person herself.[15] Within this frame, issues of class, gender, patriarchy, honor-shame, and ethno-religious identity fall away. However, one of the limitations of the SIP model is that it is designed to operate among peers. Contractor and DeChurch built their SIP model on an example of peer influence in India.[16] This limitation suggests that where strong patriarchal and hierarchical norms operate, and carry the potential to curtail the influence of peer-based networks, other forms of networking are required if an individual or a group is to be persuaded to change its mind.

12. Klein, *Women and Men*, 192.

13. Klein, *Women and Men*, 192.

14. Klein, *Women and Men*, 194–95.

15. Klein, *Women and Men*; Krackhardt, "Assessing the Political Landscape"; Contractor and DeChurch, "Integrating Social Networks."

16. Contractor and DeChurch, "Integrating Social Networks," 5.

The Overlay of Pre-Existing Networks

In Krackhardt's theory of social influence, informal friendship networks operate alongside formal work-related, organizational networks.[17] They reflect the social bonds of friendship and trust that exist among personnel outside of work, yet they can also exercise influence within an organization, for example, in seasons of change. To test this theory in the non-Western setting of KP, I considered the two major types of informal networks that exist in Pakistani society for their potential role in assisting or obstructing female influence in the workplace. The first is *birādari* (patrilineal kinship). The second is patronage.

Birādari is a system of male kinship that operates as a horizontal network of relationships within a tribe or family. In my years in Pakistan, I have observed *birādari* operate among men as a system of patrilineal connections used by those looking for social advantage for their families. Lyon, in his study of power and patronage, describes *birādari* in Pakistan as a mechanism of obligation for those who need the help or intervention of their extended family network.[18] This is similar to Sookhdeo's description of the *birādari* among Christian families in Pakistan.[19] However, there is no indication in Lyon's and Sookhdeo's research that women use this resource to exercise their influence.

It could be presumed, given the strength of patriarchy in KP, that Muslim and non-Muslim women's influence happens indirectly through the agency of the men they are best connected to domestically; their use of kinship connections in the home. Many women in KP are married to men from within their extended families, including cousins, which strengthens such relationships. This reflects something of Klein's example of the influence exercised by the USA's First Lady.[20] Although not explicitly stated, her influence—First Lady to President—is domestic: that of wife to husband. The President could then use his external relationships and power to accomplish the hopes and aspirations of his wife. In a patriarchal society, women need not be influential in themselves, it is their kinship connections that give them the ability to shape the beliefs and actions of opinion leaders.

17. Krackhardt, "Assessing the Political Landscape," 345.

18. Lyon, "Power and Patronage," 126, 154–56.

19. Sookhdeo, *A People Betrayed*, 308–10.

20. Klein, *Women and Men*, 194–95.

The second form of informal networking operating in Pakistan is patronage, where patron and client engage in vertical and unequal relationships.[21] The stronger patron uses his/her resources or influence for the benefit of the weaker client; the client reciprocates with support or assistance. The patron-client relationship involves some form of workable trust yet is also founded on obligation and reciprocity within a hierarchical social system. However, as Hine observed in her study of female activism in Pakistan, patronage can also work *against* the client.[22] She gave the example of lower-class women who were deprived of the opportunity to change the specific issues of their own subordination because of their client relationship to elite female patrons. Their voices were lost as their patrons operated as mediators and spoke on their clients behalf in the political system. This suggests that relational networks can impede as well as advance women's influence.

Pre-existing informal societal networks, such as *birādari* and patronage, are unstated in Krackhardt's and Contractor and DeChurch's SIP models,[23] where D, F, G, and H are identified as influencers because of their centrality. Therefore, I developed an adaptation of Krackardt's kite model to illustrate the intrusion of cultural networks into the formal and informal networking of an organization in the context of KP's public sphere. Figure 5 presents the overlap on organizational relationships of an elite family that operates a pre-existing patrilineal network. In the new matrix of K to Q, the person with the greatest potential to influence is P—who is also A in Krackhardt's model. She holds *cultural centrality* because of the quality of her familial relationship to the powerful head of this family (M). Although Q (who is also B) is also positioned by familial status to be a person of influence, she does not have the same level of connections within the kinship network as person P. As a consequence, her status within the organizational network is reduced, as is the influence she can exercise.

21. Clark, "Social Movement Theory," 946.

22. Hine, "The Hard Knot," 22, 340–42.

23. Krackhardt, "Assessing the Political Landscape"; Contractor and DeChurch, "Integrating Social Networks."

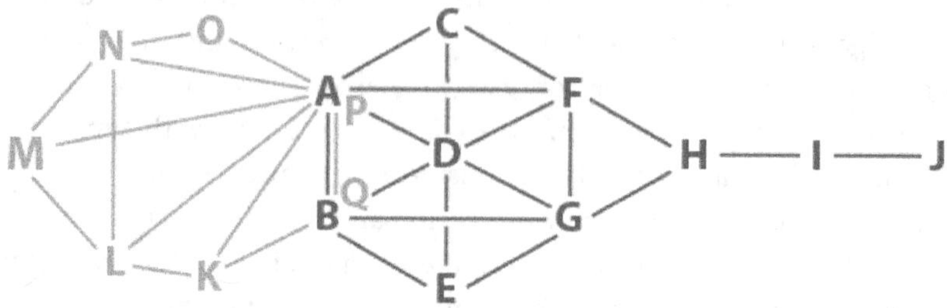

Figure 5. The Power of Cultural Networks to Provide Cultural Status Centrality. *Source*: **Expansion on the graphic of a network exhibiting a kite structure as developed by D. Krackhardt. Original graphic used with permission.**

This new model of cultural status centrality provides a lens by which to explore the influence exercised by kinship and patron-client networks. However, as I sought to apply SI theories to the lived influence of women in KP, it did not fully represent the complexity of organizational networks operating in such a hierarchical and collective culture. Women in KP have "multiple identifications" and thus seamlessly, simultaneously, and often unconsciously engage "in a diversity of publics."[24] These identifications and publics are determined by ethnicity, religion, and social and professional status.[25] Thus, women can carry power and authority within an organization simply because of the weight of the external networked structures in which they are also embedded.

Therefore, I needed a new social influence framework to provide a means by which to explore the way in which external relational networks impinge on organizational decision-making and what this means for female influence. These external networks are the powerful and influential cultural networks of ethnicity, and family, tribe and feudal relationships that form the bedrock of KP-Pakistani society. They stand outside the formal networks of organizational structures to potentially empower a woman to influence by enhancing her official, positional status within an organization. They can, for example, enable someone with a powerful family name to exert influence based on cultural deference alone.

I therefore developed a new SI framework, presented in figure 6, that synthesizes aspects of centrality in social networks and the role played by centrality in social information processing. It presents the overlap of

<hr>

24. Willemse and Bergh, "Struggles over Access," 300.
25. Ahmad, "Multiple Locations," 10.

a cultural network (K to R) on an organizational network (A to J) that provides some with the influence of an external network. It illustrates, for example, the informal impact of a woman's religion, or her family's name, their societal status, on her formal professional position within an organization. In this framework, P—who is F in the original kite model—has superiority because of her direct relationship with the person with the highest status (M) in the external network. She also retains the power of a close connection to D as the person with the most organizational connections. The same is true of N and L, who relate directly to each other, to M and to P. Together, theirs is a powerful voice, able to impact the organization they formally, and informally, are a part of. R, O and K can process their opinions through, or alternatively be influenced by, the messages coming from P, N or L.

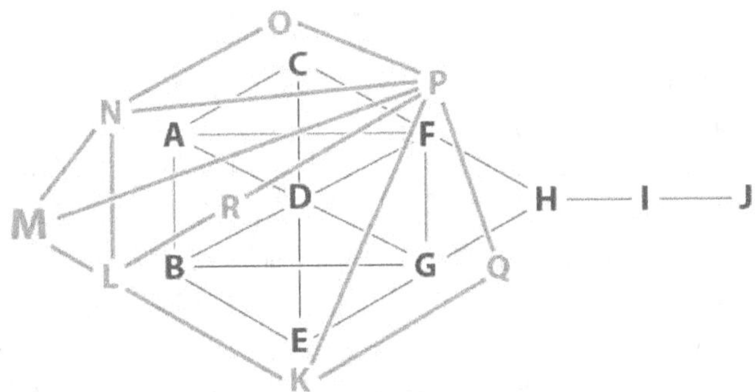

Figure 6. The Power of Cultural Networks to Determine Influence.
Source: Expansion on the graphic of a network exhibiting a kite structure as developed by D. Krackhardt. Original graphic used with permission.

The new framework also illustrates how informal, external groupings have the power to marginalize some within a formal organizational network. Persons H, I, and J from Krackhardt's original model are excluded from being organizational influencers because they are not part of the cultural network to which the others belong.[26] This could be for reasons of their religion or their ethnicity, or their gender in a majority male setting. Yet, person H, the gatekeeper of the original kite model, could become an important person for I and J, as she still exercises betweenness centrality.

26. Krackhardt, "Assessing the Political Landscape," 351.

In developing this new SI framework, I sought to address the problem of applying theories primarily developed in individualistic (Western) settings to collective societies such as KP. My framework brings to the fore those things that remain largely unstated in the original models. This includes the importance to influence of religion, gender, tribe, and feudal societies, as well as patrilineal kinship, and patronage relationships. Each of these factors impinge on female influence as a lived reality in KP. At the same time, my new framework comes alongside earlier models to underscore the importance of relationships to influence. Not only can women influence the opinion leader from positions of betweenness and closeness centrality, they can use the pre-existing networks of kinship, patronage, and ethno-religious brotherhood to institute change.

MINORITY INFLUENCE

The strength of patriarchy and other socio-religious norms in KP-Pakistan had led me to explore the use of social networks as a means by which marginalized women can strategically use relational influence. This in turn brought me to consider how long-term or permanent change is achieved. The social psychologist Moscovici proposed a theory of conversion.[27] This is a deep, long-lasting change—a conversion—that demonstrates an understanding of an issue from the minority's point of view. Moscovici argued that minorities do not have to accept a passive role and simply conform to the numerical weight of majority opinions in a show of public support. Minorities can exercise their own influence and expect to successfully convert others to their opinion. They are simply required to present their alternative ideas and new information in a way that will lead the majority to re-examine its current views.

To test his theory, in 1969 Moscovici conducted an experiment using perceptions of color.[28] It was designed to see if a consistent minority could influence a majority to give an incorrect answer. He suggested that, when confronted with a consistent and confident opinion, elements within the majority would re-examine what they held to be true in light of the views coming from the minority. If the minority views were validated as correct, conversion occurred. Building upon this research, the psychologist Nemeth argued that "Minorities do not just induce thought

27. Moscovici, "Conversion Behavior," 217.
28. Moscovici, "Conversion Behavior," 217–18.

about their message; they induce thought about the issue ... that is divergent, that considers multiple options only one of which is that suggested by the minority."[29]

The sharing of alternative ideas and new information by minority groups, and the multiplicity of responses (options) from the majority, seems to describe minority influence as exercised by secular and Islamic feminism in KP-Pakistan. For example, the successes, challenges, and failures of primarily Muslim feminist activism in Pakistan were captured in the articles included in *Womansplaining*, edited by Rehman. These articles included details of the responses from the majority in society as they reacted to the different-from-norm concepts presented to them. There was, however, a lack of detail in these articles about the work of ethno-religious minority women as they sought to influence within their own sections of society or advocate for change to others' stereotypical ideas about their community's identity. Lack of data about KP-Pakistan's non-Muslim minorities makes it difficult to determine if, or to what extent, these women use strategies that fall within Moscovici's definition of minority influence.[30] I return to this issue in later chapters, as I revisit this topic following my interviews with the ethno-religious minority respondents who were part of my sample group.

A criticism of Moscovici's study of minority influence is that it was conducted using a group of unrelated people in an unrepresentative sample group to perform "an artificial task," suggesting little similarity to the real-life scenario of minority groups trying to change majority views held by society at large.[31] Despite this weakness, Moscovici's argument that a consistent and confident minority could influence elements within the majority to change their opinions, fits, for example, with the slow but steady effectiveness of the women's movement in Pakistan that has resulted in changes to discriminatory laws. Khan, for example, described how activists, although a minority voice, refused to compromise or back down on issues they considered to be essential for individual women's rights and thus changed "the mindset of the judiciary."[32]

One of the most cited examples of effective activist influence is the 2006 changes to the 1979 Hudood Ordinance.[33] The wording of the

29. Nemeth, "Minority Influence Theory," Impact and Application, para.3.

30. Moscovici, "Conversion Behavior."

31. McLeod, "Moscovici," Minority Influence Studies, para. 1.

32. Khan, "The Politics of Activism," 38.

33. Shaikh, *Making Sense of Pakistan*, 104–6, 176.

Ordinance, tied into the lesser value placed on a woman's testimony as against that of a man's, made victims of rape vulnerable to the charge of *zina*: adultery, fornication, and prostitution. They were viewed as being engaged in illegal sex rather than as victims of physical abuse, and most were unable to seek redress through the criminal justice system. Violence against women had increased after the Ordinance was instated. The 2006 changes to the Hudood laws meant that women could report rape without fear of being prosecuted for *zina*.

In general terms, Moscovici's theory of conversion suggests that all women, as a minority group in KP, can successfully use the tools available to them to introduce new ideas designed to change majority opinions.[34] In addition, his theory also goes some way to explain why minority female influence has, overall, *failed* to change KP-Pakistani society. As Nemeth explained, a minority with an inconsistent message will have less influence than one that is consistent in its message and behavior.[35] Effective influence is dependent on the unity and strength of the minority group. Therefore, the struggle of the women's movement to effectively influence for societal change in KP-Pakistan could be due to the activists' lack of a unified position, and thereby, of a unified message. For example, some groups have decided to operate as *secular* feminist organizations. This puts them in direct conflict with those groups in Pakistan that have positioned their activism within the frame of Islam.[36] In addition, any low social status or socio-religious disconnectedness from the majority will weaken a group's ability to influence for change.

Conflict Influence

Moscovici's research also led him to suggest that "all influence attempts . . . [to] create a conflict,"[37] something that societies do not like. Conflict is understood sociologically to include the struggles that take place in society regarding issues that stratify, such as economics and gender.[38] Such struggles need not be violent. Conflict can include threats and promises, confrontational testing, and flight. It can also include the struggles that

34. Moscovici, "Conversion Behavior."

35. Nemeth, "Minority Influence Theory," Background, para. 8.

36. Khan, *Women's Movement*.

37. Moscovici, "Conversion Behavior," 213.

38. Weber, "Domination."

arise when individuals or groups pursue incompatible goals and values.[39] Goals/values are incompatible when what is of advantage to one, disadvantages the other. It is because societies do not like conflict that they work to reach an agreement. It is in this process—agreeing to end conflict—that influence occurs. According to the social psychologist Turner, who in his book *Social Influence* critiqued the work of Moscovici, conflict works to the minority's advantage. A minority can "create conflict, refuse to compromise, create doubt and uncertainty, and produce a situation in which the only solution is for the majority to shift to the new point of view."[40]

How conflict would work as an influence mechanism for individual marginalized women in Pakistan will require further research, given the strength of conservative patriarchy, socio-religious codes of honor-shame, and the positioning of female identity within Islam/religion. The suggestion coming from women's studies literature regarding successful activism indicates, however, that group or internal conflict does work in some targeted contexts. For example, the Palestinian-born academic Karmi, in her study of feminism and Islam, argued that Islamic feminism sought to influence those Muslim women who had "been caught in a conflict" between their devotion to Islam and the failure of religious practice.[41] It was this internal conflict that made these women more likely to change their opinions. This aligns with Moscovici's theory that others are likely to shift to a new viewpoint if they find themselves in a place of conflicted ideas.

Bartos and Wehr's proposal that conflict can occur in the pursuit of incompatible goals and values is suggestive of the type of situation faced by a number of women in KP-Pakistan's public sphere.[42] For example, for many families it is economically advantageous that their women gain access to education and employment. For the women themselves, it helps them fulfil their roles if they can establish equality and influence within the shared spaces of education and work. Yet, this brings them into direct conflict with men used to male privilege within the public sphere. In real terms, men are used to controlling the spaces in which they are perceived as socially and intellectually superior. One result of male resistance to female intrusion can be the verbal and physical abuse

39. Bartos and Wehr, *Using Conflict Theory*, 12–18.

40. Turner, *Social Influence*, 86.

41. Karmi, "Women," 79–80.

42. Bartos and Wehr, *Using Conflict Theory*, 13.

of women in the workplace. This was identified by Mirza in her study of female office workers in Lahore.[43] She recorded a list of conflict strategies used by the women to reinforce their honorable identity. Their aim was to thwart male intentions to take advantage of them within a shared workplace. For example, they created "a social distance between themselves and their male colleagues" by limiting, rudely if necessary, their interaction to work-related issues only. They also sought to create social distance by developing socially obligatory relationships. "They integrated male colleagues into a fictive kinship system; and they created women's spaces inside the offices."[44] They were using different expressions of nonviolent conflict as tools for influence; tactics aimed at compelling men to change their behavior, and potentially their attitudes, towards their female colleagues.

The use of conflict as an influence strategy among KP-Pakistan's ethno-religious minorities is harder to measure. The Middle East and Islam scholar S. W. Fuchs observed that some non-Muslims are striving to prove their equal status in Pakistan's predominantly Muslim public sphere by challenging the norms of public thinking, thereby creating a conflict.[45] Although his narrative is primarily about men, it may be possible to assume that some non-Muslim women are also challenging the societal norms that marginalize them and thus cause social conflict within the spaces they occupy.

Similar to Norm Influence

For the majority in society, however, a less combative strategy may help to convince them to accept the opinions of the minority. Within this frame, minority groups need to present their values—those ideas that make them different to the majority—in a manner that validates them as pro-normative.[46] As Turner explained, a group perceived as dissimilar to the majority and arguing against social norms and values is unlikely to be influential.[47] Minority groups, therefore, must work to present themselves as part of the majority ingroup rather than representatives of a deviant

43. Mirza, "Accommodating Purdah"; Mirza, *Chaddor and Market*.

44. Mirza, "Accommodating Purdah," 193.

45. Fuchs, "Reclaiming the Citizen."

46. Moscovici, "Conversion Behavior," 213, 215.

47. Turner, *Social Influence*, 99.

or counter-normative outgroup position.[48] This includes disproving any negative portrayals of themselves, and their values, coming from those who oppose them.

In KP-Pakistan, similar-to-norm influence is part of the struggle faced by feminists. They have to prove, for example, that they are not tainted by the immoral values (perceived to be) held by the West. They also have to prove that they hold to values held by society to be normative; they simply want to adapt these norms to a changing social context as women enter more spaces in the public sphere. This requires the feminist minority to be consistent, confident, immovable, and visible in a manner that at least some in society can accept. Similarly, those among Pakistan's ethno-religious minority communities who seek to influence the majority through a demonstration of shared history, political allegiances, and social identity, have to emphasize their pro-normative cultural belonging. How much women from KP's minority communities are using similar-to-norm influence is part of the ongoing discussion in this book.

MAJORITY INFLUENCE

Before continuing to explore different expressions of influence exercised by a minority, or from a minority position, it is important to understand the strength of the positions some women in KP are seeking to change. Majority opinions are persuasive and strong because they are held to be true—normative—by the majority. And, as Foucault observed, those in the majority will use the powers of surveillance and control to ensure compliance and conformity among all within their sphere.[49] In the collective society of KP-Pakistan, there is a strong expectation that everyone will avoid conflict and comply with societal norms. Muslims follow the doctrine of conformity (*taqlid*) to established beliefs and practices that operate within Islam.[50] Across the nation, the Islamization process introduced by former president Zia-ul-Haq works to bring "the political and legal systems into conformity with . . . the tenets of Islam."[51] On the micro-level, among the Pukhtuns of KP, there is a societal expectation that

48. Moscovici and Personnaz, "Studies in Social Influence," 271, 273.
49. Foucault, *Discipline and Punish*, 173.
50. Parray, "Modernist and Reformist Thought," 81.
51. Hine, "The Hard Knot," 3.

every Pukhtun will comply with the codes of *Pukhto*. As the social work scholar Aamir Jamal explained in his study of male attitudes to female education in KP, there is the expectation that every woman will conform to the controls and boundaries set by the head of her household,[52] and in this way uphold the family's *Pukhto*.

The Middle East scholar Aghaie explored the dynamics of independence and conformity for women in his analysis of the use of religious symbols and rituals by Shiʻi women in Iran.[53] In a possible parallel to *Pukhto* (and other less formalized codes operating for communities in KP), the rituals and symbols of these religio-cultural codes can be seen to promote conformity because they establish and preserve identity—for Pukhtuns and for others. Yet, Aghaie's study suggests that even within conformity on macro and micro levels, there are spaces to negotiate for change, albeit within proscribed boundaries. It is these spaces that female influence is required to explore if the values held by a seemingly immovable majority are to be changed.

Influence and Social Conformity

In the frame of social influence studies, the social psychologist Milgram developed a theory of subordination which references the existence of hierarchical societal systems in which compliance ("obedience") is automatic.[54] The philosopher Gramsci spoke of compliance as the "'spontaneous' consent" given by society to the "general direction" imposed on them, because of "the prestige (and consequent confidence) which the dominant group enjoys because of its position and function in the world of production."[55] Yet, as the political theorist Lukes noted, it is wrong to assume that consensus has been achieved simply because there is no pushback or obvious grievance.[56] In some situations, a direction has been accepted and submission occurred simply because society "can see or imagine no alternative to it, or because they see it as natural and unchangeable, or because they value it as divinely ordained and beneficial."[57]

52. Jamal, *The Gatekeepers*, 5. Men are the decision-makers in Pukhtun society.

53. Aghaie, "Symbols and Rituals," 45.

54. Milgram, *Obedience to Authority*. Milgram's theory of subordination within a hierarchical society was concisely summarized by Wren (*Social Influences*, 14–15).

55. Gramsci, *Selections*, 145.

56. Lukes, *Power*.

57. Lukes, *Power*, 28.

Coercion, that is, the enforcing of "discipline," is only needed when groups refuse to consent to the directions given by those in power.[58] This sounds like Foucault's description of the "disciplinary punishment" applied to those who offend by refusing to comply.[59]

The social psychologist Asch examined the conditions that determine the social conformity of one individual in the face of group pressure.[60] He measured the different forms of pressure that culminate in social conformity: agreement within the group even when individuals are aware that these opinions are not supported by the physical evidence. His research revealed that for many, the erosion of personal confidence by "the presumed rightness of the majority" and a fear of appearing different were enough to make a person conform, even if privately they believed the group's opinion to be wrong.[61] Conformity was, therefore, a response to the pressures coming from the majority group. This pressure, however, need not be coercive. As the social psychologists Festinger and Turner explained, a group comprised of those whom one likes, who hold similar and thus correct or valid beliefs and opinions, is influential first because one wishes for their approval, and secondly because they are viewed as a "more trustworthy source of information."[62] At the same time, however, the majority can exercise its power through its ability to reward or punish those who are dependent on them for the resources they control.[63] Turner, therefore, argued that conformity influence could result in superficial "public compliance" rather than any deep-seated attitude change.[64]

SELF-CATEGORIZATION

As I have underscored when talking of the strength of the majority, conformity to majority opinion is already a deeply established cultural norm in KP. *Pukhto*, patriarchy, *taqlid*, Islamization, and hierarchical status expect and require conformity from all within their scope. Public conformity is desirable and necessary not least because any challenge to

58. Gramsci, *Selections*, 145.

59. Foucault, *Discipline and Punish*, 179.

60. Asch, "Studies of Independence."

61. Asch, "Studies of Independence," 70.

62. Festinger, "Informal Social Communication," 272–73; Turner, *Social Influence*, 46.

63. Moscovici and Faucheux, "Social Influence," 157.

64. Turner, *Social Influence*, 37.

societal norms could be viewed as a challenge against faith and the immutability of Islamic injunctions.[65] Such collective conformity is linked to each individual's sense of her own identity based on the identity of the group(s) she is a member of.[66] In the KP context, these group identities include being a Pukhtun, a Muslim, a Pakistani, a member of a religious minority, speaking a specific language, and much more.

Writing of identity within the frame of social influence studies, Turner et al. observed that societies, cultures, and ideologies view others and themselves, as collective groups, using terms of "identical and different . . . [of] 'us' versus 'them', ingroup versus outgroup . . . etc."[67] The importance of ingroup-outgroup membership is that it enhances "the perceived similarities within and the differences between groups."[68] In addition, Turner et al. suggested that in the process of societal interaction, comparisons take place "in which the perceiver appraises self in relation to others, not from the perspective of others."[69] As a consequence, groups are shaped by the extent to which they are different from or the same as others, and by the degree to which they accept or reject external judgements about themselves.

Self-categorization is, therefore, a helpful lens through which to understand the way in which, for example, a non-Muslim sees herself as representative of her minority community in its difference to the Sunni Muslim majority. This will affect the way she influences, impacting the strategies that she adopts. Community rather than individual differences, and differences not similarities, become the determinant of her self-categorization, and these *differences* shape her beliefs, her behavior, and her influence in the public sphere. It could also lead her to separate herself from the majority, choosing to influence solely within her own ethno-religious community. In illustration, in her studies of minority Muslim communities in Ireland, the Islamic studies scholar Shanneik observed that the power of community self-categorization operating among Salafi women resulted in their self-imposed separation from others.[70]

Self-categorization theory thus provided me with the means of analyzing the *us and them structures* exhibited in KP-Pakistan society,

<hr>

65. Parray, "Islamic Thought," 79.

66. Tajfel and Turner, "Intergroup Conflict."

67. Turner et al., "Self and Collective," 3.

68. Turner, *Social Influence*, 156.

69. Turner et al., "Self and Collective," 16.

70. Shanneik, "Religion," 86.

particularly the mutual appraisals taking place between the Sunni Muslim majority and the minority Muslim and non-Muslim communities. Self-categorization seemingly operates as part of the process of Muslim majoritarianism as identified by the political commentators Ispahani and Shaikh.[71] They argue that it is within this majoritarianism that issues of Pakistani citizenship and national status are being determined. Although an investigation of Muslim majoritarianism lies outside the scope of this study, minority (self-)categorization underscores the challenges faced by non-Muslim and Muslim minorities. How they are perceived by the majority and how they perceive themselves in relation to that majority impacts their ability to influence.

In an aside, it is important to remember that perceptions change through the generations. For example, that which in the past was called a crime is now viewed as something lesser, or different.[72] Similarly, that which was tolerated in the past can now be considered a crime. At the same time, the majority in a society hold the power to resist and legislate against that which is considered to be (criminally) different, even as the *definition of difference* changes across the decades. Viewed through this lens, minority influence can be understood as an energy that challenges the truths *currently* held by the majority, even as from a majority perspective the challenge is seen as opposition to that which has always been implicitly true. This is why the minority group requires restraining or removal. Again, difference rather than similarity becomes the determinant used by both majority and minority.

In the public-sphere setting of this research, a consciousness of difference works to shape each woman's beliefs and behavior in KP's public sphere. Women are different from men. Pukhtun women are different to non-Pukhtuns. Ethno-religious minority women are different to women from the majority. Aware of the differences that exist, some women seek to create the space for what Foucault calls "new relational possibilities."[73] This is a space where influence or power occurs through relationship, rather than top-down control-submission. For other women, a consciousness of difference motivates resistance to the moral and physical controls on their lives that family and society seek to impose. Rebellion and resistance are used to eradicate this difference.[74]

71. Ispahani, *Purifying the Land*; Shaikh, *Making Sense of Pakistan*.
72. Foucault, *Discipline and Punish*, 17.
73. Foucault, *Ethics*, 1:160.
74. Foucault, *Ethics*, 1:45.

A Pakistani example of difference, similarity, and female energy was given by the Pakistani activist Saigol in her exploration of Mohajir women's sense of identity, and their consciousness of their socio-religious minority status within the nation.[75] The Mohajir are Muslims who emigrated to Pakistan from India in 1947 at the time of Partition. An Indian identity disconnects the Mohajir from being Pakistani in the thinking of some in society, even as the current generation of Mohajirs were born in Pakistan. Saigol observed of a Mohajir respondent that she talked to: "Her identity seems to be forged not only by her own sense of who she is, but also by what others say. She contests and resists the identity ascribed to her by others and, in the process, tries to consolidate who she is and what she wants to be."[76]

Saigol's conclusion was that Mohajir women participate in the (male) presentation of their community as a homogenous whole, proudly distinct from other Muslim groups.[77] The preservation of religious difference enables the Mohajir identity to be passed from generation to generation. However, at the same time, Mohajir women challenge group homogeneity as they transition between Pakistani and Indian (and other) identities depending on personality and context. The preservation of difference, balanced against acceptance by society as a whole, is something that emerges from the interviews coming from my own sample group.

SELLING INFLUENCE: THE IMPORTANCE OF SOCIETAL LEGITIMIZATION

In chapter 1, I argued that for female influence to be effective, coming as it did from those marginalized by their gender, women's *right to influence* must be verified or legitimized. I had proposed that a woman's ability to provide social proof of her *i'zət* and her status, a proof that others recognize, is perhaps the most vital aspect of influence for women in KP's public sphere. This suggests that women are required to present themselves as part of the majority, even as their message is counter-normative, may cause conflict, and those they seek to influence may be reluctant to identify with a deviant position.

75. Saigol, "Partitions of Self."
76. Saigol, "Partitions of Self," 196.
77. Saigol, "Partitions of Self," 230.

For women in KP-Pakistan, proof of belonging requires work to disprove negative portrayals coming from those who oppose them or their ideas by attacking their honorable identity; labelling them as women who have lost their *i'zət*. It is essential, therefore, that women in the honor-shame culture of KP's public sphere portray themselves as "good," that is, women of honorable status. As Fraser observed in her study of recognition, "Jettisoning internalized negative self-identities, they [members of a group] must join collectively to produce a self-affirming culture of their own. Having refashioned their collective identity, they must display it publicly in order to gain the respect and esteem of society at large."[78] In the interweaving of legitimization with self-categorization, women in KP need to replace socialized, negative self-images with positive images of self; to view themselves as honorable (i.e., good) women despite the dissonance of their counter-cultural presence in the public sphere. Then they have to sell this concept to society.

Turner noted that social influence is the task of persuading people to accept that their current ideas are "wrong," and that (your) alternative ideas are "right."[79] In the KP context, where legitimacy in the eyes of others is being sought, the emphasis is not, necessarily, on the wrongness of the original view but on the alternative idea as *better*. To use the melon field metaphor, legitimization and change occur when society is persuaded that it is *better for them* when women sit in the melon field as those who carry public sphere influence. This, in turn, depends on women's ability to (re-)tell their stories in a manner that gives societal and religious legitimacy to their claim to the right to be influencers.

Informational Social Influence

Writing within this same broad frame of legitimization, Turner observed that "'true' influence, i.e. influence leading to private acceptance and internalization, [and] long-lasting attitude change is informational in nature."[80] This information is internalized because it comes from a credible source which validates it as trustworthy. Information can also be accepted because it makes sense of "rules, procedures, . . . and

78. Fraser, "Overcoming Displacement," 24.

79. Turner, *Social Influence*, 4.

80. Turner, *Social Influence*, 37.

'taken-for-granted' knowledge."[81] Others' ability to inform and influence is directly proportional to the extent that they are "perceived as similar, expert, trustworthy, credible, etc.," and where their narrative affirms reality.[82] This includes the influence of a leader as someone socially validated as an expert, having the right to influence; one who also demonstrates a competence and credibility that others can imitate.[83]

The ability to inform and influence is important for those in the vanguard of women's presence in the public sphere. As noted in the introduction, the number of women occupying places of visible influence in KP's workplace has been growing over the past twenty years. Yet, excluding those who are involved in agriculture and crafts, they still represent less than 5 percent of a female workforce which numbers just 18 percent of women aged ten and above. Their task, together with the responsibilities of their organizational or public roles, is to prove that they can be regarded as able to influence on a par with men. Having proved similarity to the proverbial male *melons* in the workplace, they can then function in the role of trustworthy expert.

Farhad Hashmi, the founder and expert exemplar in the piety movement Al-Huda, is an example of this type of informational influence founded upon proven similarity.[84] Her influence is primarily within the gynesocial environment of the movement she started. It is her students who go on to bring change within their family circles. In her study of Hashmi and Al-Huda, Sadaf Ahmad drew on the term "experiential commensurability" coined by Benford and Snow to describe the manner in which the lived experiences of women in the movement worked to confirm the accuracy of the religious teachings they received.[85] This speaks to the success of informational influence, backed-up by role model proof, as an influence mechanism. However, as Ahmad also observed, the permanency of lifestyle-change among graduates from Al-Huda could be dependent on their future environments and experiences.[86]

Examples of women in the predominantly male public sphere of Pakistan, who informed and influenced because they were perceived as similar, expert, trustworthy, and credible are most easily identifiable

81. Turner, *Social Influence*, 152.

82. Turner, *Social Influence*, 37.

83. French and Raven, "Social Power," 266–68.

84. Ahmad, "Al-Huda," 367–70.

85. Benford and Snow, "Social Movements," 621; Ahmad, *Transforming Faith*, 66.

86. Ahmad, *Transforming Faith*, 195.

in the political field. The most obvious example is Benazir Bhutto, who influenced as Prime Minister (1988–1990, 1993–1996), and who is identified as taking on the patrilineal, political legacy of her politician father despite her gender.[87] However, Benazir Bhutto is such an exception that her influence cannot be used as representative of women in KP-Pakistan's public sphere.

THE UNINTENTIONAL NATURE OF INFLUENCE

The psychologist Schaller noted in his study of change to established norms, that influence can have unintentional consequences.[88] Thus, in the context of 1980s rural Greece, the seemingly positive influence of the West that removed stereotypical labelling of women as inferior, had the unintentional consequence of further marginalizing some women. For those working in the home, it lessened their significance as contributors to society through their domestic labors. Further study will be required to determine whether something similar is happening to home-bound women in KP. In another expression of unintentionality, A. S. Zia, in her analysis of feminism in Pakistan, proposed that the need to publicly reject the feminist message actively propelled some women, to join radical pietist movements such as Al-Huda and Jamia Hafsa.[89] For ethnoreligious minorities in Pakistan, M.-M. Fuchs and Fuchs suggested that *victim* labelling failed in its goal to end prejudicial stereotyping. They claimed that it unintentionally widened the gap of difference between minority and majority, leading to an increase in discrimination.[90]

In KP, one of the clearest examples of unintentionality is the marked increase in influence exercised by Malala Yusafzai *after* the failed attempt on her life in 2012 by those who opposed her views.[91] At age eleven, Malala, using a pseudonym, had a following as an Urdu-language blogger and activist against extremism in Swat, a district in KP. In 2014—after the assassination attempt—when she was still only seventeen, she became the youngest person in history to receive a Nobel Prize. Honored by many countries, she has been listed as one of the most influential people across

87. Bennett, *Muslim Women of Power*, 49.

88. Schaller, "Unintended Influence," 92.

89. Zia, "Contesting the Class Question," 77.

90. Fuchs and Fuchs, "Religious Minorities"; Fuchs, "Reclaiming the Citizen."

91. Yousafzai and Lamb, *I Am Malala*.

the world. Therefore, in my handling of female influence, I have to consider unintentionality as one consequence of women's involvement in KP's public sphere. Not least, as Foucault observed, those upon whom power is being acted may not choose to submit, causing unexpected or unintentional consequences.[92] The same holds true for influence.

In my exploration of the mechanics of social influence, I have looked at relational, causative and purposive female influence and its legitimization. I have identified that women can use organizational and pre-existing cultural networks to bring their ideas and values into the hands of decision-makers. I have shown that women in minority positions can use conflict to sow doubt in the majority mindset and thus bring about change. I have also established that identity—*how* a woman is viewed by society and *how* she views herself—is fundamental to effective influence. In the KP context, female identity is inseparably interwoven into the concepts of *ɪ'zət* and *sharm* (shame) and the boundaries that society puts on these key values.

92. Foucault, "The Subject and Power," 790.

5

Honor, Shame, and *Pukhto*

THE COMPLEXITY OF HONORABLE female identity in strong patriarchal cultures, and the similarities with honor-shame as practiced in other patriarchal and/or Muslim-majority nations, makes it tempting to use these systems to decode honor and shame in the KP context. For example, Mansoor's thematic analysis of honor provided me with a helpful overview of the complexity of honor-shame as a lived concept for South Asian communities in the UK.[1] As part of her PhD thesis, she thematically explored honor as a practice that is collective, cultural, and ingrained in society. She identified that honor is linked to respect, dignity, reputation, status, wealth, and a person's "image." Honor within the family, she proposed, is centered around gender-based family roles, responsibilities, and obligations; and also male control and abuse. Within the frame of Islam, Mansoor explored honor as linked to modesty, and also to visibility, and how others perceive it. She also identified that any act of dishonor brings with it negative consequences. Her research led her to propose that honor could also be shaped by "misinterpretations of the Islamic faith" because of the way in which religion is interwoven with culture. This is a sub-theme in her thesis.[2]

However, as lived concepts, honor and its converse, shame, are heavily dependent on the unique cultural context in which they operate. For my research, this is Khyber Pakhtunkhwa. Therefore, the frames of

1. Mansoor, "Exploring Honour," 142–44.
2. Mansoor, "Exploring Honour," 140, 174–76, 208–10.

Greek patriarchy, Middle Eastern views of female ontology, and honor-shame as practiced among other Muslim communities are helpful but do not provide the fine detail essential for decoding honor-shame as a cultural practice in the KP setting. I therefore approached the concepts of honor and shame through literature focused on Pakistan and especially on *Pukhto* as the predominant culture in KP. My limitation here was language: I looked only at texts written in English.

In KP-Pakistan, the common terms for honor are *ghe'rət* and *i'zət*. *Ghe'rət* is described by the anthropologist Shah, in the context of Upper Sindh, as a "natural and therefore unquestionable ideology of honor"; a cultural norm that is both contemporary and traditional.[3] As such it has no simple definition. *Ghe'rət* encompasses the performance and upholding of respect, a male guardianship of women, property and one's good name, and the required response of anger/violence to any perceived assault on one's honor. It is often bound to female behavior, and to regulating women's conformity to societal norms. Thus, Shah proposes that *ghe'rət* is used by women as well as men to justify honor killings.[4] *i'zət*, in the same way, encompasses a range of family and community sociocultural relationships. *i'zət* includes the upholding of respect, dignity, prestige, reputation, and status. Shah's study illustrates that while the differences between *ghe'rət* and *i'zət* are difficult to explain to an outsider, the distinctions between these two terms remain clear in the minds of those who practice both forms of honor.[5]

For Pukhtun women, female honor is proved through submission to the codes of *Pukhto* and the rules of right behavior established by Islam.[6] Women are viewed as those who hold "the key to men's honor," thus any "deviance" from established norms is condemned.[7] Dishonor occurs when the female space becomes a public space; that is, a place where unrelated and/or unmarried men and women meet. It could be assumed that *parda* and strict control are the sole practice of traditional, extended rural households. However, A. Ahmed's study of Pukhtun women suggests that *parda* also operates within nuclear Pukhtun households,

---

3. Shah, *Honour Unmasked*, 1.

4. Shah, *Honour Unmasked*, 57–61.

5. Shah, *Honour Unmasked*, 57.

6. Grima, *Performance of Emotion*, 127.

7. Grima, *Performance of Emotion*, 9, 164.

although the urban environment gives greater flexibility for women to negotiate their boundaries.[8]

One expression of women's right behavior within the rules of *Pukhto* is the practice of *sharm* which can be loosely translated as shame. However, care needs to be taken with this language cognate. As the social anthropologist Herzfeld observed, the process of discussing honor-shame can be complicated by the presence of words in a language that can be understood as virtually equivalent to similar words in English.[9] One such language cognate in this book involves the Pukhto word *sharm* and the English term shame.

On one level, *sharm* functions as a social guard against any inappropriate actions that contravene the established codes of honorable behavior; actions that would bring shame on the collective family. Failure to comply with societal norms and customs brings with it a loss of honor and also ostracism for the individual and his/her immediate family, just as compliance affirms honorable identity and ensures inclusion.[10]

In addition, for women in KP, *sharm* functions as a form of inverted honor, a positive virtue, that is essential to female honorable identity. Grima wrote that "women in the presence of men exhibit *sharm* by silence, subservience, and obedience, by asking no questions, lowering the eyes, refraining from eating until after the men are done, and sitting on a lower level than men."[11] The cultural performance of *sharm* thus operates as a positive practice of modesty, subservience, and honor. In April 2024, I talked about family life with Yasmin, a Pukhtun widow with five daughters and one son. She was not one of my original sample group, but someone I interviewed as part of my ongoing interest in how honor works for women in KP. Yasmin boasted to me that the only job her son has to do at home is bathe himself and clean his motorbike. Everything else is done for him. Her boast is a wonderful example of *sharm* as a positive virtue. The lower place of service taken by Yasmin and her daughters is an expression of *ɪˈzət*—theirs and the son/brother they are honoring.

Into this discussion comes an understanding, a societal known, that the work done by women carries less value than the work done by men. Moreover, while domestic jobs are honorable for women, they are shameful for men. As explained by one of the women in my sample group, when

8. A. Ahmed, *Sorrow and Joy*, 53.

9. Herzfeld, "Honor and Shame," 340.

10. Gill and Brah, "'Honour'-Based Violence," 73–74.

11. Grima, *Performance of Emotion*, 36, 37.

a boy is not active and wants to stay at home, people will ask why he is behaving like a girl. For a man to be accused of behaving like a woman is shaming language. The respondent used the term "abusive."

Ghe'rət, i'zət and *sharm* thus stand, together with patriarchy, as entrenched societal norms in KP's melon field, again with the assumption that they also directly impact the lives of non-Pukhtun and non-Muslim women. Stories of female influence cannot be told without reference to these powerful societal norms. Therefore, to aid understanding, I default to the term *sharm* where possible, rather than use the English word shame. In the same way, I use the term *i'zət* in preference to the English word honor.

In this discussion of honor-shame, it would be incorrect to conclude that *Pukhto*, which is integral to defining the concepts of *i'zət* and *sharm* for Pukhtuns, is unchanging, and that its codes are fixed. The Afghan-American scholar Kakar explored changes in identity and cultural practice among rural Afghan Pukhtuns who had become refugees in some urban areas of KP in the 1980s and 1990s.[12] Kakar discovered that the Afghan women, with male compliance, had adapted their definition and practice of *Pukhto* so that it could meld with their new status as refugees, and also be aligned with the *Pukhto* of their Pakistani urban hosts. In the process of adapting to new circumstances, their self-definition of *Pukhto* remained unchanged. They were still Pukhtuns, but as a societal group they had redefined how their *Pukhto* was to be practiced.

In 2012, a Pukhtun professor from a KP university observed to me that "*Pukhto* doesn't change, even when times change, although expressions of *Pukhto* change." That is, *Pukhto* remains the same at its core, expressing constant values. It is the practice of these values that changes. However, she felt that *Pukhto* can be destroyed by religious extremism, because it had to power to change both values and practice. The anthropologist Barth addressed this issue in his discussion of Pukhtun autonomy.[13] He suggested that where change is endorsed by a Pukhtun majority, the basic characteristics of identity start to be modified in a manner associated with honor rather than failure, thus maintaining autonomy.

12. Kakar, "Tribal Law."
13. Barth, "Pathan Identity," 133.

WOMEN'S PRESUMED POWERLESSNESS: GENDERED SPACE

Honor in Pukhtun society is centered in *parda* as a system of gendered space that positions women in the domestic sphere.[14] Abu-Lughod is representative of the academics who have written to rebut an assertion, observed as coming from Western popular media, that the system of *parda*, particularly veiling, works to render women as powerless victims of male subjugation, as those without agency.[15] While Western-style feminism may not be needed to *save* Muslim women from perceived oppression, at the same time, *parda does place boundaries* on women in KP and, therefore, its impact on women's ability to influence for change has to be considered. A Pukhtun colleague, talking to me about his culture in 2025, made this comment.

> Pukhtun women have a lot of restrictions on their lives from
> their husbands and other family members, and they do not have
> the freedom, yet they abide by these restrictions respectfully.
> Whatever their elders and family members want, they want to
> live their lives according to that.

As a Pukhtun man living in a twenty-first century semi-urban setting, he had observed that it takes strength and self-sacrifice for women to live within the very real restrictions of *parda* and *Pukhto*.

Foucault, in his analysis of discipline and punishment, observed that society has historically created "enclosures" as a means by which the powerful maintain control.[16] His focus was the prison system, as representative of the complex, hierarchical enclosures that are "integrated into the very body of state apparatus."[17] Applied to gendered space—the separation of women and men from each other in the domestic and public realms—these enclosures work to strengthen and perpetuate distinctions that most commonly attribute greater status to men. They also work to reduce "women's access to socially valued knowledge."[18] Women's domestic-sphere knowledge of cooking and childcare, for example, is understood to carry less societal value than male workplace knowledge.

---

14. Grima, *Performance of Emotion.*

15. Abu-Lughod, *Muslim Women.*

16. Foucault, *Discipline and Punish,* 141–42.

17. Foucault, *Discipline and Punish,* 115–16.

18. Spain, "Gendered Spaces," 137.

As a researcher of urban and environmental planning, Spain explored the concept of gendered space.[19] She proposed that gendered space is comprised of four components that are integrated into state and society: anthropological, design, sociological and psychological.[20] The anthropological component relates to cultural mores. Design references the spaces that separate men from women. The sociological component identifies institutions as perpetuating differences in status, based on gender. The last component, psychological, is focused on the socialization that produces gendered behavior. Spain's concepts of gendered space, comes alongside Foucault's understanding of complex enclosures or structures,[21] to show how the designation of different spaces as male-female operates in KP, and other Middle Eastern societies, and its impact on female influence.

Anthropological Gendered Space

Mernissi and Lindholm, from their studies of male-female dynamics in Arab and Pukhtun societies, observed that the cultural more behind the system of *parda* is men's need to be separated or protected from female sexuality.[22] This is Foucault's argument in practice: a separate (disciplinary) place is used by some in society to locate, access, and control another portion of society.[23] In KP, as Mernissi and Mills have argued for their contexts, male control of women is required because their nature is believed to hold the power to deceive and defeat men.[24] Male honor is thus preserved by excluding men and women from each other's spaces. Women's access to the shared spaces of education and employment, for example, are at the discretion of the senior males in their households. In terms of influence, the well-established tradition of *parda*, with its links to *Pukhto* and Islam, operates as a major obstacle to Pukhtun women's presence in the public sphere.

Given the strength of *Pukhto* and Islam in KP, it can be inferred that non-Pukhtun and/or non-Muslim women are also impacted by *parda* as

19. Spain, "Gendered Spaces."

20. Spain, "Gendered Spaces," 147.

21. Foucault, *Discipline and Punish*.

22. Mernissi, *Beyond the Veil*, 32–45; Lindholm, *Generosity and Jealousy*, 219.

23. Foucault, *Discipline and Punish*, 143.

24. Mills, "Covered and Covert."

a societal norm. This is in addition to any cultural mores coming from their own ethno-religious backgrounds or societies. However, Pukhtuns suggest that the inclusion of *parda* as a societal code within *Pukhto* makes it a stronger religio-social norm for them than for others.[25] Whether true or not, the reality is that the religio-cultural mores behind the system of *parda* make it difficult for Pukhtun women to access the public sphere. This is not the stereotypical female subjugation that Abu-Lughod is rebutting, nor is it a sign of female weakness.[26] However, it does indicate a degree of powerlessness, established in cultural norms, that requires recognition in the analysis of female influence in KP's public sphere.

The norms of *parda* also work in another way that impacts female influence. *Parda* establishes a homosocial norm in which men and women operate primarily within the frame of their own gender.[27] This makes a segregated working environment a more comfortable norm for women, and for men. Yet, one consequence of this is that women's access to the knowledge and skills available to men is reduced. Access to lesser knowledge and/or less access to knowledge impacts women's ability to strategize and to think creatively. This, in turn, perpetuates male-female distinctions. It also strengthens the belief that men are rightly attributed greater status because of their greater abilities. In addition, learned exclusion affects issues of trust and communication.[28] Therefore, men and women have to learn the skill of working together in a shared space; a skill often not taught in the home.

Design in Gendered Space

The component of *design* identified by Spain includes the architecture that physically separates genders and the "geographic" positioning of men and women in separate areas.[29] In traditional Pukhtun homes, a room (*betak*) or rooms (*hujra*) is set aside for male use. These rooms are symbolic of male power and prestige.[30] Separate voting stations for women, as well as segregated schools and colleges, are also geographic

---

25. Grima, *Performance of Emotion*, 83.

26. Abu-Lughod, *Muslim Women*.

27. Kakar, "Tribal Law," 6–7.

28. Mernissi, *Beyond the Veil*, 126.

29. Spain, "Gendered Spaces," 140.

30. A. Ahmed, *Sorrow and Joy*, 50–52; Lindholm, *Generosity and Jealousy*, 22–23.

examples of gendered space design. Design thus re-enforces the belief that the public sphere is male, the place of economic provision, and political, ideological and military power.[31] As already noted, the knowledge associated with this place of power brings with it higher social value than any knowledge obtained in the domestic realm.

In addition, the separate female space is often inferior to the space given to men. This is a natural outworking of the lower status attributed to women's gender.[32] This has implications for the physical positioning of women in the workplace. Taj, for example, in her PhD. study of women leaders in KP's educational field, recorded the complaints from her respondents regarding inadequate office spaces.[33] These spaces were designed to intimidate them, and hinder their work. Design in gendered space, therefore, carries the potential to undermine women's authority as leaders and influencers because, in the KP-Pakistan context, it can be used to place women at a lower level than men.

Sociological Gendered Space

Yet, positively, the Pukhtun anthropologist A. Ahmed, writing of the domestic sphere, argues that the system of *parda* gives "women control over their own enclosure."[34] The suggestion is that, within separate spaces, women do not have to operate in a place of submission and obedience to men but are free to be themselves, even as they remain within the boundaries of a patriarchal society. They can use these gynesocial spaces to advance female knowledge. These are spaces where religious and sociopolitical information and practices can be safely passed to other women locally, and even internationally.[35] This is a seeming parallel to Foucault's understanding of "functional inversion": the place of separation becomes a space in which skills, and morals, are taught for the benefit of society.[36] At the same time, these *sociological* structures can also work to perpetuate privileging based on knowledge. Mumtaz and Shaheed, for example, were concerned about the sociological impact of separate

---

31. Maududi, *Al-Hijab*.

32. Grima, *Secrets From The Field*, 9; Lindholm, *Generosity and Jealousy*, 220.

33. Taj, "Female Educational Leaders," 95.

34. A. Ahmed, *Sorrow and Joy*, 50.

35. Coleman, *Paradise*; Mahmood, *Politics of Piety*; Shanneik, *The Art of Resistance*.

36. Foucault, *Discipline and Punish*, 210.

female universities.[37] They foresaw that a lesser educational investment in all-female institutions, caused by entrenched patriarchal attitudes, would further disadvantage women competing against men for jobs in the public sphere, and thus enable men to retain their status/power.

Psychological Gendered Space

The *psychological* component of gendered space encompasses the act of socialization—the solidifying of a message as true or false—that occurs within a "dwelling."[38] In KP-Pakistan, the message being socialized is patriarchal, patrilineal, and hierarchical. It begins in the home but is present in the workplace. It privileges boys/men and marginalizes girls/women and yet is perpetuated by women as well as men.[39] It also upholds the traditional, conservative understanding of an ideal Muslim woman as obedient and submissive.[40] Sumaira Rehman, in her PhD. study of Pakistani female entrepreneurs, noted the negative impact on women of a socialized message of conformity. She observed that it worked to "suppress imagination and innovative ability," factors that were essential to any entrepreneur establishing and maintaining a business.[41]

Gendered space, therefore, in its anthropological, design, sociological and psychological forms *does have* a negative impact on women in KP. As women in KP-Pakistan acknowledge, *parda* as a system and a mind-set can hinder their ability to influence in the public sphere. A senior public servant, Hina, speaking in English in her online interview with me in November 2020, recalled an early encounter with a senior leader. On entering a meeting where everyone else was male, she was reprimanded by this leader for being present. He told her that the scriptures teach that "women should follow *parda*. Women are weak." While not all men are this direct, in practical terms, such attitudes inevitably curtail female public-sphere influence. This is a subject that occurred often in the interviews I conducted.

37. Mumtaz and Shaheed, *Women of Pakistan*, 86–90.

38. Spain, "Gendered Spaces," 147.

39. Isran and Isran, "Patriarchy and Women."

40. Ahmad, *Transforming Faith*, 55.

41. Rehman, "Women Entrepreneurs," 145.

THE IMPORTANCE OF RECOGNIZED PRESTIGE

The converse of male privilege in the public sphere is female influence within the domestic realm, where women can exercise very real power. The traditional position of prestige within a Middle Eastern home is that of matriarch. She represents the pinnacle of power within a system of authority that operates among women within the domestic sphere. Thus, a bride entering her husband's extended family home is subordinate to the senior women until her turn comes to occupy the position of matriarchal mother-in-law. From that place, she is able to exercise the same authority over her subservient daughters-in-law as had been imposed on her.[42] In addition, the matriarch builds strong relationship with her son(s). This develops into life-long bonds of gratitude from son to mother that are stronger than a man's relationship with his wife.[43] Yasmin's story about the way she cared for her son, told earlier in this chapter, illustrates the way in which mother-son bonds are constructed. It also documents the privileging of sons over daughters that still continues in twenty-first century Pukhtun homes.

Yasmin's story also demonstrates the way in which, in large Pukhtun families, a mother is assisted by her daughters. Lindholm had observed that the role of helper is most often taken up by the eldest daughter.[44] In adulthood, this positions the eldest sister to continue to speak with authority to her younger siblings, because she had been *as a mother* to them in their growing-up. It also gives rise to a tight brother-elder sister bond in which a Pukhtun man will go to his eldest sister for advice and financial assistance.[45]

At the same time, the recognized prestige associated with the positions of mother(-in-law) or eldest sister in Muslim/Pukhtun culture is not comparable to, for example, the status given to Greek women because of their place in the *nikokyrio*.[46] The *nikokyrio* is an economic institution that functions betwixt the home and public spheres in which men and women are accorded the same prestige. However, the roles of matriarch and elder sister are limited to the domestic realm. In addition, the cultural

42. Isran and Isran, "Patriarchy and Women," 841; Kandiyoti, "Bargaining with Patriarchy," 282.

43. Mernissi, *Beyond the Veil*, 121–22.

44. Lindholm, *Generosity and Jealousy*, 15.

45. Lindholm, *Generosity and Jealousy*, 127.

46. Salamone and Stanton, "The *Nikokyra*."

mores of gendered space attribute a lesser prestige to mother(-in-law) or sister because they are viewed as subordinate to men.[47] Therefore, any influence exercised from this space will carry less weight than male influence despite son to mother or brother to elder-sister bonds.

47. Lindholm, *Generosity and Jealousy,* 173.

6

Intrusion of the Modern

IN THE COMPLEXITY OF life for women in KP's public sphere, as well as interacting with the norms of culture and religious tradition, they are also impacted by political and economic factors. This includes the availability of global products, and the intrusion of Western ideas and concepts. There is a desire to be up to date with the latest inventions and innovations. There are those in society who want the products, the technologies, the education, and the links with the outside world that the modern brings with it.[1] However, modernism is not simply another name for Westernization: the export of Western values and cultures. In Pakistan, Westernization is associated with a modern-day imperialism that pushes on the wounds of past colonialism. Western values are to be resisted. These values are seen as coming from Western media, the strategies of multinational companies, and the policies of international and national non-governmental organizations (INGOs, NGOs). They are popularly believed to be indicative of materialism, individualism, a loss of spirituality, and moral depravity particularly in relation to women. The objection is not to Western products but to the spread of Western values.[2]

1. Maqsood, *Pakistani Middle Class*, 136.
2. Ahmad, *Transforming Faith*, 132–36.

RESPONSES TO MODERNISM

As society in KP-Pakistan interacts with the modern, and the Western, two major religious responses have emerged. The first is Islamic modernism. This is a desire to reconcile Islam with the modern approaches and products that are becoming a part of Pakistani society. The second is a push to Islamize modernity; that is, to protect twenty-first century Pakistan from outside intrusion through a return to the traditions and values of the past.

Islamic Modernism

Islamic modernism seeks a nuanced reconciliation of Islam with modernity. For many in Pakistan and the wider Middle East, it is an approach to Islam that wants to recenter it within the modern world. For some, the goal is to weave Islamic traditions, jurisprudence, politics, and education into a framework of modern science and technology in a way that will modernize Islam.[3] For others, the combination of "Islamic traditions with Western liberalism . . . generate[s] a solid defensive shield against the West" and Westernization.[4] It includes what Haddad, as a scholar of Islam and Christian-Muslim relations calls "Islamification."[5] This is the Islamizing of Western laws that is part of the process of modernizing Islam. The Islamic studies scholar Hallaq, however, questions whether "modern" (Western) societal changes, such as equal status for women (and religious minorities), can be given the religious authenticity and cultural legitimacy that Muslim populations will accept.[6]

Modern values and ideas are visibly changing societal norms for the younger generation in other, comparable Muslim societies. This was illustrated by the anthropologist Hegland as she explored the changing attitudes to the mores of traditional marriage expressed by young Shi'i women in Iran.[7] The choice of a girl's husband is traditionally handled by her parents. However, exposure to the modern in the form of education, and mainstream and social media, had empowered these young women

3. Jamal, *Jamaat-e-Islami Women*; Stowasser, *Women in the Qur'an*; Haddad and Esposito, *Islam and Social Change*; Parray, "Islamic Thought," 79–81.

4. Shehadeh, *The Idea of Women*, xi.

5. Haddad and Stowasser, *Islamic Law*, 2.

6. Hallaq, "The Shari'a."

7. Hegland, "Marriage Modifications."

to vocalize their own opinions regarding matrimony, and to resist the authority of their parents and religious leaders in the choice of a husband.

A similar resistance to the old, and an allegiance to the modern, in Pakistan's public sphere is captured in a statement by Haeri. She wrote that, "professional women demand to be treated as citizens of a modern Islamic state, with equal rights, privileges, respect, and indeed honor: honor based on their personal worth and on their professional participation in society, not on the 'symbolic capital' of female chastity and purity."[8] Haeri's research had led her to believe that women in Pakistan's public sphere are asking for a change to religio-cultural norms that would redefine their modern societal identity. These changes need not come from the West, but simply from other parts of Pakistan.

In May 2024, Hafsa, a Christian medical professional brought up in KP, spoke to me (in English) about the hold "the past" and traditional values still have on society in KP. Hafsa was not part of my original sample group, but someone I was interviewing about female honor. Still a young woman, she had also lived in Lahore and witnessed the freedom women have in that city to make independent choices and enjoy a greater sense of equality with men. She noted that in contrast, in "conservative" KP, families teach their children to respect men more than women, and everyone monitors what women are doing. Her desire was to see the modernity of Lahore enacted in the streets of Peshawar. Her influence was limited to her family and the workplace, yet at the same time, her changed values challenge the established structures and relationships of KP society.

Western modernism has an additional role in Pakistani society. It operates as a mirror that is used to reflect and/or measure social distinctives. The social anthropologist, Maqsood, in the Lahore context, had observed the ways in which the West is used as an outside audience, the *other* against which a Muslim community measures its status, piety, and modernity.[9] Traditionally this measure was used by Pakistan's established elite. However, Maqsood had observed the same process being taken up by a newly emerging, educated Islamic middle class. In this context, the West is no longer the purveyor of those values that are deemed to be harmful to Pakistani society. For the elite and middle classes, the modern West operates as "a point of reference and appeal, a source of new ideas and lifestyles."[10]

8. Haeri, *No Shame*, 41.

9. Maqsood, *Pakistani Middle Class*, 151.

10. Maqsood, *Pakistani Middle Class*, 151.

However, the West can also be viewed as representing those who stand religiously and culturally outside Islam, and who hold orientalist perceptions of Muslim nations. With its origins in the writings of Said,[11] modern orientalism references an entrenched but inaccurate view of Muslims and Muslim culture attributed as coming from the West.[12] In her book, *Pious Fashion*, the religious ethics scholar Bucar criticizes the West for its perception of veiling as symbolic of women's oppression in Islam and of fanatical Islamic piety. She begins her introduction with the statement: "Many Westerners view modest clothing as the ultimate sign of Muslim women's oppression."[13] Such stereotypical Western views were seen by Bucar, and others, as obscuring the vast variety of other realities lived out by multiple Muslim women within their own contexts.

An analysis and possible rebuttal of such perceptions as representative of the Western academic as opposed to Western popular views of Muslim culture fall outside the frame of this book. For the same reason, I do not explore Occidentalism or the legacy of Pakistan's colonial past, although I recognize that these realities impact attitudes in KP-Pakistan. However, foundational to my research is an understanding that Muslim and non-Muslim women live complex and at times contradictory lives. Clearly, there is no representative Muslim or non-Muslim woman in KP or elsewhere. Yet, in my research, I have to recognize that popular stereotypical views of Muslim societies coming from the West will generate reciprocal stereotypical views of the West by those living in KP-Pakistan. It is possible, therefore, that strongly held views of the West have impacted comments made by some of those I interviewed and, thus, affect the conclusions I draw in this book regarding the shape of female influence in KP. I follow up on this thought later in the book.

Islamize Modernity

In Muslim-majority nations, especially those with a history of Western colonialism, the amalgam of modernism, modernization, and Westernization has caused what Mernissi called a "psychological" response from some in the *umma* (Muslim community).[14] This is, in part, an uninten-

---

11. Said, *Orientalism*.

12. Abu-Lughod, *Muslim Women*, chap. 1.

13. Bucar, *Pious Fashion*, 1.

14. Mernissi, *Beyond the Veil*, 23.

tional outcome of attempts by some to modernize Pakistan, in that it has led to the strengthening of conservative religious views. Perceived as being under threat from the West, the conservative message is that Muslims need to return to the security of established traditions. *Shari'a* is recast as a "symbol of Muslim identity."[15] Traditional women are said to represent "a more 'genuine' cultural identity," and modern women become "representative of everything that appears threatening in the new and quickly changing world."[16] Thus, conservative Islamist religio-political groups, like the Jamaat-e-Islami, see themselves as essential to Islam's recovery from the process of degeneration caused by the West's moral depravity. In addition, as Ahmad observed, since the 1980s many in Pakistan have internalized a state-generated view of society established by an Islamization process that includes a conservative presentation of the ideal Muslim woman.[17] Such views, internalized by men as well as by women, will (unconsciously) impact their understanding of women's roles and their influence in the public sphere.

According to Jamal and Maqsood, Islamic and Islamist modernists aim their messages at Pakistan's newly emerging pious middle class.[18] This social class is comprised of upwardly mobile professionals who, Maqsood argues, are competing for control of the political space traditionally occupied by the secular upper-middle to elite classes. This political space is where issues of citizenship, democracy, and identity are decided. Maqsood's study of the changes that the new, modern Islamic middle class is making to Pakistani society is based on the specific demographics of Lahore. However, she proposed that her findings can be applied to the urban middle class throughout Pakistan. The extent to which Maqsood's arguments are representative of a changing class dynamic in KP lies outside the scope of my research. However, it potentially impacted the final sample group in my study, in that it contained respondents from the middle class. The importance of the modern to my research, and the parts played by conservative and traditional thought, is the way in which each of these differing yet overlapping views has the power to obstruct or facilitate influence because of their presence in the soil of KP's proverbial, public sphere melon field. These views are represented in figure 7.

15. Mernissi, *Beyond the Veil*, 23.
16. Moghadam, *Modernizing Women*, 106.
17. Ahmad, *Transforming Faith*, 137.
18. Jamal, *Jamaat-e-Islami Women*, 144; Maqsood, *Pakistani Middle Class*.

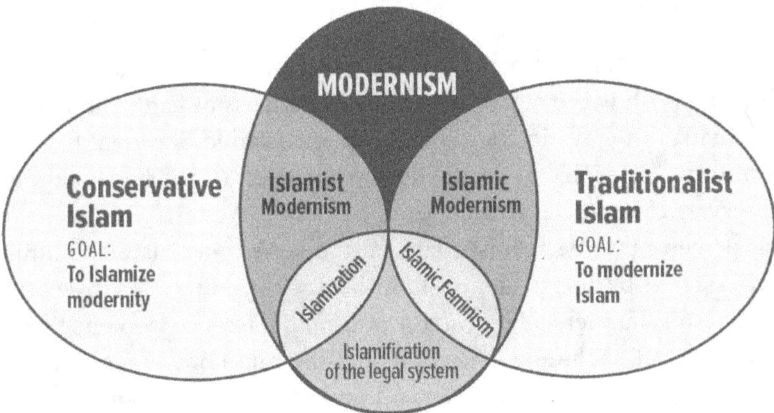

Figure 7. Responses to Modernism.

THE WOMEN'S MOVEMENT

In the 1980s, Islamization's changes to women's social and legal status became the catalyst for the modern women's movement in Pakistan. Islamization, first introduced by Zia-ul-Haq in the 1980s, is a process designed to bring Pakistan into conformity with the tenets of Islam.[19] Commentators have asserted that it began a battle between traditionalists, conservatives and modernists for the moral high ground, with women as a locus of identity for each group. It also brought a movement of women into the nation's public spaces in a way that continues to today.

In a definition of terms, however, the women involved in the modern women's movement, are not necessarily "modern women." In Pakistan, that term is most often used of women from the upper and elite classes who tend to be secular in outlook, and thus more liberal in their practice of Islam. In addition, I use the term *women's movement* to mean the many movements or groups of women active in Pakistan, and in comparable Muslim-majority contexts. Significantly, these include feminism, activism, the piety movement, and women's affiliation with religio-political Islam.

19. Hine, "The Hard Knot," 3; Weiss, *Interpreting Islam*, chap. 4.

Feminism

In her introduction to *Contesting Feminisms*, the women's studies scholar Ahmed-Ghosh wrote of two broad "theorizations" of feminism that operate in majority Muslim nations: secular and Islamic. She identified both "feminisms" as problematic for Muslim societies. In her understanding, conservatives conflate secular feminism with Western feminism and thus perceive it to be against Islam. At the same time, Islamic feminism is considered by liberal feminists to be an "oxymoron."[20] However, in broad terms, I understand *secular feminism* to reference women's links to Western input, including education, and the cause of women's rights as human rights. Also in broad terms, I understand *Islamic feminism*, also called *Islamic modernism*, to be the approach taken by Muslim feminist intellectuals who see in the Qur'an the guarantees of equal rights that had been lost through interpretations that privilege men.[21]

In opposition to expressions of feminism in Pakistan stands conservative religious thinking. In KP-Pakistan, this includes the perception that the secular (and/or secularism) is a form of atheism promoted by the West.[22] Therefore, Western-educated, often upper-class feminists are to be resisted as those presumed to challenge the very nature of a society founded in and for Islam. As a consequence, and as an influence strategy, despite the name "secular," most secular feminists in Pakistan know that the battle for women's rights has to be fought within the religious frame of Islam if mindsets are to be changed.[23] Secular feminists are, thus, those who use "Islamic modernist arguments in tandem with secular nationalist and humanist arguments" to advance women's social and legal rights.[24] At the same time, secular feminists are aware that a too narrow Islamic frame works to marginalize and exclude any "moderate or progressive religious discourse" about women's rights.[25]

Similarly, Islamic feminism operates alongside secular feminism in a tactical recognition that the issues of Islamization require "a religious response."[26] Both these feminisms illustrate the fine line between Islamic

20. Ahmed-Ghosh, *Contesting Feminisms*, 3.
21. Badran, "Islamic Feminism," 29.
22. Iqtidar, *Secularizing Islamists*, 7.
23. Coleman, *Paradise*, 131; Mumtaz and Shaheed, *Women of Pakistan*, 153–60.
24. Badran, "Islamic Feminism," 29.
25. Khan, "The Politics of Activism," 40.
26. Coleman, *Paradise*, 131.

and secular in a religiously conservative setting such as KP. Islamic feminism, in part, is seeking a more comfortable way for Pakistani women to engage in advocacy. Its goal is to challenge and change public opinion that gives the aura of being "divine" to the traditional patriarchal, societal norms that marginalize women.[27] Thus, Muslim feminist scholars and writers work to address women's social as well as religious and constitutional rights by bridging the gap between Qur'anic ideals and actual practice.[28] Traditionally, *ijtihād* encompasses a long established methodology for interpreting the Qur'an and Sunna. However, pious women are engaging in the (re-)interpretation of religious texts from a feminist perspective. They are particularly concerned with those texts that seem to justify discrimination, gender separation, and violence. For example, female approaches to the Qur'an in the English language have been undertaken by Stowasser, Wadud, and Barlas among others. In part, Islamic feminism is seeking to influence those Muslim women who have "been caught in a conflict between their genuine admiration and devotion to Islam and their dismay at its apparent denial of their status as full human beings equal with men."[29]

In terms of influence, the impact of secular and Islamic feminisms on KP's society is unclear. Many in Pakistan are uncomfortable with the term feminist because it is perceived to be Western and anti-men, although feminism as a movement has some traction among the younger generation.[30] My own conversations with open-minded male friends and colleagues in KP about the women's movement and feminism underscores this resistance. My friends referenced the overt feminism expressed in *Aurat* (women's) marches, especially the excesses of younger women's activism in the 2019 march. In the *Aurat* marches, Islamic and secular feminist protestors usually carry banners demanding the end of discrimination and violence against women. They also challenge the patriarchal nature of the home.[31] The protesters' goal is to bring into the public discourse issues of gender-identity, sexuality, and entrenched patriarchal norms that have yet to change despite forty years of activism.

27. Mumtaz and Shaheed, *Women of Pakistan*, 155.

28. Badran, "Islamic Feminism," 29; Barlas, "Islamic Feminism," 18; Esposito, *Islam*, 175–78.

29. Karmi, "Women," 79–80.

30. Saigol, "Feminism," 17; Rehman, *Womansplaining*, 7–8, 17; Khan, "The Politics of Activism" 41–42.

31. Khan, "The Politics of Activism," 41.

However, in 2019 some of the banners carried messages that were presented in language that strayed towards the crude. As the Pakistani human rights activist Mohydin noted at the time, these and the anti-social behavior of some of the protestors caused deep offence, especially as a few women publicly removed some of their clothing.[32]

The suggestion coming from Mohydin is that rather than feminism acting as an influence mechanism, it is feminists—that is, women working in male-dominated professions and their resistance to abuse—that causes change.[33] The findings of my research align with this claim. Rather than a movement, it is ordinary women in KP's public sphere who are responsible for societal change. They have influenced family to gain the right to be in education and employment, and they are exercising influence as part of their public roles. It is these local, personal and unarticulated expressions of feminism that should form an additional framework for women's studies analysis regarding the effectiveness of feminism in a religiously conservative and patriarchal society.

In addition, the suggestion that it is the *person*—not the cause—that influences provided me with a key to the identification of the techniques and strategies women are using to influence in KP. If an individual stands at the heart of influence, then in KP's patriarchal society, the strategies of *ijtihād* or private advocacy or public activism take second place to the mechanisms used by a woman to demonstrate that she has the right to be listened to and followed. However, the agency of an individual cannot be separated easily from that of women as a collective in KP-Pakistan.

Shanneik's study of Shi'i women's individual and collective agency is set in a different space to that of KP's public sphere.[34] Yet, her descriptions of individual-collective agency reflect the dynamic being discussed here. She wrote of "new" women using the opportunities given to them by the fall of Saddam Hussein to become agents of change. Part of this agency was the women's involvement in social media. They used social media platforms to express their individual-collective viewpoints with a desire to influence others. Yet beyond the influence of their messages, simply by participating in practices and places that were formerly closed to women, these Shi'i ladies were exercising role-model influence. Their presence in these spaces offered others the opportunity to reject and criticize their actions, which also served to underscore their presence in these

32. Mohydin, "The Aurat March."
33. Mohydin, "Field Notes," 248.
34. Shanneik, *Art of Resistance.*

spaces. In the same way, individual women who are present in KP's public sphere, including the sphere of social media, are opening up spaces that women collectively have not occupied before. These spaces are then confirmed by the criticism as well as the endorsement of others.

Activism

Traditionally, activism in Pakistan has been the way by which primarily upper-class women have brought the message of social change to society. Their goal has been to challenge political policies that they believe marginalize women.[35] Hine, whose PhD. research came out of her own lived experiences in Pakistan, referred to female activism as "the collective work and action of women to engage the institutions of the state and society in negotiations for change in gender relations and the betterment of women [*sic*] position socially, economically and politically."[36] The social activist Saeed identified activists in Pakistan as those who engage in public protest against legislation that discriminates against women, and who use research, consultancy, and strategic alliances aimed at changing the opinions of decision makers.[37] Since the 1980s, women have been collectively contesting Islamization as a process being used for patriarchal and political purposes that reshapes their identity and reduces their freedoms.[38] They work to identify and remove codified traditions—often equated with religious doctrines—that disenfranchise women (and other minority groups) in society.

From the beginning, activists in Pakistan have also engaged in a pro-normative offensive aimed at placing women's activism into the fabric of Muslim-Pakistani life. The goal is to give activism and activists a religious and cultural legitimacy, and to counter the assertion that female activism is "alien" to Islamic societies because of its association with the West and the modern.[39] Within the frame of social influence, this dovetails with my earlier discussion about the importance of societal legitimacy. To be influential, a message must be shaped in a way that gives it, and those proposing it, a societal legitimacy. In the 1990s, this took the form of

35. Mumtaz and Shaheed, *Women of Pakistan*.
36. Hine, "The Hard Knot," 1–2.
37. Saeed, *Tapestry*.
38. Khan, *Women's Movement*, chap. 3.
39. Shaheed, *Great Ancestors*, xi.

NGO development, as a vehicle through which the women's movement could bring social change to marginalized women. Yet, this model has been criticized by some, because it moved the women's movement away from the traditional aim of bringing change to socio-religious legislation that discriminated against women.[40]

Shaheed suggests that twenty-first century activism in Pakistan reflects the loss of young Pakistani women's confidence in the state's ability to implement real change, and also a prioritization of sexuality that is a focus of millennial activism globally.[41] In the "deeply difficult . . . complex and dangerous terrain" of activism, the intrusion of the modern, in the form of internet and social media, gives women alternative public spaces in which to share opinions, and to "out" (i.e., name and shame) individuals.[42] The suggestion is that, as an influence strategy, activism conducted on the modern platforms of social media amplifies women's voices, enabling them to reach a larger audience from a place of relative anonymity.[43] Social media also provides platforms where sensitive issues can be discussed, and it enables women to build relational networks in which they can find support.

The long-term effectiveness of activism through social media in Pakistan is still being measured. However, reflecting on the lack of visible leadership in social media platforms as well as digital activism's unwillingness to engage with state institutions, Dad and Khan concluded that social media gains were "intangible."[44] Even in the public spaces of social media, the naming of individuals could carry legal repercussions for activists, especially when their attempts to expose harassment challenged male privilege and male honor.[45] Yet, Rehman pointed to "a sense of urgency and hope . . . [and] a rising sense of confidence in collective and individual action" that she considered as positives for activism moving forward.[46] In Pakistan, activists continue to challenge the powerful religious lobby that works towards the continuation of the Islamization process. They speak out against heads of state and politicians, who they

---

40. Khan, *Women's Movement*, 285.

41. Shaheed, "The Women's Movement," 30.

42. Khan, "Politics of Activism," 40.

43. Dad and Khan, "#MeToo," 176.

44. Dad and Khan, "#MeToo," 179, 180.

45. Dad and Khan, "#MeToo," 176–77, 179–80.

46. Rehman, *Womansplaining*, 17.

believe have failed to provide and/or implement legislation aimed at improving women's rights.[47]

Although advocacy and protest have resulted in the introduction of laws that protect women, Muslim and non-Muslim, from abuse, female activism has been unable to ignite a movement that encompasses women from all classes.[48] Reasons for this include elite/intellectual disconnectedness,[49] and a failure to engage with the real issues faced by women from less privileged classes.[50] In addition, digital activism works to exclude the many (lower-class) women who do not have access to smart phones or the internet.

The social activist bell hooks, (who writes her pen name using all lower-case letters), reflecting on marginalization as a place of creativity and power, argued that the margins were a place to determinedly inhabit in order to sustain resistance rather than submit to the dominating group's expectations.[51] The international law scholar, Bennoune, in her book *Your Fatwa Doesn't Apply Here*, presents Muslim women's stories that portray this type of creative resistance. Among those she met, as part of her research into women's untold fight against Muslim fundamentalism, were seemingly *ordinary* women: "housewives, grandmothers," and "dancers." However, many of the people she lists were from socially influential levels of society. Thus, her study emphasizes that public resistance, creativity, and power is most often available to women with education, and social and professional status. Taken together with the situation for women in Pakistan, it suggests that activism as an influence strategy for social change is not easily accessible to those from the lower classes in KP and comparable settings.

There is a gap in the literature with regard to female activism in Pakistan which includes the poor representation of non-Muslim voices in the documentation of women's collective and personal action. Women's efforts to protect religious minority rights have some inclusion in the literature. Khan, for example, references Muslim activism on behalf of Pakistan's religious minorities after the arrest of Asia Bibi, a Christian woman accused of blasphemy.[52] The Pakistani social activist Saeed

47. Ahmad, *Transforming Faith*, 30–37.

48. Khan, "Politics of Activism," 38.

49. Rouse, "Gender and Identity."

50. Hine, "The Hard Knot," 14.

51. hooks, "Marginality," 341.

52. Khan, *Women's Movement*, 271–72.

included, in her collection of stories about women's struggles for their rights, the account of Pakistan's first Hindu woman senator.[53] However, the extent of non-Muslim women's contribution to activism in Pakistan remains to be documented and analyzed.

Piety Movement

One response to the intrusion of the modern into Pakistani society has been the piety movement. Unlike feminism and activism that interact with the general public, the piety movement operates within an all-female environment, as a gynesocial enclave within the male-dominated public sphere. Its significance as an agent for social change was documented by Mahmood in the context of Egypt, the educationalist Dale writing of a mosque movement in Syria, and Shanneik in her exploration of Shi'i women's piety in the Middle East and Europe. Dale suggested that women who engage with the piety movement are influenced to take on new forms of religious practice, and to move beyond traditional family ties to make new allegiances with "alternate" faith communities.[54] For the Shi'i women in Shanneik's study, participation in religious practices, including some that had formerly been male-only expressions of religious devotion, enables them to express their socio-political allegiance to their faith community.

The most prominent expression of the piety movement in KP-Pakistan is Al-Huda, an international welfare foundation originally created in 1994 by the Islamic scholar Dr. Farhat Hashmi as a Qur'anic seminary for middle and upper-class women.[55] Sadaf Ahmad identified four components to Al-Huda's ability to influence women to change their thinking and lifestyles. These are Hashmi's status in society, her role as an academic, the group's modern message, and the ways in which it disseminates that message.[56] Each of these components provide insights into female influence in the public sphere.

First, Hashmi connects with her audience as someone from the same class and lifestyle who has found a purpose for her life. Secondly, Hashmi's doctoral degree in Islamic studies is seen by her students as

---

53. Saeed, *Tapestry*, 357–61.

54. Dale, *Shifting Allegiances*, 3.

55. Ahmad, "Identity Matters"; Ahmad, *Transforming Faith*; Ahmad, "Al-Huda."

56. Ahmad, "Al-Huda," 367–70.

validating her authority to teach the Qur'an. Thirdly, Al-Huda, as a traditionalist Islamic movement, reinforces a religious understanding of the patriarchal system in which women and men have distinct roles established by Islam.[57] It uses the rules and religious knowledge already known to its female students to anchor its message in the familiar. Yet, Al-Huda's use of science and logic to present these rules and concepts remains attractive to modern, educated women who want to understand the rationale behind Islamic precepts. Students are also provided with guidelines that show them how to become better Muslims. Lastly, Al-Huda influences because, unlike Islamic education usually conducted in Arabic, its programs are structured in Urdu and English, making them accessible for working women, housewives, students, and children.

Graduating students are encouraged to use lifestyle and formal religious instruction (*da'wa*) to influence family, friends and neighbors. Some women in Al-Huda experience family resistance to their changed lifestyles as they separate themselves from the more relaxed norms of traditionally secular (modern) middle and upper classes.[58] This resistance seems to suggest that the women within the Al-Huda movement are making new faith allegiances that bring changes to traditional familial loyalties, as Dale describes regarding the Syrian mosque movement.[59]

Yet, the influence of piety in Pakistan's Muslim context has an additional element that is not part of any women's movement as expressed, for example, in activism or feminism. This is the emergence of a new middle social class that practices piety as an expression of its modern class-identity. Maqsood's research examines this class's desire to be good Muslims while also taking advantage of modern progress.[60] These women use Qur'anic schools, including Al-Huda, and *dars* (a home-based Qur'anic study group) to advance their understanding of Islam. They then put that knowledge to use within their spheres of influence. Participation in these groups is *not*, however, participation in a new faith allegiance as such. It is an expression of a collective pious yet modern class-identity. Both forms of piety—movement and class status—are thus working alongside each other to bring about societal change. Class-identity, however, takes piety out of the frame of a gynesocial enclave and places it into the frame of the state and public institutions. According

57. Ahmad, *Transforming Faith*, 89.
58. Ahmad, *Transforming Faith*, 144–46.
59. Dale, *Shifting Allegiances*, 68–69.
60. Maqsood, *Pakistani Middle Class*.

to Maqsood, this pious social class challenges the old (secular) middle and upper classes as state decision-makers.[61] This suggests that middle class piety is operating as a societal movement in twenty-first century KP-Pakistan.

In addition, middle class piety is influencing women who were never formally part of a piety movement, and who do not belong to the pious middle class.[62] Saeed identified a "social pressure" on women to express their piety through the adoption of a conservative Middle Eastern style of full veiling (hijab, *nıqāb*, and *əbāˀyə*) in the belief that this would expand their agency in the public and domestic spheres.[63] Thus, the hijab, *nıqāb*, and *əbāˀyə* are being taken-up as normative proofs, or markers, of modern women's pious identity in part because of the role-model influence of other women. This extends to non-Muslim communities as well. I have seen, for example, young non-Muslim women wearing the hijab in church because it is fashionable. I have also had discussions with Christian parents who have forbidden their daughters to wear the hijab because of its connections to another religion. At the same time, for all religious groups and communities, veiling is one way that women can publicly demonstrate their piety.

Religio-Political Islam

The fourth group within the broad sphere of the women's movement in Pakistan is female involvement in religio-political groups such as the Jamaat-e-Islami. Founded in 1941 by Maulana Sayed Abul Ala Maududi (1903–1979), JI has been identified as "one of the most influential Islamist groups in the world."[64] Its objective in Pakistan is to Islamize the nation's legal and social systems through the political process. Jamaat-e-Islami was also strategically involved in the start of the Islamization process under Zia-ul-Haq.[65]

The Women's Wing of the JI holds to the teachings of Maududi, shares the same goals as the male mainstream, but operates within its own gynesocial space. As Islamist women, members of the Women's Wing

61. Maqsood, *Pakistani Middle Class*, 54–62.
62. Ahmad, *Transforming Faith*, 155–56.
63. Saeed, *Tapestry*, 206.
64. Iqtidar, *Secularizing Islamists*, 56.
65. Jamal, *Jamaat-e-Islami Women*, 146.

reject feminist (re-)interpretations of Islam. They assert that to protect women's rights, Pakistan must preserve its identity as an Islamic nation and resist all forms of feminism.[66] The goal of the Women's Wing is to bring JI's socio-political message to other Pakistani women through *dars*, female literacy, and education, and through women's support groups.[67] Using influence strategies (perhaps) learned from Islamic feminism and the piety movement, the Women's Wing of the JI frames its conservative message within modernity. Iqtidar suggests that as JI women engage with issues of gender and honor crimes, they are modernists separated from secular feminists only by their beliefs.[68] Yet, it is these beliefs that shape the nature of the JI women's influence as Islamists.

66. Jamal, "Gendered Islam" 17.
67. Iqtidar, *Secularizing Islamists*, 143–44; Jamal, *Jamaat-e-Islami Women*, 150.
68. Iqtidar, *Secularizing Islamists*, 150.

7

Dealing with Difference

WOMEN ARE ENGAGED IN societal change through the overt expressions of feminism, activism, piety, and political association, they are also making individual and undocumented changes simply by engaging with the public sphere. Some are doing this just by being part of Pakistan's new middle class. Among these women are those drawn from Pakistan's ethno-religious minorities, including non-Muslims.

The paucity of studies that reference KP's ethno-religious minority communities has little to do with population numbers, although non-Muslims form just 0.6 percent of KP's population and just 3.7 percent of the whole nation, according to the 2023 census. The lack of academic resources centers around the challenge that religious minorities present to a province and country structured around Sunni Islam. Mernissi identified this problem in the context of the Arab world. She observed that "women and minorities are one of the indigestible huge chunks of that defiant and challenging reality an Islamic state can neither deny without asphyxiating itself . . . nor affirm without democratizing its decision-making processes and by so doing destroying itself."[1]

Where material exists about Pakistan's ethno-religious minority communities, the focus is most often on men, except when speaking of the societal abuse of women. Therefore, my own exploration into the contribution that non-Muslim women are making to societal change in KP, was hindered by the lack of literature about such women. Information

---

1. Mernissi, "Arab Women's Rights," 42.

about minority communities, and the roles played by women from these communities, are both topics that this book seeks, in part, to address. Exploring the discovered and identifying that which remains unaddressed will add to understanding about non-Muslim and other minority communities in KP.

In addition, there is the challenge of identity—how best to separate the minority from those who belong to the majority. Mahmood, exploring the "precarious situation of non-Muslim minorities in the modern Middle East," identified some of the problems that face nations and international bodies seeking to establish the measures that determine a community's minority identity.[2] These problems include issues of race, language, and culture that can be shared by majority and minority, as well as the matter of religion. Mernissi and Mahmood are thus describing the complex reality that confronts majority-Muslim nations: how to deal with citizens who share many similarities to the majority but are legally inferior because of their minority status.

RESPONDING TO ITS MINORITIES

The ways in which the Islamic Republic of Pakistan deals with its ethno-religious minority communities is complex and falls outside the scope of this book. On a societal level, however, interactions of the majority with different expressions of the minority has included discrimination and violence. Such discrimination has been the topic of academic research. It has been discussed by national and international human-rights organizations, and also by Pakistan's provincial and federal governments. One school of thought proposes that discrimination is based on caste. That is, while Muslims publicly reject the practice of caste, they have internalized the system in such a way that even those with low social status view themselves as high-caste elite when dealing with non-Muslims.[3] Within this frame, the ancestral caste of Pakistan's Christian community, for example, can still set them apart from others. The majority of Christians in Pakistan are the descendants of the people-group conversion of low-caste Hindus that took place between 1880 and 1930.[4] When I was discussing

2. Mahmood, *Religious Difference*, 51–60.

3. Devji, "Changing Places"; Singha, "Christians in Pakistan," 238; Sookhdeo, *A People Betrayed*, 190.

4. Stock and Stock, *People Movements*.

this subject with Mysha, a Pakistani Muslim and one of my research assistants, she recalled the separate glass, cup, and plate her mother kept for a Christian lady who visited in their home. In response to such attitudes, some minority women will hide their non-Muslim identities to avoid discrimination as they interact with Muslims in the workplace. This was told to me by Bushra, a Baha'i who I interviewed online in September 2020.

There was also the suggestion that Islamization plays a key part in the discrimination faced by Pakistan's Muslim and non-Muslim minorities. Khan cites the state's changes to the country's blasphemy laws: aimed at removing secularization they also promote a sense that "Islam was under attack from non-believers."[5] As explained by Ispahani, a former Pakistani politician, minorities can be understood as working against the state because they belong to other religions.[6] Shi'as can be regarded as supporting Iran, Hindus supporting India, and Christians supporting anti-Pakistan Western politics. In addition, in 2012, the Pew Research Center reported that 41 percent of those it surveyed in Pakistan believe that Shi'a are not Muslims.[7]

Ispahani is among those who propose that the legal, political, and social pre-eminence of the majority Sunni Muslim community is being communicated to the entire population through school and college level curricula and textbooks.[8] In Ispahani's view, this has "quashed the potential for critical thinking in the next generation, encouraged a false narrative of history, and introduced religious bigotry to students at an early age."[9] Faced with a majoritarian narrative, Hindus, (as just one example of the many ethno-religious minority communities), can be defensively cautious and conciliatory in their interaction with the majority in public.[10] Within the frame of influence, the arguments coming from Ispahani and others suggest that ethno-religious minority female influence in the public sphere will be curtailed by entrenched opinions and a strong majority-minority narrative.

Chaudhry's essay *Women and Poverty* is part of a collection of studies which focuses on the lives of Muslim women. In her essay, Chaudhry expressed concern for the vulnerability, and honor, of lower caste (i.e.,

---

5. Khan, *Women's Movement*, 68.

6. Ispahani, *Purifying the Land*, 25.

7. Pew Research Center, "The World's Muslims."

8. Ispahani, *Purifying the Land*, 121–26.

9. Ispahani, *Purifying the Land*, 110.

10. Schaflechner, "Betwixt and Between, 16."

poor Christian) women in Pakistan's hierarchical, patriarchal, Muslim-majority society. She observed that non-Muslim status gave low-class Christian women a greater freedom to seek work in the public sphere than their Muslim counterparts. However, in that public sphere, the intersection of what Chaudhry called "class and gender norms" made these women vulnerable to physical abuse. They were seen as those who had lost their *i'zat* for leaving their homes.[11] Although Chaudhry's observations were designed to highlight the marginalization and vulnerability of poor non-Muslim women, her comments also indicate that in Pakistan's public sphere, religious minority women can expect to be treated according to the same honor-shame standards imposed on their Muslim counterparts. The assumption can be made, therefore, that in terms of influence in the public sphere, non-Muslim women are likely to face the same obstacles as Muslim women despite any freedom of movement granted to them by their own religious communities.

How non-Muslim women are perceived by the majority population is important to my research, given that influence occurs because of an interaction between influencer and the one to be influenced. In their report for the Institute for Research, Advocacy and Development, Alam et al. explored how minorities are represented in Pakistan's mainstream media.[12] Their research concluded that although issues of discrimination and socio-political difference are covered in media reporting, the minority perspective is largely missing. They asserted that Pakistan's media fails to portray its minority citizens as contributors to the development of the nation. In addition, Alam et al. observed that the stereotypical representation of minority women by mainstream media excludes them from the general story of Pakistan.

On a state level, a 2012 report entitled *Life on the Margins* underscored the paucity of official statistical data regarding non-Muslim women.[13] Working with a sample group of one-hundred women living in the Punjab and Sindh, the authors of the report sought to understand the situation for ethno-religious minority women with regards to health, socio-economic conditions, education, female agency, political participation, and discrimination. The frame of their research was the intersection of poverty, religion, and gender. Their report concluded that non-Muslim women face a "double jeopardy": "discrimination and exploitation on

11. Chaudhry, "Women and Poverty," 109.

12. Alam et al., *Narratives of Marginalization.*

13. Jivan and Jacob, *Life on the Margins,* 26.

[the] grounds of being members of religious minorities, and on account of being women, who are marginalized citizens in Pakistan."[14]

THE MINORITY VOICE

Such research and statistical reporting highlights the claim made by the researchers M.-M. Fuchs and Fuchs that, outside of the frame of discrimination, there has been little academic attention to Pakistan's ethno-religious minority communities.[15] M.-M. Fuchs and Fuchs are among a small group of scholars, writing in English, who have worked to address this gap through their studies of the country's Shi'i, Christian, and Hindu minorities.[16] Yet, their research has remained broadly within the frame of discrimination.

The Islamic studies scholar Rieck, from his extensive study of the Shi'i community in Pakistan, observed that this Muslim group has historically downplayed its identity within the nation.[17] He proposed that Pakistan's Shi'i, with a few exceptions, have integrated themselves into society so as not to be discriminated against. However, he had observed that escalating violence in recent years has required the Shi'i community to "seek common ground with mainstream Sunni Islamist parties on political and religious issues as much as possible."[18] S. W. Fuchs suggested that Christians as well as Shi'i have sought "to reinscribe themselves onto the fabric of the Pakistani nation" as a counter to exclusionary policies and attitudes.[19]

At the same time, some from Pakistan's minority communities want to tackle majority perceptions in a way that will bring about change. One influence strategy available to these communities is public reference to historical promises that included minorities as equal citizens of Pakistan. For example, non-Muslim minorities will refer to Mohammed Ali Jinnah's speech of 1947. As the founder and first governor-general of Pakistan (1947–1948), he pledged equality for all citizens no matter what

14. Jivan and Jacob, *Life on the Margins*, 11.

15. Fuchs and Fuchs, "Religious Minorities," 2–6.

16. Fuchs, "Reclaiming the Citizen"; Rieck, *Shias of Pakistan*; Schaflechner, "Betwixt and Between."

17. Rieck, *The Shias of Pakistan*.

18. Rieck, *The Shias of Pakistan*, Responses section, para. 1.

19. Fuchs, "Reclaiming the Citizen," 17.

their personal faith or ethnicity.[20] I took a photograph of such an attempt at re-inscription into nationhood displayed on a billboard in Pakistan's capital, Islamabad in January 2022 (figure 8). It is a poignant reminder of the inclusivity of Pakistan's foundation.

Figure 8. Reinscribed into the Nation: Part of Jinnah's Speech in 1947.
Source. Billboard, Islamabad, Pakistan (own photo).

Representatives of Pakistan's religious minority communities have always worked to demonstrate their people group's loyalty to the nation. In recent years this has been included in media that focused on their contributions to Pakistan.[21] I tested this with a quick internet search. It revealed mainstream and online articles about non-Muslim heroes, and past and present contributions to Pakistani society by minorities. An article by Sumaenah Rizvi on an online platform for young citizen journalists was interesting, because, in contrast to S. W. Fuchs's assertion that minority heroes in Pakistan are "almost exclusively" male, her eclectic mix of twenty-five non-Muslim diplomats, entertainers, educationalists, and entrepreneurs contains ten individual or groups of women.[22] In addition to such efforts in the mainstream and on social media, there have been attempts by Christian academics to position Christians in the Indian sub-continent *before* the coming of Islam to counter the

20. Ispahani, *Purifying the Land*, 9.
21. Fuchs, "Reclaiming the Citizen," 7–8.
22. Rizvi, "25 Non-Muslim Pakistanis"; Fuchs, "Reclaiming the Citizen," 2.

dhimmi (protected person) status that could rob non-Muslim minorities of citizenship.[23]

At the same time, S. W. Fuchs's and Schaflechner's studies of non-Muslim minorities in Pakistan suggest that these communities have their own stereotypical views of the Sunni Muslim majority, built in part upon the same textbooks and religio-political and social attitudes that shaped views of them.[24] Using the frame of "wary and aware," Schaflechner suggested that the Hindu minority's public interaction with Muslims is based on an imagined and stereotypical view of a vast group of people believed to hold negative views of Hindus.[25] Although this audience functions in part like the Western "other," it cannot be held at a distance like the West. This other—the Pakistani majority—is current and immediate and needs to be constantly assured that its minorities present no danger to the nation.[26]

I had assumed, before beginning my research, that non-Muslim minorities would compensate for their own lack of status by drawing on external influencers through international networking, and thus apply the pressure needed for change. In his study of interfaith relations in Pakistan, Gabriel, for example, pointed to dialogue at NGO and governmental levels as providing opportunities for minorities to speak into national life, and establish points of similarity and connection.[27] However, M.-M. Fuchs and Fuchs suggest that such efforts, while aimed at helping minorities, unintentionally weaken their position, and thereby, their influence.[28] They argue that by grouping all minorities together under the heading of "victim," researchers and human rights organizations negate the many similarities that connect minority communities to the wider Muslim society. Ethno-religious minorities require public acknowledgement of a shared history, language, and culture if they are to resist attempts to have such similarities excluded from the state narrative. This includes the ways in which they are represented in school textbooks and on mainstream media. An acknowledgement of similarity is essential if minority influence is to succeed.

23. O'Brien, *Pakistani Christian Identity*; Sookhdeo, *A People Betrayed*, 29–55.

24. Fuchs, "Reclaiming the Citizen"; Schaflechner, "Betwixt and Between."

25. Schaflechner, "Betwixt and Between," 13.

26. Fuchs, "Reclaiming the Citizen," 10.

27. Gabriel, *Christian Citizens*, chap. 7.

28. Fuchs and Fuchs, "Religious Minorities," 8.

MINORITY IDENTITY

Shanneik's study of two groups of Algerian Muslim women living in Ireland provided a lens, other than that of discrimination, that I was able to use to help me understand how religious minority communities view themselves in contrast to other "religious, ethnic, or cultural groups within a society."[29] Shanneik had observed, that in Ireland, one community of "*Salafi*-oriented" women practiced deliberate isolation, what she called "self-ghettoization," in an expression of their "religious and moral superiority."[30] They separated themselves from other Muslim minority communities as well as from the majority, predominantly Catholic, Irish population. Yet somewhat paradoxically, to help establish this separation, they chose to have their children educated in Catholic schools among *kuffars* (unbelievers, infidels) rather than in available Muslim schools. In this way their children were not exposed to other expressions of Islam, and they could maintain, and protect, their own Salafi identity.

However, this self-ghettoization was not only a means of preserving their ethno-religious identity and their cultural differences, but it also provided a sense of security and superiority. As part of their superiority, these women adopted victim language, in that they identified "as victims of Western imperialism."[31] This stance comes alongside the argument that the designation of victim undermines a minority's ability to influence. In the case of the Salafi-orientated women, the victim mindset and language was part of the barrier they had erected between themselves and others. At the same time, the designation of victim was not put on them by others. These women had taken the position of victims for themselves. This is an important point when seeking to understand victimhood among KP-Pakistan's minority communities. There is a need for further study to discern whether the title of victim is simply an outsider designation, or whether it has become something taken up by Pakistan's ethno-religious minorities as an attempt to gain a (superior) place in national and international thinking.

In contrast to these Salafi-orientated women, the second group of women in Shanneik's study were from the Muslim Brotherhood. Now living in Ireland, these women deliberately found points of connection with the majority Catholic community as people of the book: those "who

29. Shanneik, "Religion," 85.
30. Shanneik, "Religion," 88.
31. Shanneik, "Religion," 88.

share a common belief in one God and a religiously grounded sense of morality."[32] Similarities in worldview and religious practice provided a "comfortable" living environment for these devout women.

To what degree these two different mindsets of separation and/or religious connection operate among non-Muslim and Muslim minority communities in KP-Pakistan is unclear. There is an indication that self-ghettoization as a means of both protecting ethno-religious identity, and retaining religious purity, can be found among Pakistan's ethno-religious minorities. Within the frame of influence, it suggests that self-ghettoization effectively limits the scope of influence to that of a person's own ethno-religious community. This would be the same for women, as it is for men. In contrast, however, where there has been a mutual recognition of socio-religious similarities between majority and minority, the channels for influence are opened-up. This could be majority influence of the minority, as well as minority influence on the majority. Such relational influence provides another application for the melon proverb with which I opened this book. Color will pass from one melon to another if they have the opportunity to sit together within the same space.

In Section I, I have largely focused on the socio-religious context in which influence operates. I have described these issues as analogous to fine woolen threads tightly entangled in a ball. My job was to unravel one thread at a time, even as each unravelling thread brought several others with it. The importance of these threads for influence is the role they play in determining the types of strategies available for women's use. They include Pukhtun identity and culture, Islam, the West, and the place of ethno-religious Muslim and non-Muslim minorities. Intertwined into them are issues of patriarchy, patrilineage, patronage, and societal status. All of these are strong societal structures that can facilitate or hinder female influence. In addition, I have shown how expressions of female status and gendered space are wrapped around the threads of socio-religious context and societal norms. They, in turn, are interwoven with threads of feminism, activism, piety, and religio-political affiliation. All of these issues have to be taken into consideration when reflecting on women's ability to influence in KP's public sphere.

32. Shanneik, "Religion," 95.

SECTION II

Women's Voices

Female Influence at Work

8

Honor

The *how* of female influence, those tactics of influence used by women in the nation's domestic and public spaces, has remained largely unanalyzed in studies of women in Pakistan. Foucault, speaking of political power, described a moment in time when not only "the concrete nature of power became visible," but there was an expectation that further "analyses of power would prove fruitful in accounting for all that had hitherto remained outside" the scope of previous investigations.[1] In like manner, *Voices of Change* is making visible the *concrete nature of female influence*—those details that were not part of previous studies—so that women's influence in KP's public sphere can be analyzed. It is part of the overall complexity of the study as a whole, that once more, as one metaphorical thread is identified and extracted from the ball of influence, it pulls out other threads as well.

Standing at the center of this book is the proverb for influence: "A melon gains its color by sitting with melons." As a metaphor it is a comfortable fit for men and male influence. A man is influenced by the men he associates with, and inversely, he also influences others. *Voices of Change* takes the same metaphor to see if it also holds true of Pakistani women living and working in the province of Khyber Pakhtunkhwa. From among the many women who are observably occupying places of influence in KP's public sphere, I spoke to forty-eight women from different ethnic groups and religions. This sample group was comprised of

1. Rabinow, *The Foucault Reader*, 58.

thirty Pukhtuns, five non-Pukhtun Muslims, including one respondent from a Shi'i sect, and thirteen non-Muslims.

My goal in talking to these ladies was to discover what are some of the mechanisms they and other women are using to obtain, exercise, and maintain influence in KP's public sphere. I also wanted to know how their ethno-religious background and/or societal status affected their influence, and the influence of the women they associated with. Only one of those interviewed, a Pukhtun, was religiously uncomfortable with the fact that, for economic reasons, she needed to work. She advised other women to remain at home if they could. Their stories enabled me to identify and then begin to evaluate the influence strategies and techniques women are using and also identify the factors that contribute to the success, or the failure, of female influence in this less studied province of Pakistan. Many of the women's voices are heard in the following pages.

Each one of the forty-eight women I spoke with was asked "What is influence?" Not every respondent gave a clear description or definition in answer to that question. However, by the end of every interview, as each woman looked at the scope of her influence, and the challenges that she and other women face, their individual understandings of influence had been articulated. This enabled me to identify and collect influence mechanisms under three broad categories or meta-themes: honor, status, and persuasion.

The category of *honor* brings together the mechanism of personal integrity and hard work, and the techniques of dedication to duty, positivity and confidence that enabled many of those interviewed to influence for mindset change. In contrast, the meta-theme of social and professional *status* groups together influence mechanisms used to ensure compliance from juniors, sometimes within the frame of patron-client relationships. The category of *persuasion* includes the mechanisms of persuasive argument, advocacy, and networked connections as ways to influence from a minority position, as well as the influence of a role model exemplar, celebrity endorser, or mentor. It also includes the widely used but little spoken of influence mechanism of *sifārish*. *Sifārish* is the act of making a recommendation or asking a favor on behalf of another. The favor is asked of someone in a position of authority with whom one has a connection. It can involve unethical behavior.

Keeping to the melon-theme as a graphic style, a summary of these mechanisms is presented in figure 9. This figure also suggests the possible importance that can be attributed to an influence mechanism based solely on the number of respondents who spoke about it. The exception was *sifārish* which was identified by very few but acknowledged to be a pervasive influence tactic in KP.

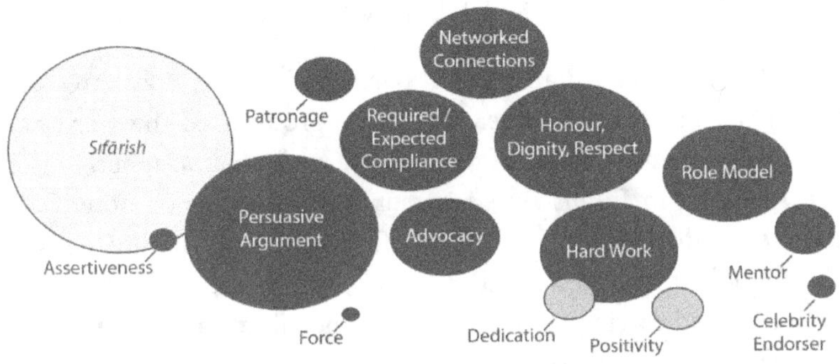

Figure 9. Influence Mechanisms.

HONOR, THE THEME

Honor, as has already been seen, functions as a lived concept in KP-Pakistan as culturally defined by the terms *i'zət* and *ghe'rət*. Its converse is *sharm*, which for women, can also operate as an expression of female honor. Honor is an attributed state of being, linked, for example, to social status or ethnic identity. Honor and respect can also be ascribed, in that they can be earned by honorable behavior. In addition, honor operates as an ethic: a strongly held set of valued principles. For example, it is synonymous with *Pukhto*: the way or code of all Pukhtuns. As such, honor underpins the proverbial melon field of KP's public sphere, for women as well as men.

In addition, in this book, honor operates as a meta-theme. The theme, or category, of honor has enabled me to group together those influence mechanisms that are centered on the concept of female *i'zət*. As a meta-theme, the broad category of honor has also enabled me to explore the differences, and the similarities, between non-Muslim and Muslim female influence. One outworking of this exploration has been a greater understanding of how women—Muslim and non-Muslim—view the proverbial melon field in which they live and work. This in turn underscores what this research has already established: that not enough is known about *ı'zət, ghe'rət,* and *sharm* as expressed by the province's ethno-religious minorities. At the same time, it also revealed that for many, female *ı'zət* in the public sphere is established by hard work.

HONOR AND HARD WORK

Although honor is such an integral part of life in KP, only three of the forty-eight women in my research sample group used the word honor (in English) when speaking of female *ı'zət* in the public sphere. Instead, those speaking in English used personal illustrations or other honor-shame terminology to describe *ı'zət*. They spoke of "dignity," "respect," and "shame." In the non-English interviews, the term *ı'zət* was often mentioned, and carried various shades of meaning. Part of the challenge of my research was identifying what was being communicated and then reproducing it in English.

Thus far, *ı'zət* has been seen to have two major strands. The first is the view that a woman should remain in the domestic sphere, and conversely, that a woman in the public sphere is demonstrating her shame. The second strand is a widespread understanding that women are the weaker sex, physically and mentally. Therefore, female *ı'zət* is maintained by avoiding those actions that bring shame to a woman's family, and in the practice of *sharm*, subservience, as a positive value. These strands are inextricably woven into each other, and both were identified by the women in the sample group. However, my focus as I explored the concrete nature of influence was not the religio-cultural norms that underpin *ı'zət, ghe'rət,* and *sharm*, although some of these practices were mentioned by the respondents as affecting female influence. My focus is the respondents' identification of honor as an influence mechanism. It soon became clear that, in their minds, honor could not easily be separated from hard work.

Dealing with a Moral Presumption

Society's expectation that women should remain in the domestic sphere because of a presumed moral flaw was highlighted by the Baha'i activist Bushra. She used the well-known Pukhto proverb, "A woman belongs to home or grave" to make her point.[2] It means, a woman's honor is found

2. Bushra recalled this proverb in English. In Pukhto it reads *khpəl kor yā khpəl gor,*

in the home; the public sphere is a place of shame for her. The inference is that only a dead woman should be found outside of her home. Bushra went on to comment that the belief-system behind this proverb was responsible for the deaths of many hundreds of women.

The perception of women's intrinsic moral weakness has already been identified. It was highlighted, for example, by Mills in regard to women in neighboring Afghanistan.[3] In KP, the view that women are shameful and, therefore, do not belong in the public sphere was identified by a number of those I spoke to as the reason for the harassment they had received in KP's public spaces. Recalling her university days, the Muslim engineer, Kiran, who I interviewed online in July 2020, commented in English that,

> in my class . . . we could not have a discussion with our classmates. Because there we were smeared upon, we were cat-called, we were faced with a lot of smirking. Whenever we spoke to the class some of the boys in the back row started to laugh at us, or smirk at us, or pass rude comments on us. . . . Because especially in . . . engineering, there is an environment that, okay, girls don't belong in this zone.

Some of the boys in the engineering class felt free to make sexually inappropriate comments (smirk, smear, cat-call) because of the presumption that the girls in the course were promiscuous, or at the very least, should not be there. Engineering was among one of many zones considered unsuitable for women because it requires close female interaction with men in the public sphere. Politics, the sciences, and aspects of the legal profession were also mentioned by respondents as traditionally unsuitable for women.

The *shame-fullness* of some careers was underscored in an interview Mariya and I had in December 2020 with Amara, an unmarried professional Pukhtun singer. We spoke on the phone in Urdu. Female entertainers are considered to be shameful by many in KP's society, so this young singer described how she worked hard to reclaim her honorability; that is, the honor that should be attributed to her as a Pukhtun. It was, in a sense, the reclaiming of her identity. She consciously distanced

---

literally "Either home or grave." A cultural rendition of the proverb is, "Home is the best place for a woman." In an alternative interpretation, Bartlotti notes that, "Applied more generally, this proverb suggests that if a man cannot possess his own home, it is better to be in his own grave." (*Rohi Mataluna*, 227).

3. Mills, "Covered and Covert," 62.

herself and her choice of songs from anything that would associate her with the designation of *sharm* given to women entertainers. Her goal was to be successful, because this would increase the number of those who respected her as a professional singer, providing her with a status that would substantially reduce the accusations that she was a very bad, that is, an immoral woman. The term used of her as a female singer was *bura*, meaning evil. She understood her influence to be the impact of her ethical songs on her listeners. Honorable success would thus broaden the depth and breadth of her influence.[4]

Maryam, a Christian medical professional, was looking for a change in cultural attitudes that would enable girls like herself, unmarried and in their twenties, to be employed in the public sphere without the immediate assumption that they had given up their honor. We spoke online in June 2020 using a mix of English and Urdu. She was one of twenty respondents, Muslim and non-Muslim, married and single, who identified as using some or all of their salaries to support their families. Eight women in this grouping said they were the sole or main financial contributor. Speaking in Urdu, Maryam commented,

> In our KPK, people say if a girl comes out of her house, she is not a good girl. . . . Sometimes families are in [economic] situations that are not so good, then girls come out of their homes [to work]. So, we should not see them with bad intentions regarding their character. We should not *degrade* them. But instead of this we should be supportive of them. . . . We should think that these girls are not certainly evil (*bura*) girls. . . . If we are agreed on this thing that girls . . . aren't bad, [then] girls can work shoulder-by-shoulder with men.

(KPK is another common abbreviation for Khyber Pakhtunkhwa.) In her opinion, a change in the majority attitude to women in the public sphere was possible, but it first required a change to the traditional mindset: that women out in public are immoral. To emphasize this, she used the word *bura*. The strength of this insult is its links to a cultural understanding that women are profoundly weak, immoral, and wicked. For the word "degrade" she switched from Urdu to English, so that I, the foreigner,

---

4. Changing attitudes in the Middle East towards singers was reflected in a discussion recorded by Hasso. ("The Sect-Sex-Police Nexus," 112.) Naming a daughter after a famous singer was a sign of greater religio-cultural openness yet it was still a shock to some, including the younger generation, because of the profession's association with immorality.

would understand the level of disrespect that women receive in the public sphere. Two other respondents also used the term degrade when speaking of the abuse women experience when entering KP's public sphere.

The Ismaili activist, Fauzia, noted that for those women, who through hard work and struggle had succeeded in advancing their careers, there was an underlying accusation that they had gained favor through sex. Mariya and I interviewed Fauzia in September 2020, using a digital platform. Speaking in Urdu, Fauzia gave a bleak synopsis of the situation for women in KP. She called it an environment where men work to "stop women from coming forward."[5] "Forward" functions as a positive term that includes not only the move out of the domestic space, but a movement from marginalization to equality, from weakness to strength, and from voicelessness to a place of influence. It was this move that Fauzia believed men in Pukhtun society worked to stop, in part because they understood it to mean a loss of honor for them. Loss of *ı'zət* for a woman who moved forward into the public sphere would bring shame on the whole extended family. Overturning this cultural norm was what, in April 2021, the Pukhtun politician Zainab, speaking in English, called "a double, triple challenge" for women.

However, many of the respondents in my sample group were confident that women can move forward into the workplace without any loss of honor. This was underscored by the Muslim educationalist Khadijah when Mariya interviewed her at her place of work. She had no doubt that women could and should be influential. Her concern was for their reputation. Speaking in Urdu, heavily mixed with English, she commented, "My *one suggestion* is that, *please*, they must take care of their dignity, their *dignity*. . . . [Use your] *strong character* to go forward and take care of your *dignity*." To emphasize her point, Khadijah repeated the word dignity; first in Urdu (*ı'zət-e nafs*) and then in English.

Dealing with Presumed Weakness

The comments made by Khadijah and others in the sample group emphasized their understanding that honor is both an attribute and a behavior. As an attribute, it is linked to professional or social status. However, as a behavior, *ı'zət* means observable female morality, dignity,

5. The word forward was also used in this same way by seventeen other women from my sample group.

and self-respect. This *I'zat* has to be maintained at all times, which requires hard work. Sixteen of the women interviewed spoke of hard work as the means by which they demonstrated that the designation of weak (i.e., less able than a man) did not apply to them. They were women who were capable and could be trusted. Trust is a key component of influence. As expressed by Safia, a Muslim surgeon whom I interviewed online in English in August 2020, they had to counter the "misconception that . . . women can't study hard enough, or . . . hold a position where they are able to do anything for even themselves." This included being trusted to make the right decisions for themselves, and for others.

The term hard work, as used by these women, contained two facets. First, they had the hard work of creating and maintaining an honorable reputation in the public sphere. Secondly, they had to work to prove themselves as professionally capable. Both facets were part of an influence mechanism used to challenge a traditional view, held by many in KP's public sphere that—in addition to being immoral—women are also intellectually weak.

Hard work as an influence tactic was part of the surgeon Safia's ongoing story. Having qualified, she became the first female surgeon in her location to take on what, to that point, had always been a male role. In that environment she encountered not only "false assumptions and bad comments" coming from a culture that had pre-judged her as a woman of poor character because she was working in the public sphere, but also the entrenched belief that she was not able to make good decisions because of her gender. Speaking in English, she explained it in these terms:

> I think that in KPK people don't think much about your work. . . . They think first about your character and if they find out that yes, she is a good character lady, or a lady with good moral values, then afterwards they try to think about your hard work. So, we have to stay a little longer for our hard work to pay off.

Hard work in this context was Safia's professional capacity.

Dealing with a similar situation, the Pukhtun lawyer, Nadia, who I interviewed online in April 2021, talked in English of the hard work involved in creating "an authentic name" or "persona" for herself. This persona—her reputation as "an authentic person"—was the reason people believed in her, employed her, and followed her advice. Her persona was established on the continuous, conscious demonstration of her good qualities as a means of ending negative cultural preconceptions. It suggested a distancing of real self from reputation, although she didn't develop this thought.

Nadia was among those participants in senior positions who acknowledged that society gave them no space for error, either professionally or personally. Any mistake can damage a woman's good name, and without that honor, her influence is marginalized or nullified. Standing behind their comments were the deep down, imbedded structures of KP society that require no explanation simply because they are. Therefore, noticeably, none of the women from the sample group mentioned that men are not required to prove integrity, ability, and decision-making capacity. Nor did they mention that society automatically attributes *ı'zət* to men while respect, honor, and trustworthiness (*ı'zət*) in the public sphere have to be earned by women.

This deep-seated religio-cultural belief in women's inherent weakness was mentioned by six of the women in my sample group. They were aware of the impact such an understanding had on their own ability to influence, to get things done. As explained to me by Zainab in her online interview, even where a woman is intelligent and well educated,

> she is still considered that she's a woman and she has limited knowledge. And because of that, . . . whatever recommendation, or suggestion, or whatever influence you want to [make], whatever things you say to the general public, there are chances that the men who are superior to you or equivalent to you, they might not even consider you . . . or what you are saying.

However, all six of these respondents immediately countered the perception of female weakness by talking of female strength and hard work. For example, Safia spoke of her work to overcome a cultural prejudice against female surgeons that she had encountered during her training. She had had to prove to her male seniors that she was just as capable as her male counterparts.

> I had to make them believe that I'm also trustworthy regarding decision-making, [and that] I am also confident to do surgeries or procedures. And I have to make them believe that I can also pursue my surgical career successfully. . . . I worked so hard that after my six-months of training, my seniors, they used to trust me more than my male counterparts. So, I made them believe that I . . . am not an option but a priority.

Her statement "I made them believe that I am not an option but a priority" was a celebration of the successful influence of her hard work. She was no longer someone they would rarely consider to perform surgery ("an option"), but someone they would prioritize.

Safia's comments suggest a deliberate imposing of her will on others. This was significant not simply because of the gender issues she highlighted, but also because she had influenced those who were senior to her within a hierarchical structure where, usually, juniors are unable to influence. She had achieved this transformation of others' thinking by the sheer hard work of being always demonstrably better than her male counterparts. The imposition of her will on those who doubted her occurred through the tactic—the influence mechanism—of consistently proving herself to be trustworthy. This undeniable proof overcame what she called the "mentality" of those around her.

Observable changes to the socialized belief that women do not have the intellectual or physical capacity to undertake male tasks was also recorded by the Pukhtun Farah in response to a question about the scope of her influence as a senior in the institution where she works. Talking in person in English to Mariya in September 2019, she framed her answer in terms of Pukhtun women's honor, demonstrated first to family and then to society.

> Because we are from Pashtuns or Pathan families so, obviously, that makes a lot of difference. Because . . . previously . . . we (women) were not allowed to work. And now when they see us, they see that we have spent a good time, and we are in a good status, better than many other woman [*sic*].

The phrase "we have spent a good time" indicated the many years she, and women like her, had worked with personal as well as professional integrity to establish and maintain a place for themselves as moral and capable women in the public sphere. Now in senior positions ("good status"), they had blazed a trail for other women to follow. In addition, her phrase "that makes a lot of difference" underscored the way in which Pukhtuns see themselves as religiously and culturally more conservative than others. The context suggests that the "they" who saw what Pukhtun women had achieved are the male gatekeepers of the domestic sphere who enable or deny female access to the world outside.

The role of the Pukhtun gatekeeper was well documented by Aamir Jamal in his book, *The Gatekeepers*, in which he sought to engage Pashtun men regarding education and "gender justice" for girls. Jamal asserted that if girls are to have education, and women go to work, then the men of their households—the gatekeepers—need to be persuaded as to the religio-cultural rightness of this change to a societal norm. Seen against this background, Farah's use of language—telling her own story through collective pronouns—was one of emphasis. She saw herself as representing Pukhtun women in the vanguard of societal change in which women are established as those with the right to influence in the public sphere.

WOMEN OF STRENGTH

One entrenched belief in KP society was expressed by the Muslim doctor Zafira, in November 2019, as Mariya and I talked with her in the hospital where she worked. Speaking in Urdu, but with a great deal of language-mixing, she said: "in our *religious* and in our *cultural* a woman is like a cow."[6] This extreme view is captured in the picture of a subservient woman who always moves her head from side-to-side in agreement, like a cow. It is impossible to say on the basis of a short interview whether Zafira always engages in language-mixing or if she was dropping English into her responses for my benefit. However, the result of this language-mixing was to turn Zafira's comment into a strong statement about her own religion and culture. She saw herself as belonging to a society that had devalued women's status to that of a domestic animal.

In response to this mindset, Zafira argued that women in the public sphere, with their multiplicity of work and home responsibilities, are "*strong*." She used the English word strong to give emphasis to her statement. To explain this strength, she used the Urdu term *sinf-e-nāzuk* (literally, the "weaker sex"). This phrase can simply describe a woman's gender.[7] However, it is also used to distinguish (weak) women from (strong) men. Strength, which is associated with honor and the right to influence, is understood to be religiously and culturally male. Therefore, strong women in the public sphere are somewhat of a cultural enigma.

6. There was a difference of opinion among the RAs regarding this idiom, although all three agreed that Zafira was communicating a belief that a woman has no value. Used here, the idiom and its meaning follow Mysha's rendering of what Zafira said.

7. On its own, *nāzuk* means delicate, fine, and graceful. It also carries the concept of fragile, describing something that is easily torn or broken. *Sinf* means gender, but the term also includes the concepts of kind, class, and genre. Together, the term *sinf-e-nāzuk* is used to distinguish women from men as a societal class, yet it also communicates female vulnerability.

Female strength, as identified by Zafira, was on one level no more than the ability to juggle work-life responsibilities. However, associated with it, was women's honor in KP's public sphere. To succeed, even on the level of simply giving instructions to a junior member of staff, women have to demonstrate a religio-cultural strength that gives them the right to influence—like men do. They need this strength if others are going to listen to and positively respond to what they say.

The exercise of strength, however, brings women into direct competition with men. This was explained by the Pukhtun legal professional, Gulnaz, whom Mariya interviewed in person in March 2020. Speaking in English, Gulnaz urged young women to "join the judiciary" as a profession. She added, "If you become scary-cats [*sic*], and sit at home because men are going to be there in competition with you, you can never achieve anything." The competition she was referring to, was not simply about who will be more successful in a job; it was about honor.

Speaking about male honor, Zainab observed, from her experience in KP's Provincial Assembly, that most men resist female appointments to senior positions for fear of being shamed. The appointment of a successful woman might highlight men's failures in the same posts and thus tarnish their/male honor. In addition, the unspoken message was that women could not expect respect, equality, or cooperation from men they had shamed. Zainab explained to me that this was the reason why she had been disowned by the majority of the men in her own extended family. They believed that her public success brought shame on them, who had done less well within the same field.

In their different ways, the respondents in my sample group demonstrated how they worked to build an influence mechanism of honor and morality that was interwoven into their proven professional expertise. However, this honor had to be publicly acknowledged for their influence to succeed. That is, others had to change their minds. The activist Fauzia, mixing English into her Urdu, expressed it in these terms: "in a *male-dominate* [*sic*] *society* . . . a woman can come forward where men *accept* this thing, that she is *respectful* for us." Fauzia was declaring that only when the respectfulness of women was accepted as being present when she was at work, as well as when she was at home, would women know that they had succeeded in changing the opinions of others in KP's patriarchal public sphere.

Using the melon metaphor, successful influence occurs when color passes from melon to melon in KP's public sphere. Influence occurs when a woman's hard work is accepted by others as proof of her personal dignity, respect, and honor—her *ı'zət-e nafs*—as well as her ability to do her job. Societal change occurs as yet others are influenced to recognize women's honor and worth in the province's public sphere. Such recognition is an expression of trust that replaces a lack of confidence in women's abilities as well as their morality.

Bluntly stated, women in KP are countering a fear that society should not be exposed to the suspect care and attention of a woman with doubtful morals. Thus, in women's efforts to convince others of their capacity in every area, public sphere honor has to be established as a state of female being. Therefore, hard work and honor are not simply the processes that lead to influence occurring, they function as a double-sided influence mechanism that can cause others to review their attitudes regarding female identity, thus leading to societal change.

POSITIVITY AND CONFIDENCE

Alongside the influence mechanism of honor and hard work come positivity and confidence. Positivity was a repeated theme within the frame of influence, mentioned by twenty-eight of the women in the sample group. These Muslim and non-Muslim, Pukhtun and non-Pukhtun women spoke of "positivity," being "positive" or they used the idiomatic term "forward." In this context, forward does not mean moving out of the home, but describes being positive regarding the future. In addition, almost half of the women interviewed used the words "confidence" or "confident" to describe how they had made self-confidence a part of their identity. For example, in her interview with me in November 2020, Eleesha, an Islamic religious instructor, speaking in English, defined confidence as a "deep down" belief in oneself as having the abilities and skills—the competence—to influence.

For Lubna, a Pukhtun working in an NGO, confidence is the quality that enables women to do many things—"like men." She chose to speak to Mariya in English when they met in September 2019. Lubna was one of the many respondents who believed that confidence or self-worth increases women's ability to operate in the public sphere as influencers. It promotes a sense of female trustworthiness against a background of discrimination and public marginalization.

Safia, the surgeon, explained it this way: "More women are going for work. They . . . are now more confident to handle different situations. At the workplace, females usually work very hard to prove themselves. . . . At the same time, I think they are able to project their image in a more positive way in their daily activities." The unspoken background to Safia's comments was the cultural expectation that women would be shy and timid in the presence of men. A position of *sharm* expressed through shyness and timidity communicates that women do not have the practical skills to undertake work traditionally done by men. Countering this expectation, a confidence in their own abilities enables women to project a positive message: that they can be trusted as having the same level of competence as their male counterparts.

Kiran was among those respondents who proactively created a space for themselves in the public sphere where their confidence could grow. She spoke of the harassment she had faced in the engineering department at university when she entered this traditionally male field. In order to feel confident about her identity she had decided to wear full veiling. She described it as "taking control of everything which I could experience as a person." She explained that,

> it is that change of environment and such strong experiences that made me realize that I should take a move and try to be more confident in terms of how am I as a person. And that way I will be more self-confident in answering back, or . . . you can say that it (veiling) was more about taking control of my life.

By "change of environment" Kiran meant the shift from the all-female environment of her school and college to the predominantly male world of engineering. She also commented that, "you cannot change the perception of society . . . But you can change their response towards you by acting positively, or by . . . addressing their concerns in a more productive way." There was no indication that Kiran, as a Muslim, belonged to a movement that encouraged her to adopt full veiling, but such influences cannot be ruled out. However, she was clear in her interview that she came from a family that did not require strict *parda* of its women.

Positivity and confidence thus operate as social proofs to be used by women in KP to strengthen their sense of self-worth and, thereby, increase their ability to influence. The women in this study had identified that a *positive* understanding of self enabled them, and women like them, to present themselves and their viewpoints in *positive* ways. This resulted in *positive* change in others. A positive self-awareness and (self-) confidence enhanced their identities as women to whom *i'zət* can be attributed even though they were found in male spaces. It also facilitated the successful communication of this change in their public identity. That is, others came to see them as operating in the public sphere from a position of *i'zət* rather than *sharm*. Used in this way, positivity and confidence were helpful devices or techniques to be embraced by all those women in KP marginalized in the public sphere by conservative, patriarchal attitudes.

GENDERED SPACE

Thus far, as I have used the respondents' interviews to present the concrete nature of female honor in KP, I have given little attention to gendered space and the practice of *parda*, especially as it interacted with the public sphere environments in which the women work. Twenty-two of the ladies in the sample group were active among the general public, or they worked in mixed settings; eleven worked in domains that were predominantly male, including engineering, politics and government service; and thirteen of the women worked in the gynesocial space of mostly female environments. Only two of the participants did not indicate the gender dynamics of their workplace.[8]

The gendering of space through *parda*, as a system of gender segregation in the domestic and public realms, is a comfortable norm for women—and men—in KP. As such, *parda* was specifically mentioned by eight of the respondents in my sample group. Among them was Shazmina, who was interviewed by Mariya in June 2019. At the time, Shazmina was a Pukhtun teacher in the predominantly female environment of a girls' school. She explained that "in Islam, Allah-*pāk* has created *parda* for women" even as he gave greater responsibilities to men.[9] In Shazmina's opinion, not only did men carry the greater responsibilities of providing for their families, but they also held women's *bakhshish* (eternal reward) in their hands. That is, men held the power to determine women's entrance to heaven. She believed that *parda* was instituted by

---

8. In addition, five non-Muslim and two Muslim respondents worked in organizations run by non-Muslims.

9. *Pāk*, literally "clean" or "holy" is an honorific referring to Allah's purity.

God as the best societal system, but it had been corrupted. Speaking in a mix of Urdu and English, she explained it in these terms:

> It is a misunderstanding to think that men are *dominant*. . . . If we *follow religion*, no man is *dominant* over a woman. But if we make our own *rules* then *naturally* people have this type of thing. If we *truly follow the rules* of Allah, then no one is *dominant*. Everybody has their own position.

Her complaint was against an assertion made by some Pakistani women, that men use patriarchy as a societal structure to dominate. She was also resistant to the attempt by man-made systems ("our own *rules*") to replace traditional norms. She didn't define what these systems were, but they could well have included Pakistani feminism as well as Westernization.

It was Shazmina's belief that if men and women occupy the gendered spaces that Allah had assigned to them within the system of *parda*, then they would have equal but different influence within their allotted spheres. These spheres are equal, because both are influential, but different, because female influence is designed to be used domestically (i.e., among other women). The implication is that the limitations *parda* places on female influence are acceptable because the system is God-given.

Among the thirteen respondents in my sample group who worked in predominantly female environments were eleven women who were employed in the educational field as teachers and administrators in all-girls schools and colleges. This included Eleesha, whose work within the piety movement placed her within an entirely female working environment. The remaining two women were entrepreneurs who had established female-only businesses. One of them was involved in an ongoing confrontation with the local authorities and their zoning laws. She needed to keep her business in the women-friendly space of a residential area. However, the law required *all* businesses to operate in the bazaar, a male-dominated space which women could not easily access because of issues of honor-shame.

The Muslim school vice-principal, Baseera, interviewed in Urdu in September 2019, described to Mariya why she had become a teacher even though her family had given her the freedom to choose any career she wanted. Teaching was her choice. She explained (using language-mixing) that "maybe I have a more *easy feel* in schools. In other places maybe I would feel uncomfortable." She seemed to be suggesting that some women did not easily fit into mixed gender environments, religiously, psychologically, or physically.

However, there was no suggestion coming from Baseera that her role as vice-principal was lesser in some way to similar positions of male leadership. It was simply different because of the gendered environment in which she worked. The public space and activities that she was engaged in, while being gender specific, still mirrored the male professional sphere. Aghaie explained this type of overlap in the context of Shi'i religious rituals: "while women's roles are similar in some ways to those of men, they are also distinct. Space and activities are often gender specific, but the two genders often interact, mirror, or contrast each other."[10] In her interview, Baseera did not provide enough details about her working environment for me to determine in what way her leadership was similar to or different from that of a man. This is a sphere of questioning for another time.

At the same time, the Pukhtun politician, Aafiya, speaking of women in KP's Provincial Assembly, described a situation of structured *parda* within a male public sphere that she chose to work against. Elected as part of a quota system to bring women into government, the expectation was that these female politicians would simply support their parties' positions in legislative voting. As a result, they gathered in the women's chambers as the reproduction of a safe, domestic gendered space in a majority-male environment. In Aafiya's words—she gave her interview in English: "Just high tea, and chit chat, and talk about clothes, and talk about designers, and things like that." This gendered space worked to separate women from knowledge and power, not least because it was ranked as different from the male political space.

Only one respondent, Hina, as a senior public servant, mentioned a shrinking public space for women in KP that was rendering them powerless to influence. While numerically women's presence in the public sphere had grown, in her opinion there were increasingly fewer opportunities for them to make a difference in society. She spoke openly and directly about what she saw as the infiltration of religious conservatism into areas of decision-making. She saw this as reducing the spaces available for women's voices to be heard, effectually silencing them. Hina told me that

> Sitting in a 2020, our spaces are more limited as compared to 1993. . . . So basically, this is a major challenge. And in terms of

10. Aghaie, "Gendered Aspects," 14.

> women, there is a lot of influence of religion. . . . Every commit-
> tee when they form it, they try to push a religious scholar.

She saw in this, the promotion of Islamist conservatism within KP that increasingly disadvantaged all minority groups, including women. In her opinion, women were no longer allowed to be the catalysts for change that they once had been.

In contrast to the majority of respondents, five of the women in my sample group proposed that there is little difference between male and female influence. Two of these women spoke of male and female in religious terms, both genders knowing their boundaries and influencing within them. For two others, societal change had led to the presence of confident females in the workplace, able to influence on the same level as men. Just one respondent, Baseera, who, as noted above, worked in an all-female space, proposed that "women have greater *empowerment* . . . and greater influence." She used the English word empowerment to emphasize her point. Baseera gave two reasons as to why women have greater influence. First the traditional respect that women receive in the public sphere, that puts them at the head of every queue. Secondly, she commented that the prioritization of women in KP gives women "a great deal more *importance*" than men. She used English to underline her belief that women in twenty-first century Pakistan are being treated as important. This seemed to be a reference to programs of purposive equality designed to include more women in the government, public service, and the spheres of private business and NGOs. The reasons for purposive equality in organizations, including Pakistan's adoption of a quota system to bring women into politics, lies outside the scope of this research. Those in KP-Pakistani society who resisted such movements may have perceived them as promoting Westernization.

Zainab, however, noted that although women profited from the opportunities provided by schemes such as the quota system that brought women into government, there was a "stigma" attached to those who obtained positions through that route. Her experience had shown her that women brought into positions of influence by purposive selection were "not considered equal" to their male peers. She called this "a very big challenge." For Muslim and non-Muslim women to break through multiple layers of societal marginalization is a huge challenge, requiring them to draw on all of the resources available to them.

9

Suspicion of the Different

ONE AREA THAT STILL needs to be addressed, before moving to look at other ways in which women in KP exercise their influence, is where ethno-religious minorities fit into the relational structures that facilitate influence. As has been established, there are many areas of overlap in regard to language and culture, yet great differences between majority and minority, not least in how these communities perceive each other. Of the forty-eight women interviewed as part of my research, thirteen belonged to non-Muslim minorities (Christian, Baha'i, Sikh) and one respondent identified as an Ismaili (Shi'a). A consciousness of difference to and exclusion from the Sunni majority was spoken about by all of these women. Their interviews contained stories of the marginalization they had encountered because of a majority suspicion of their religious identity. For example, the Christian nurse, Raima, who Mariya and I interviewed in Urdu in September 2020, spoke of the bigotry (*ta'sub*) she had experienced as a child attending government primary and high schools. She gave the example of a Muslim-only drinking water cooler that Christians were not allowed to touch. She went on to add that she had not experienced such discrimination as an adult.

The Christian teacher Samira, who I interviewed in July 2020, spoke of her experience as the only Christian in her workplace. She described herself as the vice-principal in a government school in a KP village setting. Although she did not say so, in such a setting the majority, if not all of the pupils and staff would have been Muslim. She had been due, as the one with professional seniority, to take on the role of principal when the current incumbent retired. However, there was a protest by the staff about her appointment, and instead the Muslim sports teacher was made head of the school. In the staff hierarchy, this appointment was designed to communicate to Samira that she was less than the least of all the teachers. The education department later changed this in-house appointment, but Samira remained vice-principal.

Sexual harassment related to religious ethnicity and the pressure to convert were also issues described by some of the non-Muslim women in my sample group. Kora, the Christian teacher I interviewed on a digital platform in July 2020, described some of the troubles she had faced because of her minority status when living and studying at university in Peshawar.

> Muslim families teach their daughters to stay away from Christian girls. Even my friends, they frankly told me that, "Our parents don't want us to stay with you . . . or talk to you." Because they are afraid that we might convert them. . . . Muslim boys are different. They harass Christian girls, they exploit them, they try to convert them. . . . So, I have suffered a lot of harassment when I was in university. I . . . had to live there in a very diplomatic manner.

Her comments about exclusion and harassment echo similar observations made by Jivan and Jacob in their study of non-Muslim women in Pakistan. They wrote that women from such minorities are vulnerable to "discrimination and exploitation on [the] grounds of being members of religious minorities."[1] Fauzia also spoke about the problems faced by women from her minority community, because of a widely held belief that Ismailis are not Muslims. In illustration, she told several stories about the bigotry and harassment that her own family had experienced as Ismailis that included accusations of criminality and immorality.

Bushra also mentioned women's vulnerability to what she called "religious obstacles." That is, the harassment, kidnapping, and forced conversions of Hindu, Sikh, and some Christian women by Muslim men. As a Baha'i activist advocating for minority and women's rights, Bushra used radio, television, and other platforms to speak against such discrimination and abuse. She noted that the response of the Hindu and Sikh communities to a perceived threat from the Muslim majority was

---

1. Jivan and Jacob, *Life on the Margins*, 11.

"keeping the doors closed." That is, they protected their girls by keeping them at home. However, this also meant that these girls had little access to education and a career.

In response to suspicion coming against their communities, six of the respondents in the sample group talked of using positivity, together with personal and professional integrity, to change mindsets in public-sphere environments. Two were Christian teachers who worked in all-Muslim girls' colleges. They described how they exercised influence by being positive in their responses to negativity and suspicion, and by using hard work to demonstrate devotion to their jobs. Their aim was to change negative stereotyping against their religious minority coming from Muslim colleagues, students, and parents. They both reported some success as local attitudes towards them changed. One of these teachers, Kora, who had talked of the harassment and exclusion she experienced at university, spoke of her influence on her female students. She said,

> I exercise my influence through my behavior. I inspire them. Do you know that they are really very much amazed by our character, our behavior, our sincerity, our devotion. That we are very much devoted to our work. And we do our work with very much sincerity, according to them. . . . They are curious that how is my life going, how is my personality, how I got manners from, from where I studied, from where I get guidance, from where I get support. . . . So, I exercise influence by knowledge, by guidance, by supporting them, by being positive with them, by encouraging them.

Kora's use of the possessive adjectives "our" and "we" in this and her earlier comments demonstrate that she was aware of her need to prove the honorable identity of her Christian community, while also establishing her own personal morality and professional capacity.

The other four respondents who talked of using positivity and integrity to influence others were non-Pukhtun Muslims. They spoke of the ways in which their identities, for example, as Punjabis or Kashmiris living in KP, reduced their status, and consequently diminished trust in them by the Pukhtuns among whom they lived and worked. They were required, therefore, to prove themselves as people of integrity before their influence would be accepted. The engineer Kiran described this exclusion in terms of "alienation." She was a Hindko-speaker seeking to work alongside Pukhtuns in KP's public sphere. Talking about Pukhtuns, she said, "They have this strong . . . attachment with their language and with their culture, and they kind of isolate other people who don't speak the same language, or they don't have the same culture." Kiran went on to explain how this impacted some of the work meetings she attended.

> If I am giving a suggestion, which is superior to another sugges-
> tion that is given by a male, that suggestion would not be taken.
> Right! But . . . after sometime, . . . when someone else (male) said
> it, who was . . . a Mohmand, that position was very appreciated."

She ended her comments with a slight laugh. The Mohmand are a Pukhtun tribe. They were named by Kiran to highlight the extent of her isolation as an outsider. Kiran's slightly exasperated observation that her opinions were heard but not acknowledged, in some ways gave her indirect influence. Her ideas *were* taken up when later presented by a Pukhtun man. There was no indication, however, that she turned this into the influence mechanism of planting ideas for others to use later. Her focus was the irritation of being ignored and not credited with an idea accepted by the group.

Keddie, in her study of minorities in Iran, noted that in the Middle East linguistic and ethnic differences are more significant than religious divergence in modern times.[2] In the same way, although religious divergence was not in play, Kiran in my study seems to be suggesting, that linguistic and ethnic differences are at least as significant as gender in the alienation she experienced. This is because her Hindko identity placed her outside the tribal network of her Pukhtun colleagues. Taken together, her gender as well as her ethnic identity rendered Kiran unable to exercise direct influence in meetings that contained a majority of Pukhtun men.

Eleesha, the Muslim religious instructor I interviewed, had moved to KP from another province in Pakistan. She was married to a Pukhtun but still commented that "it's taken many years for me [to be accepted] . . . because I was a person who was not a Pukhtun when I came into this society. . . . You have to prove yourself." She did not expand on what "have to prove yourself" involved, but the suggestion was that she had worked hard to demonstrate that she was a person of integrity on a par with Pukhtun women. Prior to her acceptance into Pukhtun society, her opinions had carried lesser value.

The interviews revealed that not all the resistance to women's presence in KP's public sphere came from Pukhtuns, or from a tension between the Muslim majority and ethno-religious minority communities.

2. Keddie, "The Minorities Question," Religious Tolerance section, para. 6.

Non-Muslim women faced resistance to their public sphere presence coming from their own communities that was centered around female honor and women's behavior in KP's public sphere. Such resistance bore many similarities to the opposition described by the Muslim respondents in my study. For example, Maryam, a single Christian woman working in the medical field, recounted to me how, while at university, she had wanted to blog.

> So, at that time I was not allowed. Like in KP we are not! I was doing *parda*, covering my face in the university. So, I was not allowed to post my pictures on social media. Even if I write something, so people will come out with something else. Like, "You are from KP. You are living in a very small city, and you are posting things like this! You are not allowed to."

As a woman from KP, living within the dominant culture of *Pukhto*, she veiled her face to demonstrate her honorable character.[3] However, the "people" she referred to, who objected to her blog, were seemingly from the wider Christian community. They felt empowered to tell her what she was not permitted to do; and she submitted. This demonstrated the power of societal norms in KP to determine women's acceptable behavior whatever their ethnic or religious background. Maryam's conclusion was that women who want to use social media for social comment need to live elsewhere in Pakistan, not in KP.

Maryam's experience suggests that on some issues, there is little difference between the norms of the Christian and Pukhtun communities. However, there was not enough data from the results of my study to demonstrate whether the conservative attitudes Maryam had encountered had been culturally "borrowed" from Pukhtun society. There was also not enough data to determine whether similar controls operate for other non-Muslim minority women in the province. In addition, I was unable to determine whether the reverse was also at play: that is, minority women who consider sections of the majority as lesser. Hegland, for example, in her study of Shi'i women in northwest Pakistan, recorded a gathering of urban, Muslim women from the minority Mohajir and Qizilbash ethnic groups, who "considered rural Pukhtun women to be beneath them."[4]

3. There was no sense in Maryam's comment that she was openly questioning why she, a non-Muslim, needed to follow conservative Pukhtun veiling. However, that thought may have been behind her comments.

4. Hegland, "Mixed Blessing," 184.

It could be assumed that, as those standing outside the majority Muslim community, non-Muslim minority women and their communities would support each other. However, a lack of understanding of each other's religious communities was expressed by two minority participants. They talked of the prejudice they had encountered trying to interact with Christians. Bushra, as a Baha'i, had been shocked that Christian "church workers" had stopped their young people from attending a community project she had established aimed at empowering minority youth. She said, with a sad laugh, "These educated people create such problems in the [*sic*] society." The "educated people" were the Christian leaders, who, in her opinion should have used their status and influence to facilitate co-operation across minority communities, rather than suspect her of trying to convert their youth. Her comments underscore the great need for more research into KP-Pakistan's ethno-religious minority communities and their interactions with each other as well as with the majority. One aspect of such research has to be the issue of status and its interconnectedness with trust, and thereby with influence.

10

Status

Just as the theme of honor brings together the concrete mechanism of *i'zət* combined with hard work and the tactics of positivity and confidence, so the theme of status and status-based compliance reveals the interconnectedness of the very real issues of patriarchy, religion, *Pukhto*, and patronage that operate in Khyber Pakhtunkhwa. To understand the role status plays in public-sphere female influence, I once more have to deal with the metaphorical ball of entangled religio-cultural threads. Through the respondents' stories and reflections, I was encountering the traditions and values that underpin patriarchy and societal status in KP's public sphere. It is these norms and values that help shape the ways in which women in KP approach influence.

OBSTACLES

In order to comprehend the ways in which professional and social status function in KP-Pakistan, it was important for me to understand the societal boundaries which operate as obstacles because they challenge a woman's right to be involved in the public sphere. In this book, I have proposed that hierarchical patriarchy, as a system of societal norms, is deeply rooted in religion and culture in the province and the wider nation. It operates as a significant force in KP's proverbial melon field for Muslims and non-Muslims alike; and all but four of the forty-eight women in the sample group addressed this issue. Male domination is the element that makes sense of the situations they were describing, although only one of the respondents used the word patriarchy in her interview.

The scholar-practitioners Richards and James observed in their study of patronage in the Bible, that "*In a culture, the most important things usually go without being said.*"[1] Patriarchy in KP operates in the same way. It is something that women deal with on a daily basis but do not overtly acknowledge. My questions, especially about male-female influence, and the obstacles that women face in exercising their influence, became the spur that prompted the women to talk about the issue of patriarchy. Where a term was needed, the women used variations of the phrase "male dominated society." Over half of them spoke of a society in which men are superior, and where women occupy a subordinate place. They spoke freely of male privileging, required female subservience, and marginalization. They also talked of socialized attitudes. For example, the Pukhtun politician, Zainab, commented that, "for some reason they (men) feel that we (women) do not have the intelligence, or exposure, or knowledge to have important positions, or to hold that specific office. And they undermine you." By exposure she meant practical experience.

Eleven of the women Mariya and I spoke to, five Pukhtuns, two non-Pukhtun Muslims, and four non-Muslims, specifically mentioned KP and Pukhtuns as the reason for male domination in the public sphere. For example, speaking in Urdu with English language-mixing, Tamina, a Pukhtun registrar in a teaching hospital, made the matter-of-fact statement "that our *society* is a *male-dominated* one. That is influence. Male's *influence* is more. Their *say* and their *behavior* and everything." As Mariya and I interviewed her in November 2019, it became clear that, in her opinion, men have greater influence simply because they were male. Rubia, also a Pukhtun, who we interviewed in the same month, recounted from personal experience that, "In our society, . . . even if you are on a very good post or something, and you have a man who is comparable to your post, their influence is more." Her teenage daughter, who was also present during this interview, agreed.

The question that generated the most comments about patriarchy in KP asked the respondents to describe the difference between male and female influence in the public sphere. Two of the Pukhtun women in the sample group used the opportunity this question provided to give

---

1. Richards and James, *Misreading Scripture*, x.

a religious rather than a cultural definition of male dominance. They assumed that I, as a foreigner, stood outside the norms of culture and religion as practiced in KP. Their answers were shaped at ensuring that I knew what is right from wrong. One of these ladies, Fahima, who I interviewed in November 2019, gave her forthright opinions in Urdu but with a great deal of English language-mixing. Speaking in the medical institution where she worked in a senior capacity, she said,

> *Publicly* we see *definitely* that *male dominance* is very much greater. There are many *factors* in it, and the biggest *factor* which is *exploit* [sic] the most is religion. . . . To men Allah gave in religion *full dominance*. [But] they use this *influence* in a wrong way. . . . In our *culture* and because of our *lack of education*, I must say illiteracy, because of that we (society) are using it (male dominance) in a wrong way. . . . If we look at our religion, our Prophet's teaching, there should be nothing like what we call *influence*. *Male* and *female* have their own places. If we remain in those places, there is no *question* about *influence* coming into it . . . because as a *female* I will recognize my *limitations*. And . . . the *male* [sic] will recognize their *limitations*.

Fahima used English to provide extra emphasis to the points she was making and also as an influence mechanism. Her use of English was to convince me of the truth of what she was saying. Fahima wanted me to understand that it is uneducated men in society who are misusing the dominance God has given them to oppress women. Whereas, in her opinion, the teachings of Islam made space for men and women to live productive and fulfilled lives alongside each other, without men needing to influence (i.e., dominate) women.

Although the research demographics identified Fahima as middle class, it was not possible to determine whether she belonged to the newly emerging, Islamic middle class in urban Pakistan identified by Maqsood.[2] Her comments reflected a traditionalist mindset that was resistant to the West's perceived push for global gender equality structured according to a Western model. Yet, at the same time, Fahima's role as a senior leader, and her comments about socio-religious practice in KP-Pakistan, indicated that she believed in gender parity mediated through Islam.

In addition, Fahima was responding as much to the issue of gender as to the topic of influence, and thus she represented those in the sample group who struggled with the concept of female as distinct from male

---

2. Maqsood, *Pakistani Middle Class.*

influence. In her understanding, men and women have different, God-given places and roles, what she called *limitations* (i.e., boundaries). Within this system, responsibility (*full dominance*) for the family is given to men. In Fahima's opinion, if Islam is taught and practiced properly there would be no question of influence (i.e., male domination) because everyone would know their right places. Her comments echo those of the teacher Shazmina speaking of *parda* as a societal system instituted by God. It underscored the need for women, who sought to be influential in KP's public sphere, to interact with a widespread belief—held by women as well as men—that men's right to control women was established by God.

Hina, responded to this mindset as an activist, which she combined with her public service role. She recalled how, as a young woman in a high-level meeting, a senior government figure, a man, had told her, "This is written in the Qur'an that women should follow *parda*. . . . Women are weak." His point had been that it was religiously wrong for her to be present in the meeting. Hina commented, however, that, when "they start to use religion, so I try to learn more and more about religion." The "they" in her comment referred to conservative voices in KP society. Her goal was to counter religious objections to women as public sphere influencers with arguments that gave religious reasons for their right to do so. She told me that she gathered information from other religions as well as from Islam to enable her to speak out on behalf of all women in KP.

The association of influence with dominance is an important finding in my research. In addition to Fahima and Hina, other respondents also recalled situations in which men were positioned by culture and religion to dominate (i.e., influence) in the public sphere. For example, the entrepreneur, Daania, who talked in English to Mariya in September 2019, spoke of the barrier patriarchal attitudes are to her own "dominance."

> Where it's a man-dominated society . . . the men who do not want your dominance, . . . they will not accept your strengths to be acknowledged. I felt them to be an obstacle initially, but I believe with the passage of time you prove yourself that feminality [*sic*] is not your weakness but it's your strength.

The phrase "do not want your dominance" underscores male resistance to her influence as a businesswoman. Her dominance is her right, as a woman, to be accepted by men as one who can influence from a place of strength, just as men do. Daania's strategy is the imposition of her will through the visible, extended public proof that her feminine gender ("feminality") is without the weakness of *sharm* and lack of intellectual ability attributed to it by society. She is challenging the view that women are created as the weaker sex.

Later in her interview, Daania listed some of the specific obstacles she has to deal with, which she identified as being rooted in KP's public sphere environment. These obstacles include non-cooperation from male-run government departments, threats, and attempts to close her down.

> The environment doesn't allow you or it restricts you to exercise your influence as a female and as a female entrepreneur. So, I have felt many a times constrained, but I believe that the hope and the struggle to keep doing and keep working for the community, unless and until there is a hazard which stops you completely. . . . It's been disheartening sometimes, where you feel that the people they don't co-operate. They do not wish you to work as an independent woman, and sometimes you get threats from the community as well. Sometimes you get the legal obligations that as a female, or as the head of the institution, you are not supposed to work beyond your means.

By hazard, she meant serious threats against her personally. The phrase "beyond your means" refers to the cultural and legal barriers that stopped a business*woman* from doing something that was acceptable for a business*man*.

Bribery was mentioned by just one of the women interviewed as the only viable solution when all other forms of influence have failed. The purpose of a bribe is to influence another to do something illegal in order for the one giving the bribe to gain what they want. The difficulty of investigating this technique to achieve one's goals was the reason I decided not to develop the theme of bribery as an influence mechanism. However, it stands as one concrete measure that women can take to ensure that their goals are achieved.

Nadia, a lawyer, was among those in the sample group who commented on the obstacle *Pukhto* was to those women who wanted to be actively involved in the public sphere. She commented, "As you know, the Pukhtun society, *alhamdulillah!*[3] We people are so much restricted to our code of ethics." She was referring to doing *Pukhto*, that is, living out one's Pukhtun identity, of which the rules of *Pukhto*, the tribal code, are a central part. She did not unpack her observation any further except to

---

3. *Alhamdulillah*, means "praise God."

call *Pukhto* a "double-edged sword," suggesting that as a type of religious system, it could both empower and restrict women.

Aghaie also considered the power of a socio-religious system that could both restrict and empower.[4] His study of Moharram symbols and rituals followed by Shi'i women living under the Qajar dynasty in Iran made it clear that these symbols and rituals were not *other* to their faith. These symbols and rituals, like the codes of *Pukhto*, operated as that in which they were deeply invested, and which were also a part of their identity. The rituals portrayed women and girls as submitting to "appropriate" male authority, but also as those who courageously rebelled against "inappropriate" male attempts to dominate.[5] They were those who could speak out for a cause, and who were responsible to educate their children in the ways of Islam. Aghaie commented, that "Moharram symbols and rituals provided opportunities for pious women and girls to define their gender identities along religious lines, while at the same time asserting direct and indirect influence [over men], expanding their social networks, increasing their social status, and expanding their participation in certain aspects of public life."[6] While Moharram rituals cannot be equated to the code of ethics which is *Pukhto*, Aghaie's study suggests that it is possible to find within the structure of religious practice those points of empowerment that provide women with status and authority outside the home.

However, in Pakistani society, a hierarchical patriarchal system operates in which it is the right of *every* adult male to tell *every* female what she is or is not permitted to do. This was described by Alishba, a Pukhtun NGO worker, who wanted to video an incident in her village that interested her. Speaking to me in English, in July 2020, she recalled how she clashed with what she called "the main culture" of KP and the restrictions on women that flowed from that. "As I opened the camera, someone (male) came and said, 'You know, you cannot do this. You are a woman and just get limits on yourself to what your norms are.' So, I had to obey, you know. You cannot always argue." "Your norms" are the cultural limits all women are expected to adhere to.

Alishba did not explain why a man from her village saw her behavior as contravening the codes of *Pukhto*. It may simply have been that she was out in public. Or that in a video she was capturing images of men and

4. Aghaie, "Symbols and Rituals," 45–61.
5. Aghaie, "Symbols and Rituals," 48.
6. Aghaie, "Symbols and Rituals," 61.

women, which some Muslims consider to be religiously inappropriate. Her purpose in telling the story was to illustrate the types of obstacles that women face in the public sphere where every aspect of their behavior is monitored and judged, and where women are expected to automatically comply. In this instance, Alishba chose the easier route of submission, implying, however, that resistance was sometimes a possibility.

SOCIETAL STATUS AT WORK

Alishba's experience is a window into the patriarchy that operates in KP. This patriarchal system is also hierarchical in that it ranks society into positions of senior-junior. Alishba was expected to obey because her gender made her junior to the man who ordered her to stop what she was doing. The cultural norm of ranked societal status in KP-Pakistan is complex, incorporating the earned status of a profession, social status ascribed by class, gender, age, experience, and personal maturity, as well as gender.

Professional Status

Seventeen of the women Mariya and I interviewed spoke of influence in terms of power or being positioned to be powerful. To use the metaphor of the melon proverb, successful influence originates from those melons who carry the weight of societal status. Yet, although thirteen of the women who linked influence to the power of a post were well educated, and thus could expect to use their professional status, two were from unskilled working-class families. Six of the seventeen were from middle class backgrounds, and just nine had elite or upper-class status. Two came from religious minorities.

Twelve women from this diverse group described influence as either synonymous to power or linked to the authority of a recognized professional position and/or social status. The importance of position and power was underscored by Zainab when I asked her to describe what is influence. She came from an influential family, and had worked in activism, but she and several other women had moved into politics because it positioned them to influence with greater authority. They had realized that,

> if you want to influence you need to have some position, you need to have some power. It can be your PR (personal relationships),

> it can be your status, it can be status in the community, it can
> be your position that you're holding. But it is important to have
> that position in hand. And normally this is how it works. . . . If
> you want to influence people it is important to have a registered
> body or a platform to work from. Or to be recognized. You can
> have some position. That can be a party position, that can be a
> political position, that can be a position in local government,
> . . . something that is recognized. Because if you do not have a
> platform, you can still influence people, but it requires a lot of
> struggle.

Her use of the word status—a position of power held within a community or organization—has to be interpreted against KP's hierarchical social structure. Within this structure, elite and upper-class women carry the authority to influence on the basis of their family name. Yet, as Zainab noted, elite social status on its own is not able to influence in every situation, because it does not carry enough authority. In another part of her interview, she spoke of her investment into activism as an attempt to boost her influence. However, activism did not have the public endorsement or recognition that resulted in societal change. Joining a political party, and participating in provincial government, had provided her with a publicly recognized structure. It gave her a position, and with that status came the right and the authority to get things done—to be a person of influence.

The same message was repeated by the two other politicians interviewed as part of this research. They also came from elite and upper-class families and spoke about the influence of their family name. However, the addition of a recognized political position had enhanced their already considerable abilities to influence. For Aafiya, this additional status literally gave her the power to get things done. Speaking in a celebratory tone, she told me that now, when she was made aware of work that was "stuck-up in offices," all she needed to do was make a phone call or personally visit that official and everything became unstuck.

These political respondents were not alone in their understanding that women need the power of a recognized position, a place of dominance, in order to influence. Baseera switched from Urdu to English to describe influence as "*womens in power.*" Moving back to Urdu, she stated that influence equates to the extent "of my *ekhtıārāt.*" *Ekhtıārāt* means both power and authority. That is, she could influence according to the power/authority of her position as vice-principal. This type of power-based influence was described by the senior medical professional Zafira through the Urdu proverb, "He who has the stick has the control."[7] The stick is literally a *lāt'hi*, which is also the name for the batons carried by the police in Pakistan. The proverb is saying that the strongest person is the one in command. Applying the proverb to her position, she said: "This *influence* is because of my *post* . . . in being the *head of my department*, and I use this *influence* to *carry out* my work." For her, the power to control that was implicit in her position *was* the mechanism she used to influence. She went on to describe how this authority ensured that all those junior to her followed her orders. It also removed any obstructionism that might arise because of her gender.

Not everyone interviewed supported the use of the proverbial *lāt'hi* as the best long-term influence strategy for women. While use of a stick enabled control, it was also viewed by Shazmina as diminishing the respect of the wielder.

> If we give *respect* then we can complete our task or work easily
> in love. If we use a club; the club is okay, it works on a *temporary*
> basis to bring people down, but with that hate develops in their
> hearts and they lose *respect*.

Speaking in Urdu, Shazmina used the word *ḍanḍa* (club) to describe the use of position to bring people down, to force them to be submissive to another's control. The *ḍanḍa* is the type of weapon used by security guards. Her comments spoke to a form of coercive power that seemed to have little to do with women's attempts to influence from a position of authority. However, Shazmina's response—she was answering a question about the scope of her influence—indicates how tightly power and influence were intertwined in her mind and, by implication, in the minds of others who link influence to status, and thereby to dominance. Shazmina, however, was rejecting the sustained use of a metaphorical *ḍanḍa* as an influence mechanism. For her retaining respect was essential if women were to influence. She emphasized the point for me by using English for certain key words: *respect* and *temporary*.

However, for the majority of the seventeen women that Mariya and I interviewed who spoke of influence in terms of power, the use of the power implicit in a post was an essential influence mechanism.

7. This popular Urdu proverb says *jiski lāt'hi uski bhens*. Literally, "Whoever has the stick has the buffalo." It is commonly used in situations where there is competition for control.

They could not influence without it. They saw professional status as *the* means of gaining compliance from those junior to them. Fahima, who worked as the head of a medical department, explained that "My influence is around my responsibilities . . . And it is acceptable because of my *position* or my *post*. Whether they (junior staff) agree or not, they have to accept it." The power attributed to her post legitimized her right to expect compliance within an organization where female influence was a relatively new phenomenon. This influence, she went on to explain, was "not related with *gender*. . . . Because of the *position* I am at, people have to *obey* me. *That is a must*. They have to do it. Whether they do it by heart or not by the heart." Compliance was non-negotiable in her mind, be it done willingly ("by heart") or unwillingly ("not by the heart"). These comments link Fahima with the man who told Alishba to put down her camera. As seniors operating from a place of dominance, they both expected automatic and absolute compliance from those junior to them.

Zafira, who had used the stick metaphor, also spoke of the influence mechanism of required compliance, engendered by her post, that negated the marginalization associated with her gender. She told me, "I think instead of my *gender*, my *post* has the biggest role in it. *Kamāl!*" Her comment was made with an ironic laugh. In this context, *kamāl* (literally, excellence, superiority) could be understood to mean, "as if by magic." Zafira was emphasizing that it was not the excellence of her gender but the superiority of the title she bore that, magically, caused compliance.[8]

The way in which the mechanism of required compliance was linked to a job title, no matter how humble, was illustrated in an interview I took with Humaira in September 2020. Humaira, a Pukhtun, had never received an education. Widowed, she worked out of necessity as a security checker at the gate to a hospital. She spoke to me, and Mariya who provided translation, in Pukhto and Urdu using the online platform a colleague provided for her. Out of respect for her education level, we did not use the term *ekhtīār yā asr* when speaking of influence. This more formal term lay outside her comprehension level. Instead, we used the word *tāqat*, meaning both power and authority, as a concept she could more easily understand.

---

8. Someone who has worked hard but wants to be humble will say of their achievements, "It wasn't my *kamāl*, it was just how things worked out." At the same time, the term carries the colloquial meaning of "magic." This is the meaning attributed to Zafira's use of the word *kamāl* by one research assistant.

In a comparable way to Fahima, Aafiya, and the other women in the sample group who held positions of senior leadership, Humaira also viewed her job as providing her with the power of position and status that required compliance from others. Specifically, this was the conferred authority to admit or refuse entry into the hospital compound that was contained in her post.

> If I tell them, there is no doctor [so you can't come in], they say, "You are not a *doctor* here. You are just a *dai* (hospital attendant) here!" I am telling them, "That I am sitting here! They have given me permission. They have asked me to sit here for something!" But if they do not listen, then I go and ask the *chowkıdār* (security guard). And then the *chowkıdār* comes after that, and they do listen to him.

The word *dai* literally means midwife or birthing attendant, but in this context was being used idiomatically by others to emphasize Humaira's low professional and social status. It communicated that she had no real authority to prevent the entry of people who were ranked above her. Her counterargument was that her position carried with it all of the power of the hospital administration: "They have asked me to sit here for something!" At the same time, although Humaira viewed her position at the gate as equal to that of her male colleague, the *chowkıdār*, in the public eye, his role as gatekeeper or guard was understood to have greater authority because of his gender. A *chowkıdār* is always male. Recognizing this cultural norm, Humaira drew on his male authority to affirm her professional right to expect compliance from those at the hospital gate.

At the same time, a high-ranking or senior position could enhance a woman's influence by simply reducing the number of people she was junior to and, therefore, expected to obey. As Fahima explained to me, "Now, . . . because of my *position* there is no sort of *influence* on me." That is, there was no-one in a position of dominance above her who could require her compliance. In a similar vein, Tahira, an entrepreneur who Mariya interviewed in Urdu in April 2019, recalled the years when she was a junior employee. She laughingly commented that as "an *under*" she had not been able to influence. The word *under*, used as a noun, means a junior or subordinate. Tahira now runs her own business, and has no one over her, to tell her what to do.

In the reverse of this, Roshni, an influential Pukhtun lawyer with upper class status, observed that when she moved out of her role in senior leadership in private practice to act as a legal advisor to an NGO, her influence was immediately curtailed. She told Mariya in her interview in July 2020, that positioned in the NGO as someone with junior status, she was required to ask permission from others and to comply with their orders, whether she agreed or not.

Being Assertive Without Being Male

The exercise of compliance as an influence mechanism as described by the respondents in the sample group also carried with it aspects of personal assertiveness. Interestingly, four of the women who talked about this subject approached it through the term "misbehave." To misbehave is not simply to behave badly. In KP-Pakistan, the term encompasses a range of forceful behavior used by men as well as women. Misbehave is therefore a reference to culturally inappropriate behavior. At one level this can be simple obstructionism—being difficult. In her interview Humaira called such behavior *shokh* (literally, "naughty"). However, misbehave also includes actions that are loud and abusive. It includes shouting at those who are junior to you. Baseera, in her school setting, called this type of behavior *ziādti*, a term that encompasses the idea of abuse as well as acting inappropriately. *Ziādti* describes the type of behavior that can be used by someone in authority who is taking advantage of their position to do something bad against another person.

Aware of the option to use the power of one's position to be forceful, five of the ladies in the sample group reflected on their own and other women's assertiveness. Humaira, for example, acknowledged that when others refused to comply with a request delivered "with respect," she had to use the power of a raised voice and a forceful personality. These are behaviors not traditionally associated with women in public spaces. They were, however, a necessary part of her job as a hospital gatekeeper. In the same way, the senior medical consultant, Rubia, argued that "sometimes you have to be assertive. . . . I would lead people softly, but at times I feel like that will affect my influence. Because people will say she is so soft so just forget it." Being "soft" is a traditional and appropriate female trait for (Pukhtun) women in KP. However, it is also associated with weakness and the designation of *sinf-e-nāzuk* which diminishes a woman's capacity to demand compliance. Therefore, implicit in Rubia's reflections on being assertive was the idea of behaving more like a man. That is, she could influence from a place of strength—like a man.

The struggle was how to be assertive without being aggressive. These women recognized that coercive force (the club) or a raised voice would be associated with misbehaving, and result in a loss of respect and, thus, long-term influence. The delicate balancing act of assertive female influence was explained by Hina.

> I'm assertive but I am not aggressive. Because . . . in a polite manner you can go further. Because if you are working for rights, it does not mean every time you have to show your anger. . . . Although some people, I don't know why, they consider me so strong. . . . But, you know, it might be that this is my image of being really assertive on certain issues. But somehow, I don't feel assertive, I don't. I talk to them. I never shout on people. . . . I believe, if you are soft in your argument, and not aggressive, you can win your task. Because . . . if you become aggressive, sometimes you lose your stamina. So, in a settled way, if you are moving with your negotiation or with your argument, so you can convince people.

Hina's use of the phrase "in a settled way" refers to a calm and measured approach to advancing ("moving with") one's negotiation or argument. However, she also used the word stamina in reference to the strength and resilience needed to achieve one's goal. As a woman in leadership, she recognized the power of her strong—even forceful—personality. Yet, she consciously distanced herself from the type of power that was associated with force and by implication inappropriate maleness.

Four of the five respondents who reflected on assertiveness occupied leadership roles that demanded mandatory compliance. Humaira was the exception, as a *dai*. In their jobs, they all chose to tone-down the mechanism of power to make it something softer in order to retain respect, even as they sought to command submission. In addition, Hina's comments implied that a softer approach helped to temper the strength of their personalities, making the commanding power of their posts more palatable to a KP society still adjusting to women in authority. As explained by Zafira, with a smile and a slight laugh as she talked about strong women, "They said that she is *sinf-e-nāzuk*, but no, everywhere she has to be *strong*."

These women, and the others who linked influence to the power of a position, understood that professional status, established on a publicly legitimized platform or post, carries weight and authority. As these public roles were traditionally male, use of such weight and authority felt uncomfortable. At the same time, this weight enabled them, and women like them, to use the influence mechanism of status that requires compliance. For a few, compliance was obtained through measures analogous to control through the use of a stick, or enforced submission by means of a club. Others, however, sought to gain compliance through a controlled assertiveness that enabled them to retain the softness of their gender. The social diversity among the group of seventeen respondents who spoke in this way, also suggests that status-based compliance is available for *all* professional women. At the same time, Humaira's recourse to the male *chowkıdār*, to bolster her authority as a *dai*, also suggests that a low social status could negatively impact the success of the mechanism, whereas for those with higher status, compliance was easier to obtain.

Social Status and the Use of Patronage

The three participants among the sample group who I had identified as having elite status by birth belonged to feudal, land-owning families that practiced a system they called "philanthropy" or "social work." They were clear that on one level, their influence was interwoven with the cultural system of feudal patronage in which they operated as patrons. The words patron and patronage were not used by any of the participants in my research. However, eight of the women spoke in terms that were reflective of patron-client relationships. For example, patron-client language appeared in a description of the traditional feudal relationship of land-owner with villager given by Aafiya as she talked about her "social work."

> I organize a lot of events also, like for women in my village. Very, very poor women. It's a feudal village so they never even think that they can ever respond or fight with or do anything against the *Khans*. . . . My mother used to go and help out the village women. She was a great social worker. . . . So, this thought came to me, okay, my entry point here is for literacy into women. Because they're totally illiterate women. So, I said, the Holy Qur'an is the best then. . . . I said, I want fifteen young girls every month. They'll sit here. Each one will read two paras . . . and we'll finish the Qur'an in an hour or so and then we'll have tea, and we have discussions, and I'll also make them play some games and things like that. So, I got them out of their houses and sitting

> with me in my home and no difference between me the feudal
> [landowner] and they are the poor people.

Khan is a general term for feudal landlord. The phrase "never . . . do anything against the *Khans*" illustrated the expectation of compliance on both sides of this traditional patron-client relationship. The interviews with Aafiya, and the two other elite women in this study, also demonstrated that they had expanded this type of traditional patronage-cum-social work to include NGO activism, education, and politics—to which, as elite women, they brought an expectation of compliance.

However, later in her interview, Aafiya exposed one of the negative effects of client-patron relationships; where clients simply comply with the patron's requests because of the rewards associated in this relationship. For twenty years, she had been working with male colleagues dealing with issues of female emancipation and empowerment within Pukhtun society. However, these men still kept their wives confined by *parda*. She commented that they seemed to agree with the values they disseminated, yet years of interaction with that message had not changed their thinking. This lack of personal buy-in indicates the power of *collective* thinking and *collective* commitment to traditional socio-religious values, that as individuals they felt they could not work against. In addition, *parda*, standing at the center of *Pukhto*, may have made it more resistant to change than other values, such as health and hygiene.

The lawyer Nadia was one of the eighteen women I had identified as holding upper-class status. Her comments about creating a "persona" for herself—her reputation as a woman who could be trusted—have already been explored as part of the discussion about honor and hard work. However, her remarks can also be understood as expressing patronage. For example, she observed that successful outcomes to requests for her assistance generated loyalty from those (clients) who trusted in her (as patron). This created "a very loyal and a very highest persona" which was why others (clients) "listened to" and "believed in" her. This was helpful for her; in that it increased her reputation, her persona, as a successful influencer and thus established her as a patron with the power to get results.

The results coming from the limited scope of my sample group of forty-eight women were focused largely on patronage from a patron's perspective. Four women, for example, spoke of the cultural expectation that they would use their professional contacts and networks to work on others' behalf at an official or organizational level. Among them was

Hina, who for a time had worked for an INGO. She spoke of the belief among her contacts and family members that she would use her senior position in the INGO to provide them with jobs, or release funds for their projects or business ventures. The collective understanding was that she was positioned as a leader, a senior, and thus could expect compliance to any request she made on behalf of others. From the stories told by Aafiya, Nadia, Hina, and others, I concluded that patronage operates as another position or status-based influence mechanism. It is available for women just as it is for men. As an influence mechanism it holds advantages for the patron as well as the client, as illustrated in Nadia's story.

Female Lineage

Although *birādari* was not mentioned directly by any of the respondents in the sample group, there were indirect references to the outworking of patrilineage. They talked of the power of father, brother, uncle relationships that could advance or hinder their ability to access the world outside their homes. Patrilineage was that under-addressed expression of male privilege in the province that women have to deal with if they are to gain male support. Its presence in their lives was incorporated in their stories, as the women spoke of KP as a male-dominated society.

However, as I indicated when discussing social influence, *birādari* is a networked structure that can come alongside attempts to influence because it involves the extended family or the tribe. It can overshadow an organization and provide privilege to individuals who otherwise were not positioned to exercise influence. Nagina, who Mariya met in June 2019, talked in Urdu of a female equivalent of the *birādari* network. She worked in a school where the principal was her cousin.

> If there is someone else's work or my work, *obviously* she will prefer my work. For example, she will listen to my point first. If I have any *problem* or *issue*, she should deal with that first. Now I am not saying that if I am asking a favor for a wrong thing, she should help me first. But if, really, I need help for something, or I don't understand a thing, and many other people are waiting to speak to her, having a cousin is a *plus point*. I can talk ahead of other people.

Nagina's role in the school was that of a junior; she worked in the kindergarten. However, her influence was that of a senior, simply because of her lineage. As a result, her point of view was considered above those who were organizationally senior to her. In her interview she went on to describe how she obtained permission to act in a way that was contra to school policy, simply because of her relationship with her cousin. This type of kinship network was also evident in Samira's story, where the Muslim staff gathered together to convince the out-going school principal to appoint the sports teacher as her replacement. The corporate decision of the informal tribal network held greater power than the formal decision made by the organization's head.

Taking Advantage of One's Position

An additional facet of status, particularly for the elite, was the power to act counter-culturally to achieve their goals. Transactionally, the deficit of a counter-cultural act was more than offset by their social status. Such status was able to legitimize their actions and demand compliance from those invited into the activity. For example, Aafiya, who described herself as a "freelance person," broke the boundaries of gendered space to entertain male guests associated with her work. For this, she appropriated the male-only space of the family *hujra*, their male guest facilities. This counter-cultural use by a woman of a traditional male space was something that someone from a lower class was unlikely to attempt.

In contrast to the elite respondents, none of the eighteen women who identified as upper-class spoke of influence in terms of their social status, even as it was clear that many of them belonged to families and tribes with influential names in KP. While their focus was on how they influenced professionally, their interviews revealed that they could also take advantage of their social status. For example, Ribca, who belonged to a prominent non-Muslim family, was able to accompany her father on his overseas business trips because of his social status. In our online conversation in July 2020, she explained this to me in English.

> For me to broaden my horizons, to come out of this culture to
> see how the world is, I started travelling with them to experience
> these different countries, the different cultures. . . . I used to . . .
> sit with them in his meetings. I used to listen, and by listening
> you learn a lot.

The exposure of those trips with her father and his staff led to invitations to address international forums, which in turn gave her the opportunity to use informed, persuasive argument to challenge and change Western mindsets about Pakistan, being a Pakistani woman, and belonging to a religious minority. It also positioned her as someone whose opinions the UN and other global institutions wanted to hear. The implication was that upper class women, like elite women, have networks they can tap into, plus family names they can use to exert additional influence where needed. Their social status also expanded the scope of their influence to include spheres unlikely to be entered by those from the middle and lower classes.

The impact of elite and upper-class status on influence was explained to me by Safia. Although she did not equate influence with dominance, she was one of very few respondents who directly addressed issues of social status, clearly positioning herself among the upper class of KP-Pakistani society. She commented that "in the public sphere, women can in fact influence according to their social circle, according to the norms of the area they are belonging to, and definitely [from] their capabilities and the position they are holding in society." This suggests a rigidity of social and professional boundaries within a hierarchical senior-junior society, where women could (only?) influence within the parameters of their class or their job. Safia's point, however, had been to underscore the fact that women can be influential, rather than highlight boundaries to female influence.

Aafiya, perhaps because of her elite status, was even more direct in her assessment of KP-Pakistan's hierarchical social structure and its impact on male and female influence. When asked to describe influence, she replied,

> In Pakistan, it's very, very obvious that there is a rich class and there's a poor class. There are the leaders and the influential ones and there are the ones who are totally dependent. They're followers and somehow, they seem, sorry to say, not to have the brains to think of how they can get out of the life they are leading.

She seemed to be implying that as a societal norm, this rich-poor division required no further explanation, such was the leader-follower, senior-junior, patron-client reality of the world in which she worked. Within that world, women in KP with elite and upper-class status not only had the weight—the power, authority, connections—to lead, they had the exposure to experiences and events that in Aafiya's opinion lay completely outside of anything those from poor families could even imagine.

Middle and Lower-Class Status

It is not surprising, therefore, based on Aafiya's comments, that the limitations of a low(er) identity on female influence was not a major theme in the interviews given by those respondents I had identified as coming from KP's middle and lower classes. One theme that did come through was the problem of dealing with obstructionism for those who did not have the backing of an elite family name. Education had enabled Alishba to leave her lower-class background to become a medical professional, placing her in the middle classes. However, this professional status was not enough when dealing with a government bureaucracy that also considered the reward power implicit in elite and upper-class status. She told me:

> When you tell them that you do not belong to that rich family,
> then . . . the respect level in the thinking of people comes down.
> There, they think as you do not come from that rich family, they
> need not support you, or they need not encourage you.

Her comments provided an insight into influence exercised within a hierarchical collective society that looks to a family name (i.e., reward power) when considering compliance. Middle and lower-class women do not have the name, status or reward power and, therefore, cannot expect compliance outside of their places of work. Often, where there is obstructionism, they have to look to other tactics or people to provide the influence they cannot.

The effect of a rigid system of hierarchical compliance was also highlighted in the interview with a Christian nurse, Parveen, who Mariya and I interviewed online in September 2020. She was one of three women from the sample group who appeared to hold junior status as a permanent position rather than a steppingstone to advancement. Parveen's role was one of responsibility within her department, but as she talked about influence, she described the position as one of structured hierarchy and required compliance. This had not prevented her from being a mentor to nurse-trainees, but there was nothing in her interview that indicated organizational or cultural support aimed at cultivating independent thinking and decision-making, or the opportunity for her to influence her seniors.

MATURITY, AGE, AND EXPERIENCE

At the same time, factors of personal maturity, age and experience could not be excluded from the exercise of influence. "Middle-aged or older women . . . seem to have greater experience and confidence in navigating patriarchal social systems, whether in the family or in the larger society."[9] Length of service, in addition to age, is also a factor. For example, two of the women in the sample group spoke of the resistance they encountered when they first joined an organization, even though they occupied positions that required automatic compliance.

Naila, a lawyer, who Mariya interviewed on a social media platform in July 2020, explained in English how maturity, age, and experience are judged within the legal profession by clients considering whether to hire a woman or not, given that most lawyers are male.

> People somehow calculate the level of your influence, and then they say, okay, now this person should be followed because she has such of an experience, so much of education, and now, it looks good too that she has that knowledge . . . People say that the more you are getting aged or the more you are growing, that idea or that position would be given great weightage. . . . So, with the passing of time, . . . influence increases.

That is, in Naila's opinion, a woman's *ability* to influence is linked to the process by which others recognize her *right* to do so. Maturity, experience, and length of service ("the passing of time") contribute to this process because they enhance professional capability and make it more trustworthy. There was also the element of cultural respect for age implied in Naila's statement, although this was not developed by her. Her focus was on personal maturity as an influence tactic that women could use. Thus, her advice to all women in KP was that they cultivate maturity as part of their identities, even if they did not have much education. "If she is not an educated woman, for example, she should at least make herself be that woman who has the maturity levels. Not saying that she should be a serious woman, no. But . . . her say should have a weightage." In this context, "serious" means occupying a recognized position in the public sphere, which Naila acknowledged was not available to everyone. Her advice was for women to cultivate that level of personal maturity that gives weight

---

9. D'Souza, *Partners of Zaynab*, 123.

to her opinion, "her say." This was the maturity of dignity and wisdom, which she called "decent," meaning respectable, and morally good.

However, the word "compromise" was also used by seven of the women in the sample group as a quality they had learned through experience. As explained by Eleesha, from her role as a teacher of Islam, this was not a compromise of "values and ethics," but an ability to come to a place of mutual "understanding" that facilitates influence. Eleesha was not among those women who used their social or professional status to influence, yet she joined those women who had learned from personal experience when to step back from a conflict rather than try to push through a point of action. Bushra, when talking of compromise, referred to the dangers of taking offence and planning revenge. She called it "taking a grudge" which could also work against the possibility of any future influence. As someone from an ethno-religious minority, she commented, with a brief chuckle,

> You have to step back, just your future talks or for your future plans, for the survival of your community, or for the survival of your women in the society, you have to step back at certain points. When people are not ready to hear you, when people are in a position to oppose you, then obviously the wisdom is to step back, instead of coming and taking a grudge and working against them. I personally think that getting step back is better than getting involved in a conflict with them.

A SENSE OF INDEBTEDNESS

Coming alongside personal experience was a sense of indebtedness. Spoken of by five women, this indebtedness was an expression of their desire to, in some way, repay those who had supported them in their struggles to reach a position from which they could influence others. Three of these five women spoke of a responsibility to give back to their families for their sacrificial support. However, for two of the women, there was an obligation to the wider community. Nadia, for example, spoke of her indebtedness to those who had supported her political candidature.

> I considered myself that I am indebted to my people (her supporters), who repose their trust in me through their vote. . . . I was strongly indebted to them. . . . I am lost for the words that how I can repay them, how I can deliver back to them.

For Nadia, a sense of indebtedness operated as a spur to be active and visible in the public sphere, and to use her position to influence on behalf of others.

EDUCATION

Coming alongside experience, education was referenced by the respondents as a major route for female influence. The power of education to change women's standing was mentioned by thirty-two of the women in the sample group, not all of whom used status as their preferred influence mechanism. Six of them saw education as something that enlightened and enabled women, building character and shaping personality. For example, Eleesha, whose role in the piety movement included Islamic character-building training (*tarbı'ya*), believed that "the proper education and the proper background" gave women a much better chance of impacting society. A proper education, for her, was not the pursuit of a degree, but the right mix of religious and secular subjects that enabled each woman's natural abilities to flourish.

Seven of the ladies specifically commented on their ability to think independently and/or they promoted independent thinking as a goal women should aim for. The school administrator Farah, for example, expressed her appreciation of the British nuns who had overseen her education at a convent school.

> They taught me life-skills which are so much deeply rooted in me that I live with them, with those beliefs and things. And then the same things I am passing to my family, also. Like . . .[being an] independent thinker. I know what I have to do and what I have to achieve in life. . . . And that makes me stand out from the rest of the crowd.

The nuns' influence, in Farah's opinion, had impacted the characters and the personalities of their many students as something they took with them into adulthood.

However, although Farah worked in a job where independent thought was appreciated, her comments pointed to a society in which such behavior was not necessarily encouraged. Bushra, for example, explained that Pukhtuns do not want, she used the word "allow," women to be influential because that placed women in positions where men were required to listen to—and comply with—their instructions. She noted that from infancy, "people put this in their children's minds that being women is an act of abasement and shame to have. So definitely when it comes to public and getting influence by womens [*sic*], so people don't allow this. . . . Pukhtuns don't like women to be influential." She considered this to be one of the reasons why men oppose female education.

Against this background however, education was not simply a route to bring more women into the workplace. Education functioned as an important tool, taken-up by secular and religious social-action groups, to improve the quality of women's and girls' lives.[10] It was also mentioned by six of the women in the sample group as women's legal right, guaranteed by Pakistan's Constitution. At the same time, eight of the respondents explained how uneducated women contributed to the socialization of the same patriarchal message that marginalized them. For example, Zainab noted that,

> if we want to change the mindset of people, . . . if we want to accept women to have the same influence as men, . . . we need to give them (women) respect. And that respect needs to be taught at a very young age. I feel that it is high time we focus more on men. We . . . complain about how men treat women but not realizing that it is the mother who taught him that. . . . It wasn't intentional! It wasn't intentional. But it is the small little gestures that sort of raised . . . a boy into a man who considers women inferior. . . . So, I guess, it is important that we need to teach . . . these young mothers how to change that behavior and how to treat their children equally.

Her phrase "small little gestures" summarizes the many ways in which boys are privileged within the home; a socialization that is reproduced as male privileging in the public sphere where it negatively impacts female influence. She emphasized the lack of awareness that women have about what they are doing by repeating the phrase, "It wasn't intentional!" Zainab was tapping into a narrative that envisioned a future society that accepted women as valuable contributors to the public sphere. This would be a society without workplace harassment and domestic violence. In Zainab's opinion, this society would be achieved by educating girls, who as mothers would educate their children to have respect for women: boys to respect their mother and sisters, girls to value themselves.

Nadia paraphrased a slogan that highlighted NGO and government attempts to change patriarchal norms by emphasizing the importance of

10. Khan, *The Women's Movement*, 295.

female education. She quoted, "Give me the good mothers so I will give you the good nation."[11] The idea being promoted is that an educated mother will socialize a message of gender equality within the home and ensure that *all* of her children are educated, positively impacting the development of the next generation. The slogan, and this concept, are captured in figure 10.

Figure 10. "Educate a Girl and You Educate a Generation."
Source: NGO Sponsored Poster Advocating Education for Girls, Islamabad, Pakistan (own photo).

Education's ability to provide women with professional qualifications that raised their social status was not spoken of directly by any of those Mariya and I interviewed. However, using the filters of education and their fathers' last jobs, the implication was that for five of the women, four non-Muslims and one Muslim, education and/or a career had raised their social status. Four of them had transitioned from a lower

11. This slogan was also quoted by the Christian teacher Kora: "If you educate a woman, you educate a household; but if you educate a boy, you just educate one person." The official version states, "Educate a boy and you educate a person; educate a girl and you educate a generation."

socio-economic background to that of middle and upper class through higher level education. Just one respondent, with little formal education, had made the same transition using her business acumen. In terms of societal influence, however, the findings indicated that middle class status was not enough to offset lower class origins, at least in dealing with bureaucracy. As the NGO worker, Alishba had noted, when people learned of her lower-class origins, their respect for her went down. Yet, she also told me that there was a recent trend in KP whereby people had started to respect women for their successes in education and employment. In this departure from traditional norms, *i'zət* was being given to women based on their achievements, which in turn was establishing for them a status and reputation beyond that of family name, or lack of it.

GENDERED STATUS

I had expected to find in the interviews some reference to public-sphere influence that reflected the power exercised by women in the domestic realm, particularly that of a mother or mother-in-law. As the household matriarch, it was a mother(-in-law)'s duty to control the behavior of her daughters(-in-law) and maintain the honorable name of her family.[12] Thus, not unexpectedly, thirteen of the respondents named their mothers as having played a part in their journey to the professional position they currently occupied. Eleesha also spoke of the role of a mother or grandmother as someone who influenced the "moral values" of her family.

However, only three women in the whole sample group talked of bringing *mother influence* into the workplace. The oldest of these respondents, who worked in an all-female environment, had built a professional (not social) matriarchal relationship with her younger staff in which she treated them as daughters, and they treated her as a mother. This was a comfortable and familiar arrangement that worked because of their gyne-social workplace. It mimicked, to some degree, the domestic environment.

Kiran, the youngest among the three women who spoke of familial influence in the workplace, described how, when she was working as a university lecturer just a few years older than her students, she had co-opted the respect due by sons to their mothers and applied it to her all-male class. She called her students "*beta*" (meaning, "my son"). *Beta* established them as children and positioned her as mother—the older,

12. Isran and Isran, "Patriarchy," 841.

senior figure who was to be obeyed. She commented that it caused her students to realize that "she is our teacher, she is an elder, and we cannot cross that line [of respect]." Although a young, single woman, Kiran had co-opted aspects of traditional mother status within a patriarchal culture to enhance her professional public sphere influence. The addition of mother status to her professional role of lecturer worked to curtail harassment by her male students because it increased her right to speak with authority.

In Pukhtun society, the position of eldest sister also contains the right to influence family, even married male siblings;[13] and five of those interviewed referenced sister influence within the home. Eleesha, for example, talked of how, as an eldest sister, she was able to influence her family using the power of suggestion. However, only one participant, Gohar, a banker, spoke directly of bringing sister status into the public sphere. She gave her interview to Mariya in English in September 2019. Her experience had shown her that female bank staff could become those unthreatening and familiar sister figures to whom the customers could relate. She attributed the success of women in the banking world to this "softer" (female) approach. It made clients ready to listen to their advice and be influenced by them.

Although public-sphere mother and sister status co-opted aspects of women's gendered standing within culture, the positions of mother or sister were not influence mechanisms in themselves. They were an additional tactic that could be used alongside the positional authority already held by the participant. They worked to enhance influence because they carried a degree of familiarity that made them comfortable in certain circumstances, such as a university or bank. The ability to draw on traditional, gendered status added cultural weight to the influencer's professional status and also set boundary lines of respect that protected their honor. There was no mention by the respondents of influencing using any other familial relationships, such as aunty.

OBSTRUCTIONISM

I began talking about status by looking at the obstacles that women face to their influence in KP. I end by looking at cultural obstructionism. The interviews revealed that, despite the hierarchical societal norm of

13. Lindholm, *Generosity and Jealousy*, 127.

expected/required compliance, anyone (male or female) in a junior position could obstruct a senior (male or female) through the cultural practice of *tang* (obstructionism). *Tang* is an idiomatic term used of deliberate resistance to authority that ranges from laziness to non-compliance. It appeared in the interviews as the respondents talked of dealing with jealousy, bureaucracy, and lazy staff. They also referenced the use of *tang* based on the religio-cultural premise that women are weak. As expressed by the educationalist Mohsina, in her interview in Urdu in September 2019, "They think to themselves, 'It doesn't matter. What can she do? What can she do?'" Although she did not add, 'she's just a woman,' that was the implication. The "they" who were using *tang* to obstruct Mohsina were junior staff, both men and women. Her repetition of "What can she do?" perhaps indicated the lived experience of helplessness in the face of entrenched obstructionism. Similarly, it was Zainab's experience that at a leadership level, men made "uncomfortable" by a woman in the "superior" position of committee chair would simply stop working. Two other respondents also described obstructionism from staff intended to cause them to fail in their jobs.

Interlinked with patriarchy, male obstructionism had the power to completely negate a woman's influence. Zainab described an incident in which her influence was overturned by the stronger voices of her male peers. She had used an established parliamentary system to report the violation of her political privilege caused by the disrespectful, non-compliance of a male civil servant. That man was suspended from his job in accordance with governmental rules. However, using his connections, he contacted two of Zainab's male parliamentary colleagues. They spoke to her superior, who reversed the decision, and the man was reinstated. She commented that such situations of male privileging happen "very frequently. It's not rare, it's common."

Zainab had used this personal illustration as an example of women's powerlessness within a system that gave preference to the male voice. At the same time, it highlighted the successful use of her positional influence and her ability to upset the status quo, even though that success was short-lived. However, she continued her story to indicate that obstructionism need not lead to a complete failure. "So, what we do is that when we feel that we have failed and we cannot influence our specific people or a specific group, or a specific person, then . . . obviously, . . . we try and convince people who can influence them." Zainab could use her own networks, or possibly *sifārish* connections, to find and utilize the person with the stronger voice to overturn situations of failed influence. Her use of the collective pronoun "we" suggests that this was a common route taken by women when faced with the obstructionism of male privileging.

At the same time, and significantly, women's presence in the public sphere speaks of changes in patriarchal attitudes. The women I interviewed were working in these public spaces with the permission of the men in their households. As noted by the Pukhtun Qamar when she talked to me online in October 2020, it is a girl's/woman's father, brothers, or husband who have been "given the power of making decisions for her." Qamar was working as the head of a public-health program. She attributed her success in the public sphere to her father.

> He believed in me, and he gave me an opportunity to be what I want to or aspire [to be]. Like, for example, I wanted to be working side by side with men, and I was the first woman in my family who started working with men. . . . I was not literally at the time thinking of money, fame, or something like that. But there was something in me that made me believe that I can do work side-by-side with men. And for that my father definitely was the influencer.

In all, almost half of the thirty-one women who included in their interviews an expression of thanks to their families for their support, mentioned a father and/or husband. Notably, no one in the final group identified as being in the public sphere without some sort of male support, with the exception of one non-Muslim respondent who was supported by her mother. The two key words they used were "supportive" and "cooperative." For example, Zafira in her advice to other women, recognized a woman's need of male support, no matter how strong her personality. Speaking in Urdu, with lots of language-mixing, she said that women

> need . . . a *support system*, . . . her *parents*, also her *siblings, brothers*. For women, without the *support* of men, it is very difficult. Her *husband* has to be supportive. . . . Her *male* children have to be supportive of her. *So, without support*, if she thinks that she has to do work, then I think her *character* has to be *strong* [enough] that she can cross all these *barriers* and *hurdles* by herself. And if not, then a *support system*.

Her reference to "barriers and hurdles" was to KP society, although in her interview she did not specifically mention male domination.

In addition, on a less direct level, the success of male family members could also increase women's professional status in KP's public sphere. Women can share in the honor and status attributed to a family's good name. Thus, Nadia recorded how the support of her successful younger brothers made her feel stronger as a politician. "Because it is a Pukhtun society, a masculine type of society, so they value masculinity more. So, my . . . brothers' good reputation . . . gives me a lot of strength and gives me a lot of support." The implication was not necessarily that Nadia's, or Zafira's, capacity to exercise influence would be diminished without male support, but simply that the struggle to obtain and maintain influence would be harder, requiring a formidable strength of character. There was no mention in the interviews that the converse was also true. However, when speaking of the influence exercised by a role model, there was the suggestion that women's visible success worked to enhance male reputations.

11

Persuasion

Honor and hard work, personal integrity, devotion to duty, positivity, confidence, and status-based compliance have been identified as the influence mechanisms and tactics available to women in Khyber Pakhtunkhwa's public spaces. They have been underpinned by the familiar roles of mother and eldest sister, or enhanced by age, maturity, and experience. Also, a strong argument has been put forward for influence to be understood as domination. As such, it is exercised, respectfully if possible, by those whose professional or social status require those junior to them to submit. However, the definition of influence as senior-junior compliance was presented by just seventeen of the forty-eight women in the sample group. Thirty-one others spoke of influence in terms of relational transference or impact.[1] This is a notable split in the sample group's understanding of what influence is and how it functions in KP's public sphere.

For the thirty-one women who did not describe influence in terms of power, influence is exercised through advocacy and persuasive argument used to some extent by those whose personalities and visible success

1. The reason why the opinions of these thirty-one respondents were not presented ahead of those from the other seventeen women is due to the way in which I have grouped the twelve major influence mechanisms into broad meta-themes, as well as the complexity of religio-cultural norms in KP-Pakistan. The way in which I am able to use stories from, for example, Safia and Eleesha, across the themes of honor, and status, as well as persuasion, is an illustration of the ways in which they and many others take up influence tactics as required. Their use of influence mechanisms was not dependent on how they chose to define influence as a concept.

have established them as role model exemplars, celebrity endorsers, and/ or mentors. As those in the public eye, there is a significant overlap with issues of status and *i'zət*. These women also included the roles of networking and *sifārish* in their descriptions of influence. Alongside many of their stories, were accounts of resistance and even failure to influence.

THE TRANSFER OF IDEAS

The religious trainer Eleesha was clear in her definition of influence. It "would be my talk or my ideas transferred on to someone. . . . It is basically my thoughts or my aspiration that I carried on to the other side." She spoke as someone whose life had been positively influenced by the teachings of the Al-Huda piety movement and its founder, Farhat Hashmi. She was now actively involved in encouraging others to consider the religious lifestyle that Al-Huda promoted. Within this frame, influence can best be known by the effect it has on its recipients. Thus, twenty-four of the thirty-one women in this grouping answered the question "what is influence" by explaining what it had achieved. They used words like "impact" and "effect." Mohsina, the educationalist, spoke of the way she had been influenced at the start of her career by "a close *interaction*" with those who supported her professionally. Using language-mixing to make her point, she described influence as "the *impact* or *effect* on others in any way. A little bit *positively* or *negatively*, it has an *effect* on others. Then they *change* their *behavior*. Then they *change* the way they work."

Safia, whose struggle to be accepted as a surgeon has already been told, described the power of societal interaction in the context of her job. "As a health-care provider, I come into interaction with . . . men and women. So, . . . *I am changing* (her emphasis) the misconception that people have about women in our setup." "Our setup" is a reference not only to her place of work but to KP as a patriarchal society. Her daily interaction with patients and their families is the environment in which she works to influence others by replacing their current ideas about women with new ones.

This transfer of ideas involves knowledge, where knowledge is not simply the passing on of information. For twelve of the women in the sample group, knowledge included an astute observation of people and situations. Knowledge gained from observation enabled them to effectively use persuasive argument as an influence mechanism. Speaking in English in an online interview in July 2020, Laaila gave advice to others based on her own strategy as a legal professional. "If you first observe the situation and then you act accordingly, you will influence others very easily."

Zainab, the politician, identified persuasive influence as "selling" an idea or a project to those with decision-making authority. The educational administrator Khadijah called this type of influence "*convincing power*." Although her term included a reference to power, it had nothing to do with coercion or status. Rather, it was, in the example she gave, the gathering of facts that would enable her to achieve her goal. In this case, presenting a situation to the school director in such a way that she could be persuaded to reduce the fees for a family in financial need. This type of advocacy as an influence mechanism was also identified within the frame of activism by three of the respondents.[2] Among them was Qamar, a manager in a government health program directed at public awareness. She described her work as advocacy used collaboratively to build a momentum for positive social change. She wanted to avoid creating a conflict with those who did not agree with her. She asserted that, "People who don't agree with you, you cannot improve. But you have to advocate. And advocacy and opinion-change, or maybe social change, is not an easy process." The phrase "cannot improve" was a reference to forcing people to change their minds, which as Shazmina had identified was a temporary solution. The use of a metaphorical club could result in not just a loss of respect for the person demanding compliance, but an increase in long-term opposition.

The terms "exposure," and "awareness," or descriptions of access to experiential knowledge, featured in the interviews given by fifteen of the women in my sample group. The importance of exposure to female influence was underlined by Daneen in November 2019 as she spoke with me about influence. "The more exposure you have, the better influencer you become." She was speaking from her own experiences as a school principal. Exposure in this sense is an awareness of issues beyond formal education, data collection, or knowing one's rights. It forms part of the tactical knowledge that women use in the exercise of persuasive argument. It equipped Ribca, for example, to confront stereotypical thinking about Pakistani women at international forums. Exposure is required because of a presumption of female naivety regarding the ways of the world. This

2. In the overlapping of influence mechanisms, these three respondents were part of the group of seventeen women who linked influence with power, and the group of twelve women who talked of the role knowledge plays in effective influence.

lack of experiential exposure causes Pukhtun men to question women's ability to hold important positions in organizations or government.

Although women can use convincing power to advocate and persuade, there was one corollary added by Mohsina as she spoke about the effectiveness of persuasive argument as an influence mechanism. Speaking in Urdu, she used the word *asr* meaning "effect" or "influence." "When you talk about the KP *environment*, there is less *asr* in women's words than the *asr* that is in men's [words]." That is, in her opinion, female influence remains less effective in KP's public sphere than male influence. Without the weight that is associated with male influence, it cannot achieve the same results. The exception being gynesocial working environments.

PERSONALITY

The roles played by confidence and positivity, age, maturity and experience, and the balance of assertiveness and softness in the exercise of influence have already been identified. Intertwined into these factors, and into the respondents' identities as women making a way for themselves in the province of KP, was the aspect of personality. The medical consultant, Rubia, for example, described herself as having "been given a personality which has a positive aura . . . that influences people." Although not every participant was this forthright, each one of the forty-eight women in the sample group reflected to some degree on how their temperaments had helped them to influence, or how they had been influenced by others' attractive personalities.

These women talked about confidence, resilience, focus, persistence, integrity, empathy, and an ability to learn from mistakes and disappointments as well as successes. They demonstrated a strength of character that enabled them to push against societal norms in the belief that their goals were beneficial to others. Twenty of these women spoke of their strength of character as an essential part of their identities. It helped them to be listened to and trusted. In addition, those in leadership spoke of their ability to be independent thinkers; women who were not restricted by negative public—or domestic—criticism. These attributes, together with a formidable character and the ability to seize opportunities, were recognized as helping them, and other female leaders, forge a strong public identity. This trustworthy and strong public identity was what the politician and activist Nadia called "an authentic name."

VISIBILITY

Within the frame of *convincing power*—persuading others to take for themselves that which you believe to be true—the lawyer Roshni described influence as an investment of self into others' lives.

> Influence is convincing people. . . . Mostly influence is taken as a power word, you know. It is the power of winning hearts through actions, your deeds, your words. And they can change the life of people. It can also make a permanent impact. What you are, you . . . dig into the world of people.

She used the metaphor of "digging" to underpin the depth of personal investment and the type of permanent impact she saw powerful influence having in others' lives.

All of the women that Mariya and I spoke to in the course of this study were in places of public visibility. They were part of that small minority in KP (under 5 percent of KP's female population aged ten years and over) who were visibly engaged in employment outside of the home. Their visibility provided them with opportunities to "dig into" others as role models, celebrities, and mentors. Thirteen of the forty-eight spoke specifically of how their leadership roles in the public sphere had positioned them to influence other women, especially the younger generation. Twenty-two of these women talked of the importance of role model influence in preparing other women to succeed. At the other end of the continuum, ten of the respondents recognized that they had been influenced by successful women as role models or mentors.

Role Model Exemplar

Returning to the melon metaphor, some versions of the proverb state that, "A melon catches color having *seen* another melon."[3] This suggests that influence occurs because of observed behavior. Those in junior positions, for example, learn by observing a senior. Tamina described the *seen* influence of junior-senior interaction in the context of her job. Although she gave her interview in Urdu, she put the key words into English. This was for my benefit but also to make an emphasis. "At my *workplace, obviously*, the *seniors* [influence me]. I take *influence* by their *knowledge*, by

---

3. This version of the proverb was quoted in Urdu by Tamina: *kharbuza kharbuze ko dekh ker rang pa'kārta heh*. The verb *dekhna* means, "to see, to watch, to look at."

their *clinical skills*, [etc.]. And if someone (junior) is *influenced* by me, then *obviously*, . . . everything will be observed in me."

The words "impressed" and "inspired" were used by women in the sample group to describe influence that was based on what you see in others. Some used the Urdu words *tāsir* and *matāsir* meaning to be affected or impressed by, to have respect for, and to admire.[4] Sumayyah, answering the question, "What advice would you give to women who want to be influential in KP's public sphere?" brought together the issues of self-confidence, *i'zət*, and professional excellence that enable women to be role models. Sumayyah is the principal of a school.

> The most important thing is the woman has to believe in herself. That she can do it. Because in the public sector and the private sector, only you will survive if you have that self-esteem and if you believe in yourself. If you believe in yourself, you will make other people believe in you as well, because you will be confident, you will be communicative, you will be able to speak your voice. And all these things matter. But if you are [not] submissive, I wouldn't say authoritative, but if you make yourself heard in a good way, you win people over. . . . You impress other people. . . . If you are honest with your profession, and if you do things with your heart and your mind in it, eventually everyone will notice you. Your work will speak for you. You don't have to influence others; they will get influenced themselves.

The phrase "you don't have to influence others" is a reference to using force or forcefulness to make others accept you and what you are saying. Oddly, she also said, "if you are submissive" which seems to imply being a gentle persuasive influencer rather than a forceful one. Therefore, I have assumed the absence of *not* was a slip of the tongue and added the negative. Submissive in this context would mean women taking the lower place of *sharm* that includes not speaking out, and not directly talking to men. However, it is possible that by the word *submissive*, Sumayyah meant someone asking for submission in others; she goes on to use the word authoritative. In this case, a better transcription would be "But if you are submissive (i.e., require submission in others), I wouldn't say authoritative, ..." The thrust of her advice is, however, that a confident,

4. As we talked about how best to render these words, the RA Mysha explained how *asr* (effect, influence) is the Arabic root of *tāsir* (effect) and *matāsir* (affected or impressed by).

articulate woman who is good at her job and has a following of people who believe in her, will be an influencer.

The question regarding advice that led Sumayyah to talk about personal excellence as that element which impresses and influences people, caused Zainab to talk about being a role model. I have included just a fraction of her lengthy response and used it as a frame by which to consider the power of female visibility. This is her advice, as a politician, to other women in KP's public sphere.

> Number one is that you become a role model. And the moment you become a role model, you need to understand that . . . you sort of can influence people and with that you need to be very careful what you do. Because if people can praise you for your good traits, people will rip you in pieces if you commit a mistake. So, there are challenges in becoming a role model, because it's not just that you are representing yourself. You are representing a community, a group of women. . . . At the moment we are considered as representing 51, 52 percent of the population. But we are also representing . . . those young girls who want to join politics. So, I feel that once you have become that role model, you need to watch what you are doing. You cannot mess around because if you commit a mistake, you are not only blocking waves (i.e., preventing progress) and . . . compromising your credibility, but you're also creating problems for the youth who want to join politics. . . . Because of our culture, society, and norms, it is considered that good women don't join politics. So, if you want to change that, I feel that, you know, once you become a role model it is an extra, a double effort that you need to stay between those two lines and, you know, how to keep yourself composed, and how to keep yourself correct all the time. Because you are under the spotlight then. You are representing those people. . . . People can give your examples and can convince their elders if you become a good role model. But, if you make a mistake, you can destroy everything for those upcoming young girls.

Zainab's words highlighted the sense of responsibility felt by all of the women in the sample group who held senior leadership positions. They were compelled by their visible success in the vanguard of social change to exercise the influence of a role model exemplar, to demonstrate the veracity of professional female success, and the authenticity of personal integrity in the public sphere. Their success as women of proven integrity was that of trailblazers. As such, they opened the door to professions for those embarking on their careers. This was especially true for careers within fields held to be shameful for women, like politics.

Zainab's advice also underscored the precariousness of women's positions in the public sphere. Their vanguard visibility left them with no margin for error either professionally or personally. Any mistake would compromise integrity and create problems for the next generation. Zainab used the term "blocking waves" to indicate the power of one mistake to stop a movement for good from happening. Her advice to role models was to "stay between those two lines." That is, to stay on the path of composure and correct behavior. A role model could not respond negatively to provocation or obstructionism. She had to be "correct all the time," meaning that she could not afford to make those wrong choices that would compromise her personal morality. The activist Fauzia referenced the widespread belief that successful women advance their careers through what she called "*negative*" relationships. She used the English word *negative* in her Urdu comments so that I would understand her point; successful women are believed to use sex as an influence technique. Part of the purpose of honorable female role model influence was to overturn such stereotyping.

Zainab also referred to visibility as being "under the spotlight." Successful women were to use their visibility to be living, expert exemplars that others could reference. The power of media to spotlight a well-positioned role model was mentioned by Roshni. She spoke of the influence she exercised through her radio and television appearances as a lawyer. Women had told her that "we have gotten influenced, and we have decided that we will come into the field of litigation, and we will not spend our lives sitting behind a desk." Following her example, they wanted to work in open court rather than practice law from the safety of an office. Roshni also spoke of the fathers who had been influenced by her visible success and were "encouraging their daughters" to pursue a career in law.

This is a remarkable success, worth underscoring. Roshni was implying that these heads of families had been influenced by her, even though she is a woman who has broken *parda* and *Pukhto*. Watching her on mainstream media, they had judged her to be someone who had retained her *i'zət* while also achieving notable success, even fame. The influence she extended was strong enough that these fathers chose law as a career for their daughters, even as, in KP, law is considered to be unsuitable employment for women.

Among the twenty-two respondents who spoke of the importance of role model influence were six women from the Christian, Baha'i, and Sikh communities. These ladies echoed the sample groups' understanding that exemplar responsibilities were part of women's visibility in the public sphere. Bushra, for example, identified herself as a "role model" for women in her Baha'i community, and the Christian Ribca talked of the international opportunities she had to speak out on behalf of *all* Pakistani women, as well as the nation's Christian minority.[5]

In addition, all six of these non-Muslim women saw themselves as exemplars for their own ethno-religious communities to the Muslim-majority. This most often occurred naturally through interaction at their places of work. Ribca, who occupied a leadership position, observed:

> I used to teach medical students. . . . So, being a Christian, and trying to . . . help these kids realize their full potential. . . . It ends up having this effect that these kids become tolerant towards Christians. They start respecting Christians. Because they don't have a lot of contact. . . . They don't know Christians in authority. So, imagine a Christian woman being in authority, . . . helping them to become the best that they can be. That leaves a tremendous amount of respect in their hearts. . . . In that way, it did leave an impact, and I am grateful that I got that chance.

Role model influence, therefore, for these ethno-religious minority women came alongside the mechanisms of positivity and devotion to duty that were part of their honorable identity. They were able to influence for a change of mind regarding their faith community for the *individuals* they interacted with. However, what remained unclear from the interviews was the degree to which these non-Muslim women's visible professional and personal success in the public sphere could influence Muslims in a broader sense. There was no evidence given that, for example, they could change community thinking in the way that Roshni had when Pukhtun to Pukhtun she influenced fathers to approve of the law as a suitable career for their daughters.

---

5. What Ribca did not address was how Muslim Pakistanis viewed someone from a religious minority speaking as a representative of all Pakistani women.

Celebrity Endorser

Roshni's success as an influencer, however, may have been more than simply her position as a visible role model; an ordinary woman touching other people's lives through her success. As someone who appeared on mainstream media, she brought with her celebrity status. Naila, who identified herself as an influential social media blogger as well as a legal professional, understood celebrity influencers to be those you see and want to copy. She included in her list of celebrity influences actors on television, social media personalities, and teachers. She described from personal experiences what it means to be a celebrity on social media platforms in Pakistan. "It means that people look up to you, and then they learn from you, and they get influence from you, and then they start doing whatever you are doing. So it is that you have an effect on them."

Other respondents also recorded how they had been influenced by Pakistani women who were famous for their online presence. In addition, they named historic figures, recent political personalities, their own famous fathers, and successful professional women as having influenced them. Eleesha, for example, provided an illustration of the powerful influence a celebrity teacher and media personality could have on others. She spoke of Farhat Hashmi, the founder of the Al-Huda piety movement, as one whose teachings and lifestyle had given a purpose to her life. Hashmi had shown her how to "become a beneficial person." Being "beneficial" involved influencing others as she had been influenced.

The difference between a celebrity endorser and a role model exemplar has to be interpreted against the background of women's recent emergence into the public sphere. For example, the women who followed Roshni into litigation did so not simply because her visible success was something they wanted to copy. They chose that career because they accepted her endorsement, as someone who appeared on mainstream media, that this field was one that women could enter without damage to their or their families' honor. In a sense, she was a recognized celebrity endorsing the legal profession as a *brand*. The power of a celebrity endorser also cut across ethno-religious divides. Maryam, a Christian, for example, was an avid follower and admirer of a female Muslim influencer. She endorsed her approach to life; and bought her products. This is the more traditional form of branding that celebrities bring alongside their influence.

In terms of person (who), process (why), and mechanism (how), the interviews have shown that a position of successful and honorable visibility, especially for women in leadership, facilitates the influence mechanisms of role model endorser and celebrity exemplar for Muslim and non-Muslim respondents alike. However, Maryam noted that even for those at a celebrity level there is criticism. Not only are there topics that no one should discuss in public in KP-Pakistan, but there are also those things that women specifically, because of their gender, are not allowed to say publicly. Maryam told me that people will say, "why are you talking about certain topics, which are not allowed in our society."

In addition, family attitudes and class status may have made it difficult or even impossible for a woman like Maryam to become a celebrity endorser, despite her passion to be someone whose opinions are on social media for others to engage with. Potentially, as a Christian, she has greater freedom than her Pukhtun contemporaries. However, she did not have the support of her family/community to blog. They were fearful of what might come upon them as a community through her visible online presence. Also, as a member of the lower to middle class, she lacked the opportunities that were available to someone like Ribca, who belonged to an upper-class family.

Mentor

Returning again to the melon proverb, the type of melon mentioned is a *kharbuza*, a yellow muskmelon. Literally, the proverb says, "A muskmelon gains its color by sitting with muskmelons." This could be understood as a metaphor for the influence of close contact as found in mentoring or grooming. "Grooming" is a commonly used positive term in Pakistan, meaning guidance and training. As Safia explained, junior doctors "look up to seniors for their professional grooming." Daania used the word "icon" to describe herself in relationship with her staff, as those junior to her. She was one of very few female entrepreneurs in KP and was acutely aware of the way people looked to her as both a role model—an icon— and someone who, in her words, "nurtured" the younger generation.

Mentoring was spoken of by eleven of the women who took part in the study. Six of them, including Hina and Farah, commented on the mentoring they had received from their teachers. Three of them, in senior positions, mentioned their own mentoring of younger women.

This included teaching them how to behave in a majority male space—a sphere that women were newly entering. Their comments acknowledged how little there was at home, or in segregated education, to prepare girls to interact appropriately with men.

In addition, the banker, Gohar, equated influence with the process of being mentored by a person who embodied in her life those elements that made one want to change because they challenged current ways of thinking. Her own mentoring had come from women who were different to her in their ideas and thought processes. All of this was captured in her definition of the word influence.

> Influence is basically . . . your thoughts, your behavior, your attitude, your work ethics, the way which you handle yourself. And it is communicated to another person who finds it, and gets impressed by it, or tries to change or adapt to what you show or how you behave. . . . Influence. It means to mentor somebody. To help somebody. To change somebody. Influence is like you are bringing a sort of small change in a gentle way.

The effectiveness of mentoring as a strategic influence mechanism for women in KP was explained to me by Romika, a Pukhtun, and a senior leader in an INGO, who I interviewed online in English in March 2021. She described how government institutions had used mentoring to support newly qualified female engineers.

> When they started coming into the government institutions, it was a very difficult time for the institutions themselves and the community where there was no acceptability. And then some of the government institutions, what they did, they placed those females with those visionary people who were mentors. That gave them the strength. And they were kind of the change makers for them. And then slowly and gradually, those females who were first put in the office space to do only official work, now they are at key positions at the field level and supervising the districts.

The implication was that these "visionary mentors" were female pioneers, the first women to take up government posts, possibly in fields other than engineering, who paved the way for the next generation. No longer are female engineers restricted to the *parda* style safety of an office job, but they can expect to gain managerial positions in the field, in charge of men.

However, neither Romika or any of the others in this grouping of eleven women, talked of differences in mentoring styles from first generation pioneers to second and now third generation mentors. Nor was it clear from Romika's comments to what extent the change in mindset within the government departments, allowing women greater access to the field, was due to other influence tactics available to women, in addition to mentoring. However, these eleven respondents were clear that mentoring was always exercised professionally, by proven and mature women in positions of seniority, in the nurture of their professional juniors. They were confident that it resulted in long-lasting change.

RESISTANCE AND FAILURE

Alongside mentoring, within the wider frame of persuasion, ten Muslim and three non-Muslim women in the sample group spoke of their efforts to change entrenched societal practices that harm women. These practices included domestic violence, workplace harassment, early marriages, inheritance rights, and the sexual abuse of religious minority women. All of these respondents were involved in high level committees, including Pakistan's National Commission on the Status of Women. Thus, they were positioned to influence decisions being made at legislative levels in KP, and also federally. They recounted how they had used persuasive argument to establish rehabilitation programs and women's shelters. Where needed, they had also changed strategy to use their professional status to help individual women receive a fair hearing in the face of official obstructionism.

However, Zainab and Romika described both the issues and the contexts they were dealing with as "tricky." The adjective tricky encompasses what Khan calls, in her analysis of the politics of activism, a "complex and dangerous terrain."[6] Complexity and danger arise because of the entrenched nature of patriarchal norms, and the strength of resistance to any attempts to change them. Romika, speaking of failed influence, told me: "When it comes to the matter of the policies and the procedures, it's a very tricky thing." Tricky, at this level describes being unreasonably thwarted in her attempts to influence for change within the INGO where she worked. It is impossible to determine from her comments how much such failure is due to the same levels of socio-religious resistance and gender-based obstructionism that Khan documented in the context of

6. Khan, "Politics of Activism," 40.

female activism. Romika may have simply used the adjective to describe organizational red-tape and inertia.

Zainab's experience is closely aligned to that of Khan's. Zainab used the word tricky to describe both the failure of successive governments to implement pro-women legislation and the difficulty women experienced in trying to access their rights. She used the example of inheritance. Despite being enshrined in state and Islamic law, female inheritance on the death of a relative is strongly resisted by KP's male-dominated society, which makes it difficult and dangerous for women to claim what in law is rightfully theirs.

The impact of such resistance on would-be influencers was noted by Qamar in terms of her own struggle to influence as the manager of a program designed to improve domestic living conditions for women. This included dealing with the issue of domestic violence. She spoke to me of the helplessness it engendered in her, when, despite a massive amount of trying, nothing could be done to change the mindsets that enable the abuse of women in the home.

> So, . . . you see where you feel helpless. And your influence, it is a lot of efforts, . . . not just because of the advocacy or sensitization efforts. It's beyond that. It is something inbuilt. The violence, . . . the socialization background and a misinterpretation of your Islamic teaching. And power, and position, and relationship. . . . These are a few things . . . [where] you think that your influence is not as good as you want.

Her comments point to the resistance by powerful, conservative elements within KP society and the "inbuilt," (i.e., cultural) norms against which female advocacy can feel inadequate. Resistance included, in her experience, male violence, and the use of power, position, and male networks to obstruct any attempts to bring about change. The result was the continued marginalization of the female voice, and a sense of helplessness.

Yet, there was no indication from any of the interviews that a lack of personal agency required the respondents to use cunning and deceit as influence mechanisms, even though these characteristics were attributed to women by popular folklore and traditional religious belief. In fact, nine of the forty-eight women Mariya and I spoke to declared that they *had never failed to influence.* Two of the nine explained that they took care over what battles they fought and only exercised their influence when and where they were confident of success. Just one participant declared that when situations arose where failure seemed likely, she left her job! From an analytical viewpoint, this strategy seems to illustrate a failure to influence rather than an example of never failing.

Five of the women declared that they had never failed in their influence because they chose not to categorize unsuccessful attempts at influence as total failures. Instead, they reclassified them as God's will, or as an obstacle to be challenged. The school principal Sumayyah unpacked this process when she talked to Mariya in September 2019:

> I cannot think of anything that I haven't been able to do. I think I am quite good at problem solving. And if one thing doesn't work out, I will try another way, and another way, and another way. And in the end, I do get what I want.

As summarized by Zainab, "If you are focused and you're resilient, you eventually learn how to influence. And that can be you influencing them directly, or you looking for people who can influence. So, things get done."

NETWORKING

The use of people and networks to "get things done" is one of the repeated themes that emerged from the interviews, although only three women used the term "network." Nine elite and upper-class women, Muslim and non-Muslim, spoke of being part of groups of like-minded individuals, all linked to social change. For example, on a professional level, Romika recounted that the success of her INGO project was directly linked to the connections she was able to form and maintain. No connections meant no influence, in her opinion. "If I am talking about the government stakeholders, the more you are with them and the more good connections you have, the more you will exercise your influence." Also key were the "gauge" of a woman's influence and the "level" her role. That is, to influence, a woman needs to bring a level of status to the network that positions her as someone who should be listened to; this is her gauge. Romika's professional position placed her among senior decision-makers, where aided by her upper-class status, she was able to use both organizational and informal networks to successfully discharge her work responsibilities. Although not made explicit in her interview, these informal networks may have included those of *birādari* because of its links to both family and Pukhtun identity. Networking seemingly provided Romika with a route by which she could circumnavigate the trickiness of organizational resistance as she worked to influence for societal change within an INGO.

The types of networks identified by these nine women, in addition to the informal links of kinship and social status, included those of social work/activism, academic research, and politics. In addition, the older women in this group brought to their current posts a multiplicity of networked connections established in the past. Also within this group were women whose past and current national and international exposure linked them to powerful forums including the National Assembly, national commissions, regional women's groups, INGOs, and the representatives of foreign governments. These respondents were aware that their participation in powerful networks made them less easy to ignore. According to Nadia, such connections got laws passed.

In the same vein, Qamar described her involvement in a network of senior, well-connected women. Each woman was successful in her own right, but it was by working together that they could get their requests into the hands of "like-minded policy makers and parliamentarians" as the men working directly with legislation. "Like-minded" here means, supportive of the women's views and values. Networking in this context, therefore, took the form of group membership. It was as a group together that the women had the weight to pass on proverbial color to others, and see their influence achieve individual and, ultimately, societal change. Importantly, however, networking also serves to highlight even senior women's marginalization in KP. As Qamar explained, "Without their (male) support, women cannot bring or influence any agenda in their life." She was referring to women's lack of decision-making capacity in the domestic and public spheres. In her opinion, such marginalization of women exists not just in Pakistan, but "around the world." Male support is therefore essential because high-level decision-making remains in male hands.

This need for male support, and the lack of decision-making capacity, places women in KP in the position of *client* in a societal patron-client network that works both horizontally and vertically. For example, Zainab had used her networked influence to facilitate a project for underprivileged children. At that time, in her words, a "nobody" in the professional world, she had coerced local government authorities, and used her peer networks until the project had the permissions and the funding it required. She attributed her success to her "family background" (i.e., her elite status). Her success was based on the power and authority implicit in her family name, her connections to other families of similar status and wealth who worked on her behalf behind the scenes, and her use of connections to high-level decision-makers and national leaders in her patrilineal kinship and friendship networks.

Middle and Lower-Class Networking

Without the power and authority of a family name, and often positioned socially and professionally as clients or juniors, women from the middle and lower classes could not necessarily expect compliance from others. Therefore, they had to find other ways to persuade people to their point of view. However, only two women from these strata of society spoke of using networks to increase their influence. One was Fauzia, who spoke of herself as someone without social or professional status. She considered herself to have influence because of the social activism network of which she was a part. She described that connection as her primary influence mechanism.

> I am not on a big *post*, nor do I have a big position, but I have re-
> lationships like that. Praise God that I built it this much strong,
> that if there is a concern I just need to call someone, and all is
> done. . . . After that every problem was solved by itself. I can only
> tell you this: that this is influence.

Fauzia made up for her lack of status, as a middle-class Ismaili woman, by being networked into a group where she had built relationships to individuals with societal clout. These women had the authority and power Fauzia lacked. At the same time, however, her activism brought her into direct conflict with her own elders. She described it as a battle on three fronts: her right to speak out as a woman, her right to represent her faith community, and her right to challenge prejudices in the Pukhtun mindset.[7]

The mechanism of networking provided the means by which Fauzia, and women like her from the lower and middle classes, could access the authority commanded by those with high(er) social status. From Fauzia's example, it seems that their access was as clients seeking the support of a patron. However, once part of a network, women from low(er) social and/or ethno-religious minority backgrounds could tap into the power

7. Fauzia had also indicated that no one in her family supported her involvement in activism.

contained in the network, as well as contribute to a group that spoke with a powerful collective voice. It mirrors the experience of upper-class women who also needed the collective weight of a network to achieve change; and who also came as clients to male patrons and decision makers.

However, within the frame of the limited numbers of my sample group, the interviews showed that upper class and elite women are more likely to be part of networks than women from the lower and middle classes. Their accounts indicated that social status, at least in part, determines access to powerful networks able to exert influence. However, this requires a quantitative survey to determine the accuracy of my suggestion. In addition, my interviews did not explore the quieter, community-based networks that are achieving change on a smaller, local level.

Sifārish, Recommendation Culture

Lack of access, and other limitations on their personal or professional influence, can require individuals to request a favor through the cultural practice of *sifārish*. This is the act of asking a favor, on behalf of another, from someone in a position of authority with whom one has a connection. The favor is often, but not always, asked on behalf of a relative. The influence mechanism is the *act* of recommendation; of making a request on another's behalf. As an influence strategy, it is not dependent on a successful outcome. *Sifārish* can involve the person in authority breaking the rules in order to grant the favor. The designation good (positive) or bad (negative) attached to *sifārish* is determined by the nature of the assistance the other person is being recommended for.

Ribca observed that "the *sifārish* culture . . . exists in every department and every field" throughout Pakistan. Yet, given the prevalence of this type of influence, just one woman in my sample group mentioned it directly, and only three women referred to it indirectly. Four others, including Ribca, only talked about *sifārish* because I asked them specifically about this cultural practice. Ribca described the influence mechanism of *sifārish* in both positive and negative terms from her own experiences, and also from her professional role in the medical field.

> It has its pros and its cons. Why I say that is because, you know, with *sifārish*, the people who don't work as hard, they tend to come . . . ahead. But at the same time, those people who have been working hard for something, . . . they are left behind. So

> even in those cases, sometimes you need a *sifārish* . . . to do the right thing . . . you have to do it. You have to, because otherwise they are just held back. So, . . . it's not a good thing, but sometimes to do the right thing, you have to do it. It depends on, I think, the person for whom you are doing it. For example, if I am in a position where I am checking patients. We give them numbers [so they are seen in order]. . . . But if a colleague of mine comes in . . . and says that there's a really old lady . . . but her number is about number ten, and you are checking patient number one, so could you please check her first. So that is a *sifārish*.

In Ribca's description, the recommendation made by her medical colleague was on behalf of a 90-year-old lady; that she be seen ahead of other patients because of her age. This was good *sifārish*, because Ribca was influenced to bend the rules on behalf of a deserving person. Bad *sifārish* occurs when a person is influenced to flout the rules simply to advance someone who does not deserve such help. As Ribca pointed out, bad *sifārish* enables some to progress by getting a job or gaining a professional advancement without putting in the hard work that would have legitimately qualified them for the position. As a consequence, those who had worked hard to advance their careers were left behind and had no alternative but to find someone who could recommend them to a person in authority willing to (potentially bend the rules) and prioritize them above others.

For two respondents, however, the practice of negative *sifārish* was *synonymous with influence*. One of them, Khadijah, spoke of "influence" as something she would never allow to be used in her place of work, although she was happy to use influence (i.e., *sifārish*) elsewhere. This view of *sifārish* as a negative practice may be the reason why the majority of women in the sample group chose not to mention this common influence mechanism in their interviews. When I spoke with my RAs about *sifārish*, Idris was reluctant to identify it as an influence mechanism. Influence for him is a positive exercise, while *sifārish* is a wrong use of relationships, and something society should not engage in.

SECTION III

Analyzing the Voices

12

Honor's Role in Female Influence

WOMEN ARE CHANGING THE traditional ways of thinking and behaving in Khyber Pakhtunkhwa. Girls are coming into KP's public spheres of education and employment because of the influence of older female role models, especially those with a media presence. Networks are providing ways by which women can persuade others to change their minds; and goals are being achieved, despite resistance and obstructionism. Yet it is clear that, however women choose to influence, their *ɪ'zət-e nafs* and their status are key factors in the process.

"The terms 'honour' and 'shame' have been used to represent an enormous variety of local social, sexual, economic and other standards. The significance of these values in each culture should not be minimised."[1] This holds true of the presentation of honor and shame, as found in the province of KP, even as it was first said by Michael Herzfeld of the Mediterranean region. Presenting concepts such as *ɪ'zət*, *ghe'rət*, and *sharm* through the filters of another language and culture is complex. In many contexts, the English-language glosses of *honor* and *shame* are inadequate to communicate the lived experiences of another culture and attempts to categorize hinder rather than help the processes of cross-cultural analysis.[2] In an effort to bridge the gap, and communicate depth and breadth of meaning, one approach has been to use stories. Accounts of real events not only unpack what honor-shame mean within a specific

1. Herzfeld, "Honour and Shame," 339.
2. Herzfeld, "Honour and Shame," 339; Taylor, *Linguistic Categorization*.

181

culture but also explain the different shades of meaning captured by the language of that culture when talking of these lived realities. Story can also be used to underscore a specific perspective within a culture.

My perusal of books about honor-shame written in English by Pakistani authors, available from an Islamabad bookshop, revealed a multiplicity of titles that use story to explain honor in Pakistan from a female perspective. For example, *I Should Have Honor* is Khalida Brohi's quest to present honor-crime through an autobiographical, non-academic lens. Nafisa Shah's *Honour Unmasked* is an academic approach to understanding the relationship between honor violence (*karo-kari*), and the law and politics in the Upper Sindh. Shah uses testimony—stories of actual events—to illustrate the lived reality of honor in specific Sindhi communities. The journalist, Mehr Tarar's *Do We Not Bleed?* also uses story to present the everyday issues of honor that impact women's lives in twenty-first century Pakistan. Honor for Tarar is most often understood to be a father's, brother's, husband's or son's honor "all connected to how a woman lives her life" with the associated tension of conforming to "'accepted' standards of morality." Haeri, however, in her book that tells the stories of influential, professional women, suggests that honor goes deeper than a woman's compliance to societal codes, and is also more than any symbolic attribute of purity or chastity. She argues that professional women in Pakistan, visible in the public sphere, desire their honor to be founded on who they are as people—their actual rather than their symbolic worth, as those who bring value to society.[3]

These are the issues that the forty-eight women in my study were also grappling with. Purity and chastity, women's *i'zət-e nafs*, were important to them, not as symbols but as a demonstration of worth. They used story, together with idiomatic and proverbial language, to communicate the embeddedness of *i'zət* in culture and women's condition, and the impact this had on their/female influence. For the Pukhtuns in my study, honor is an ethical attribute, enshrined in *Pukhto*; yet it is also their behavior and the state of their being. The women from other ethno-religious groupings talked in similar ways about the importance of their respect. Unsurprisingly, therefore, the presentation of female dignity, the assault on that dignity in the public sphere, and the measures taken by women to preserve and promote their honor are core elements of many of my respondents' stories.

3. Haeri, *No Shame*, 36, 41.

My research moved beyond simply recording stories to consider the use of honor, together with hard work, as an *influence mechanism*. This honor mechanism challenges the traditional perception of female purity and chastity, but not to see it removed. For everyone of the women who took part in my research, female purity—they used the words dignity and respect—remains the "'natural' foundation for social and moral order."[4] The challenge that these women represent to traditional mindsets is their push to extend the boundaries of female purity. Consciously and unconsciously, they have brought women's *i'zət* into the public sphere. More than this, they—and observably other women in KP—have taken on roles and responsibilities that were formerly the preserve of men.

It proved helpful, therefore, when analyzing female *i'zət* not to limit my presentation to the English term honor, but to partner it with words such as respect, dignity, and trust. Dignity encompasses right behavior, which in turn speaks to the right to be valued and respected for one's own sake. Respect contains a recognition of the value someone brings with them because of who they are, as well as the contribution they are making. Trust is a response to observed dignity and respect.

Nadia, in her interview, described the creation of an authentic name as something she set out to achieve through her honorable identity, her *i'zət*. *I'zət*, used together with hard work, is a key influence mechanism for her. The term *authentic* is descriptive of someone who is seen to lead "a meaningful moral life."[5] An authentic name is an expression of female honor and also a "claim to worth" that brings with it "the social acknowledgement" of that worth.[6] Thus, the public endorsement of worth stands at the heart of honor. The challenge for women is seeing their honorable worth endorsed in a space that traditionally brings dishonor on women. As described by Safia, in her struggles to be accepted as a surgeon, once a woman's moral authenticity is established, she can continue to use the mechanism of honor and hard work to persuade people that she has the mental capacity to perform tasks that are traditionally male. Safia's task is to reproduce the ideal of female dignity in the public sphere in order that society would acknowledge that dignity and grant her the worth of an honorable reputation. That is, there would be a public acknowledgement

4. Haeri, *No Shame*, 36.

5. Maqsood, *Pakistani Middle Class*, 62.

6. Malina, *New Testament World*, 31.

that "her actions conform[ed] with social oughts."[7] Only after that would any demonstration of her professional abilities be considered.

Foucault's analysis of truth provided me with another tool by which to approach the duties and obligations, the social oughts that are contained in the cultures and communities the women in my study belong to.[8] These are the often-unspoken rules of society that they are required to submit to, in order to influence. Foucault described the processes that take place as a society uses its power to frame the truth about a topic. (He chose as an example the way in which society handles the separation of the insane from other people.) Foucault observed that society creates a code by which to monitor and judge people. Judgement is based on adherence to this code. He wrote that this code "rules [the] ways of doing things (how people are to be graded and examined, . . . etc.)" and produces "true discourses which serve to found, justify and provide reasons and principles for these ways of doing things."[9]

In the KP context, the primary truth regarding female honor in the public sphere is formulated by the code of *Pukhto. Pukhto* is then reproduced in and/or supplemented by the respondents' own socio-religious communities as they formulate their own codes. Societal judgement of female identity and behavior takes place against these codes. The challenge facing Safia in her struggles to be recognized as a surgeon is how to influence KP society so it would recast the truths it adheres to in order that the codes it uses to monitor and judge women can be redrafted. This would require society to replace a "field of knowledge," a societal mindset, with another knowledge or truth. Society would then have to accept the associated shift in power relations associated with that new knowledge.[10]

One part of women's success in changing public mindsets is demonstrated on a practical level by the respondents in my study. They had entered education and employment with the support of key members of their families as those who had already been influenced to adjust their traditional stance on women in the public sphere. The terms supportive and cooperative used by these women encompassed a shift in (male) mindsets that had enabled them to enter spheres that were formerly closed to them. This shift in power relations also enabled them to take up positions of responsibility that were formerly designated as unsuitable for

7. Malina, *New Testament World*, 32–33.
8. Burchell et al., *The Foucault Effect*.
9. Burchell et al., *The Foucault Effect*, 79.
10. Foucault, *Discipline and Punish*, 27.

women. This is important. It suggests that for Pukhtun women, *Pukhto* is not only being successfully negotiated, but also permanently changed in the urban and settled areas of KP.[11] Due to the diversity of my sample group, the suggestion is that the equivalent codes, operating among the other ethno-religious identities in KP, are being changed in a similar way.

In other comparable situations, the language of revolution has been used. Afary used revolutionary terminology for example, in her analysis of the ways in which young Iranian women were persuading their parents to support approaches to marriage that would not have been tolerated by earlier generations.[12] The same sort of language was used by Hasso of female activists in Bahrain.[13] The women interviewed for my study, however, did not consider themselves to be part of a revolution, even where they were conscious of their involvement in influencing for societal change, or were directly involved in activism. The key issue for the respondents was not the platform on which they stood, but that they retained their cultural identity and honor while occupying that place of engagement with KP's public sphere, be that study, work, or religious, social or political involvement. It is for this reason, therefore, that none of the Pukhtun respondents viewed themselves as having lost their *Pukhto*.

Barth, writing in 1969, studied the maintenance of Pukhtun honor, their identity. He argued that while lineage and *Pukhto* provided that identity, it was maintained by the activities of *melmastiā* (hospitality), *jirga* (council) and *parda* (seclusion).[14] "These three central institutions combine to provide Pathans with the organizational mechanisms whereby they can realize core Pathan values fairly successfully."[15] For the men of Barth's study, these are the values against which the performance of identity is measured and judged. They are also values that are shared by other ethnic groups in Pakistan; the peoples living on KP's borders. Barth argued that Pukhtun identity changes when the performance of *Pukhto* is poor, and where other "alternative identities" coming from surrounding areas, including Afghanistan and the Punjab, are available. His examples were of a loss of autonomy, and situations where Pukhtuns need only keep the

11. Barth, "Pathan Identity," 133–34.

12. Afary, *Sexual Politics*, 360–61.

13. Hasso, "The Sect-Sex-Police Nexus," see 119–20.

14. Barth, "Pathan Identity," 120. Barth's definition of *parda* is through the lens of male virility, whereas the women in my study talked of *parda* as central to their honor because it shows submission to male seniority and to *Pukhto*.

15. Barth, "Pathan Identity," 123.

minimal requirements of *Pukhto* to retain their identities as Pukhtun.[16] It could be argued, therefore, that in my study, those Pukhtun families who broke *parda* and allowed their women access to the public sphere had simply taken on practices coming from the Punjab and elsewhere, and were poor in their practice of *Pukhto*. The implication being that something similar is also happening to the non-Pukhtun women; that they, too, are poor in the practice of their ethno-religious codes.

How women in KP reach the public sphere requires ongoing research, including the issues of effective persuasion and a decline in the value given to societal codes. The importance of women's demonstrable honor as both the result of and a catalyst for societal change, however, cannot be understated. It reflects the success of the mechanism of honor and hard work exercised in KP's public sphere by Muslim and non-Muslim women. It also suggests that it is the public endorsement of a woman's honor that makes her a credible influencer, which in turn reflects growing confidence in the new identity and behavior of women. Viewed through the lens of social influence theory, this is true influence. That is, influence that has led to "long lasting attitude change."[17] In real terms in KP, women's voices backed by women's behavior, have persuaded some in society that there is a benefit in allowing (certain) women to exercise influence in the public sphere. Others have then conformed to this societal change, because they understand it "to provide evidence about reality."[18] Women working and influencing within the public sphere is something that they/society can now accept as a norm, with no loss of honor, dignity or respect attributable to those women, or to their families. This is a new message that KP society is having to grapple with.

THE ROLE OF GENDERED SPACE

Resistance to the new message of women's honorable presence in the public sphere, as spoken of by the respondents in my study, was seen to come from those in KP's society who saw no benefit to a female presence in the public sphere. In 1939, the conservative Islamic scholar, Maududi, described *parda* "as a title for the set of injunctions which contribute *the*

16. Barth, "Pathan Identity," 132–33.

17. Turner, *Social Influence*, 37.

18. Turner, *Social Influence*, 37.

most important part of the Islamic system of community life."[19] (The emphasis is mine.) In his understanding, "the free intermingling of the sexes" opened the floodgates to licentious and obscene behavior.[20] Thus, according to Maududi, it was a man's responsibility, "as governor in the family," to ensure that "women's sphere of activity should be segregated from that of a man's."[21] Almost 80-years later, Aamir Jamal's research into girl's education and gender justice in KP, showed Pukhtun men—the governors and gatekeepers of their families' honor—grappling with the same issue of *parda* and their male socio-religious responsibility. The challenge for these twenty-first century men was how to ensure the segregation of women from men by which honor is maintained whilst also allowing their daughters access to the public sphere for education and possible employment.[22]

The power behind segregated space as a societal system was identified by Foucault within the framework of discipline and punishment.[23] He observed that the powerful in society have historically created enclosures to maintain order, and to ensure the supervision and control, the productivity, and the safety of individuals within certain designated spaces. These spaces included factories, schools, prisons, and towns.[24] Foucault argued that these spaces created a hierarchy or ranking, whereby each element "is defined by the place it occupies in a series, and by the gap that separates it from the others."[25] These places were ideal concepts, yet they were also real, functional spaces, which Foucault, believed had enabled the rise of capitalism. In the same way, *parda* as a system of gender separation is an ideal, a truth, for many in KP-Pakistan, but at the same time it operates as a functional space within society. As such *parda* is not simply an ethical goal, part of *Pukhto*, but a reality that all women, not just Pukhtuns, have to negotiate to some level.

In my analysis of gendered space, Foucault's theory of enclosures, although a useful lens by which to understand the implementation of codes on sections of society, was inadequate to analyze how *parda* as a socio-religious choice impacts female influence. Of those interviewed

19. Maududi, *Al-Hijab*, 18.
20. Maududi, *Al-Hijab*, 3.
21. Maududi, *Al-Hijab*, 159.
22. Jamal, *Gatekeepers*.
23. Foucault, *Discipline and Punish*, 141–42.
24. Rabinow, *The Foucault Reader*, 17.
25. Foucault, *Discipline and Punish*, 145.

for my research, only four Muslim and four non-Muslim women talked about *parda*. This suggests, firstly, that *parda* impacts Muslim and non-Muslim women alike, and secondly, that as a topic, it is not necessarily associated with influence in KP. Thirdly, *parda* may also be one of those societal norms that require no discussion because they simply are.

At the same time, these eight women presented opposing views: that *parda facilitates* female influence; and that it *obstructs* influence. According to the first view, *parda* is part of a structure established in and by Islam that facilitates female influence. This was clearly expressed by the Pukhtun educationalist, Shazmina, in her statement that "Allah-*pāk* . . . created *parda* for women." She was indicating that women in the public sphere want to follow the "narrow path" of piety and "acceptable behavior" as part of being "a good Muslim."[26] Shazmina's comments may reflect a resistance to perceived secularization, just as in the Iranian revolution the hijab and *chador* (veil) took on a "political and ideological hegemony."[27] However, her comments may equally have been in response to my Western research and/or an expression of her involvement in a conservative women's group such as Al-Huda or Jamaat-e-Islami. Whatever the underlying cause, Shazmina's understanding of *parda* stands as an expression of some women's acceptance of norms that seemingly work against what others might define as women's human rights and freedoms.

Dramatically, a female activist, protesting publicly in Bahrain, was recorded as asking, as she was arrested, "Are you going to charge me with a violation of honor?"[28] Her crime was being in the company of men to whom she was not related. The association of honor with women, and the positioning of this honor within female-only spaces, is a constant tension for men and women, as women enter the public sphere, be it in Bahrain or KP. One solution is the construction of female-only spaces. The Pukhtun anthropologist A. Ahmed proposed that these spaces work for women because they give them "control over their own enclosure."[29] Although she was referring to the design of Pukhtun homes, her argument can also be applied to gynesocial spaces in the public sphere. Within these spaces, women are protected from accusations of impropriety, and from any physical harassment. In addition, they are separated from any religious or cultural restraints implicit in working with men, such as expectations

---

26. Ahmad, *Transforming Faith*, 4.

27. Afary, *Sexual Politics*, 270.

28. Hasso, "The Sect-Sex-Police Nexus," 128.

29. A. Ahmed, *Sorrow and Joy*, 50.

of *sharm*, and the restrictions of *na mahram*. These are the men before whom a woman must keep *parda*.

They also do not have to deal with men who are made uncomfortable by being required to work with women. It is part of my own story, as the executive director of an organization in KP, that men were often uncomfortable dealing with me directly. They could look my husband in the eye, embrace him, and relate to him man to man. As a female director, and my husband's boss, I was somewhat of an enigma. Similarly, Iram explained that the role of female admissions was created in the school where she worked to help mothers coming to register their children. They "did not feel comfortable sitting in the office with a male alone. There is nothing bad in it, but our environment, our culture is not like this, that a woman should come and just have a negotiation or talk with a male staff." The aim was to make women feel comfortable in the public sphere. For the same reason many offices will have separate seating areas for men and women. Women also need separate washrooms, prayer areas, and rest spaces, because women cannot sit down to relax in the same room as men.

Therefore, as the vice-principal Baseera explained in her interview, she chose teaching as a career because it guaranteed a comfortable, "easy feel," all-female working environment.[30] An all-female space also enables women to move into positions of leadership and control they might not occupy in a mixed environment where men may object to women being appointed in leadership over them. Female leadership in separate female spaces, in interaction with gender peers, enhances women's "confidence, competence, feelings of self-worth, and prestige."[31] In turn, confidence and competence enhance women's ability to influence.

The second of the opposing views about *parda* coming from the interviews was that gendered space obstructs, rather than promotes, female influence. The feminist Spain, in her examination of the relationship of space to gender, knowledge, status, and power, had identified four components that perpetuated the privileging of men in society.[32] These were the cultural mores, physical design, societal institutions, and socialized behavior that operate across the three sectors of family, education, and the

30. It cannot be presumed that all of the thirteen respondents working in majority-female environments chose their workplace *because* it provided gendered security. At the same time, such choices were not impossible. It may be that Baseera was simply the only one to talk openly about it.

31. Hegland, "Mixed Blessing," 185.

32. Spain, "Gendered Spaces," 137, 147.

labor force. She argued that in societies that practice gender segregation as a societal norm, women's status is lower than in societies that have more integrated domestic and public spaces. A consequence of lower status is exclusion from the knowledge that gives the power to control. Where power is used to manage and control people, then knowledge is essential because it enables the wielder to be effective in his/her use of power.[33]

In my research, this viewpoint was captured in Aafiya's critique of female parliamentarians who, following gender segregated norms, were separated from the heartbeat of political legislation in the female only space of a women's lounge. Aafiya, shocked by the barrier this presented to female influence, worked to bring women together to engage with political activities. She was part of a spearhead within the KP Assembly to take a male sphere—governance—and convert it into a shared space. In addition, Aafiya's elite status had enabled her to physically appropriate the male-only space of the family *hujra* for her socio-political activities. Aafiya's actions were indicative of a move towards an emancipation that challenges male interests. However, Hina, working in a similar area to Aafiya, referenced a growing conservativism in KP-Pakistan that was marginalizing women by reducing the number of places in which they could resist patriarchy and push back against the gendering of spaces and activities. Although Aafiya, Hina, and others in the sample group held men responsible for the reduction of female spaces at a decision-making level, it is possible that this conservatism was one outworking of a growing Islamist middle class, and a subsequent loss of influence by the elite and upper classes. If an accurate assessment, it would mean that women as well as men will be involved in any future marginalization of women in KP-Pakistan.

THE ROLES PLAYED BY CONFIDENCE AND POSITIVITY

In social influence terms, the confidence to be in the male space, doing those things that men do, is an expression of (self-)confidence directed at a task. It is "a belief in one's ability to undertake a *specific* action to achieve an outcome."[34] Greenacre et al. proposed that people with "social self-confidence," that is a strong belief in one's own ability to interact well with

33. Gordon, *Power*, xviii–xix.
34. Greenacre et al., "Self Confidence," 3.

others in an organizational or social setting, are more likely to emerge as "natural opinion leaders . . . able to influence the decisions of peers."[35] In KP, social self-confidence and the move into the male-dominated public sphere is heavily intertwined with issues of honor because of the religio-cultural codes to which women and their families subscribe.

Sadaf Ahmad's conversations with Al-Huda students recorded the sense of freedom and security they felt when they adopted full veiling as an expression of *parda* they could bring into the public sphere.[36] Observably, a growing number of women throughout Pakistan now choose to wear full, Arab-style veiling as an expression of purity. Veiling facilitates confidence when interacting with men in the public sphere. Thus, I have seen in Pakistan's capital city fully veiled women jogging in a public park. Among the respondents in KP, the decision to veil was best described by Kiran who, dealing with issues of harassment at university, put on the əbāʾyə and hijab to create a comfortable space for herself where her confidence could grow. It gave her a sense of freedom, of taking back control, and regaining her confidence. However, Ahmad argued that the act of veiling in itself did not function as an influence mechanism. It did not, in her opinion, alter "the power structures within society . . . that give men carte blanche over women's bodies."[37]

A part of Kiran's ongoing story is that her decision to wear hijab cost her an internship at a Western university. Her male supervisor would only send her if she removed her headscarf; something she chose not to do. The complexity of *parda* is that, for some women, it operates as a type of resistance, of taking back control and restating one's honor. While for others, like her supervisor, it is to be resisted. Kiran did not talk of his motivation. He may have believed that the confidence and positivity she would need to study overseas should be expressed in a decision to take off the hijab. Equally, he may have been among those who see in Arab-style veiling the expression of an external power that seeks to control. In Kiran's case, her veiling/piety could have been perceived as an expression of extreme/extremist views, especially as she interacted with those less familiar with Muslim customs in a Western country. It seems from his request, that the supervisor viewed Kiran's hijab as an external religio-cultural symbol that she used to communicate "conservative notions of respectability and propriety," but one that did not necessarily represent

35. Greenacre et al., "Self Confidence," 4.

36. Ahmad, *Transforming Faith*.

37. Ahmad, *Transforming Faith*, 170.

her true motivation.[38] As a symbol it could be more easily discarded, enabling her to travel overseas.

Yet even if worn symbolically, the use of hijab and other forms of veiling come into every day life to empower women with an honorable identity in public. KP society recognizes it as such, much as they might do, in other contexts, a nun's wimple and habit. For the wearer, hijab is a statement of religious purity that can, as it did for Kiran, provide the wearer with confidence. The empowerment of *əbā'yə* and hijab has impacted Pakistani women who travel to the Gulf and other locations in the Middle East. There they have observed there "the mobility offered by the hijab."[39] It facilitated female freedom of movement and employment in mixed gender settings. The implication was that this use of hijab could be reproduced in KP-Pakistan replacing *parda* as a system of complete gender separation. This suggests that the increasing use of hijab among Pakistan's middle classes contains the ability not simply to provide women with confidence to be in the public sphere, but to reshape the traditional boundaries of gendered space with all the potential this has for female influence and ongoing societal change. Jamal and Maqsood's research is therefore seemingly documenting aspects of a modern restructuring of *parda* as a moral system in KP. This is a major shift in the understanding and application of *parda*. It requires a deeper analysis of change and its impact on people within the framework of power and societal practice. Further study is also needed to understand why the use of the traditional burka, *chador* and dupatta is not able to provide the same message as the *əbā'yə* and hijab. There is a need to gain a deeper understanding in how the wearers of hijab and other forms of veiling balance the restrictions that veiling represents—as a central expression of *Pukhto*—against the empowerment that these expressions of *parda* bring.

Confidence and positivity were key to Kiran's ability to function at university. Confidence is the cultivation of a belief in oneself as capable; positivity is the communication of this belief. Together, they work to facilitate influence for women in mixed or predominantly male environments where issues of honor-shame are being worked out, as illustrated in Kiran's story. Confidence and positivity are also expressions of belief in one's community identity. This was identified most clearly by the non-Pukhtun, ethno-religious minority women in my study who used the

---

38. Hasso, "The Sect-Sex-Police Nexus," 120.

39. Jamal, *Jamaat-e-Islami Women*, 156–57.

influence mechanisms of confidence and positivity to overturn stereo-typical thinking about themselves and the communities they represent.

This same sense of personal and corporate confidence and posi-tivity forms part of Saeed's accounts of women of influence in Pakistan contained in her book *Tapestry*. However, the ethno-religious minority women included in Saeed's compendium were not there as representa-tives of their faith communities. Saeed was celebrating the role played by influential women in Pakistan who were part of opening up a new space in the public sphere on behalf of *all* women in Pakistan. These women, Muslim and non-Muslim, like the respondents in my own study, were communicating that women's visible, physical presence in the pub-lic sphere has power simply *because* women are found in a space that had previously been closed to them. That they were there, in the public sphere, is influence in and of itself.

13

Influence from a Place of Difference

My interviews with the forty-eight women from KP identified that their influence *is* directly connected to their marginalization at deep, religio-cultural levels. One of the major forces in female marginalization is hierarchical patriarchy, that ranks women as societal juniors. My research, therefore, has to consider how women negotiate and/or resist the hegemonic socio-religious power of patriarchy that operates in and influences every sphere of life in KP-Pakistan. The women in my sample group called it male domination; a patriarchal social system that continues to shape their identities in KP's public spaces, as it had generations of women before them. It is this identity that some of the respondents in my study were seeking to redefine. Others were unconsciously contributing to this redefinition simply by being visibly employed in KP's public sphere.

The issue of marginalization, while impacting all the women in my research, takes on an extra dynamic when assessing the mechanisms of influence used by women from KP's non-Muslim minorities. Thirteen of the women in my sample group fell into this category. Foucault, writing of the development of discipline and punishment in Europe, described the mechanics used by a state to separate from the majority those it considers to be different.[1] His comments aid our understanding of the impact that issues of difference have on society, both the majority and those discriminated against.

---

1. Foucault, *Discipline and Punish.*

> Generally speaking, all the authorities exercising individual control function according to a double mode; that of binary division and branding (mad/sane; dangerous/harmless; normal/abnormal); and that of coercive assignment, of differential distribution (who he is; where he must be; how he is to be characterized; how he is to be recognized; how a constant surveillance is to be exercised over him in an individual way, etc.). . . . All the mechanisms of power which, even today, are disposed around the abnormal individual, to brand him and to alter him, are composed of those two forms from which they distantly derive.[2]

These two aspects of power—branding and coercion—Foucault understood to be shaped by social, cultural, and symbolic factors that determine what is or is not normal, deviant, and possibly dangerous. The exercise of power and control was comprised of the tangible and intangible resources accumulated by individuals and state institutions. These resources became so deeply embedded in the social fabric of everyday life that they functioned as "self-evident" norms that society found "difficult to abandon."[3]

Within the frame of my own study of female influence, these observations by Foucault seem to explain how Muslim majoritarianism and tribal discrimination are expressed in relation to the non-Muslim and non-Pukhtun communities in KP. Ethno-religious minority communities have been collectively *branded* as different, and separated from the majority, by those whose societal power determines what is "normal" and/or acceptable. These designations, reproduced in school and college curricula, become understood as the norm by much of KP society.

Within the broader frame of what is labelled "the Muslim world" the designation of minority has been documented from diverse angles using a wide variety of case-studies. For example, Keddie's research focused on Iran and documented the religious, linguistic, political, tribal, nationalistic, class, and ethnic differences that separate Muslim and non-Muslim minorities from the Muslim majority.[4] Mahmood investigated the role of the state in establishing religious difference and equality in Egypt and the wider Middle East.[5] Afary included in her research the ways in which

---

2. Foucault, *Discipline and Punish*, 199–200.

3. Foucault, *Discipline and Punish*, 232.

4. Keddie, "The Minorities Question."

5. Mahmood, *Religious Difference*.

non-Muslim communities are impacted by decisions made by the state, and their resistance to these decisions.[6] Hasso has investigated male and female Shiʻi activism as part of revolution within the micro-context of Sunni-ruled Bahrain.[7] These studies are part of the background against which I have set my own research; to discover how non-Muslim women, as well as Muslim, are influencing for social change in KP.

Ispahani is among those who have documented the impact of Muslim majoritisation on society in Pakistan.[8] She documented the move by the state to re-label the Ahmadi as non-Muslim, and the current marginalization of Shiʻi communities. She also referenced discrimination against other non-Muslim minority communities. However, as M.-M. Fuchs and Fuchs argued, a focus on discrimination can artificially place Pakistan's non-Muslim minorities into an "ahistoric" vacuum in which they are viewed as disconnected from the rest of society.[9] For opinions to be changed, and stereotypes overthrown, issues of similarity need to be emphasized. In my study, Ribca talked in her interview of working to establish those points of connection with Muslim medical students. She also spoke passionately of her work to break down stereotypical ideas, held by individuals in international communities and institutions, regarding Pakistan's minority communities. However, my sample group was too small to determine how many non-Muslim women are active in similar ways to Ribca.

One reason for the lack of information about Pakistan's minority communities may be attributable to population numbers. Non-Muslims form under 4 percent of Pakistan's total population, and therefore, their political significance is small. Thus, an ahistoric vacuum, a continued focus on discrimination, little political significance, and the marginalization of women may account for the paucity of non-Muslim women's voices in research on KP-Pakistan.

Simon Fuchs went some way to address the vacuum on information about minorities with his insights into the actions of Christians and Shiʻis to reclaim their status in Pakistan.[10] He had observed that these communities use three core strategies aimed at changing majority attitudes: their historic contribution to the nation, their current loyalty, and the

6. Afary, *Sexual Politics.*

7. Hasso, "The Sect-Sex-Police Nexus."

8. Ispahani, *Purifying the Land.*

9. Fuchs and Fuchs, "Religious Minorities," 8.

10. Fuchs, "Reclaiming the Citizen."

promotion of religious piety. However, none of the non-Muslim women that Mariya and I interviewed spoke of using their influence mechanisms to prove their loyalty to country or their right to be treated as equal citizens. An exception may have been Ribca through her use of international platforms to speak on behalf of minority women in Pakistan. At the same time, this direct approach may have been possible only because it happened outside of the country.

The non-Muslim women in my study used the influence mechanisms of positivity, personal integrity, and devotion to duty to demonstrate their loyalty to their organizations and to counter negative stereotypical views of their religious communities. Yet, on a micro-level, these women seemed to be using approaches that parallel Fuchs's findings. They were emphasizing similarity to counter socialized prejudices that portrayed their communities in a negative light. For example, the Christian teacher Kora described how she used her behavior to inspire her Muslim students who were reportedly amazed by her character. This comment pre-supposes that the students held socialized negative views of Kora's minority community. In social influence terms, this is a similar-to-norm social influence strategy that removes the need for conflict. Minority groups simply need to present their values, as Kora did, in a manner that validates them as pro-normative.[11] This works to disprove any negative stereotyping of their and their communities' values coming from those who oppose them.

Foucault had observed that those in power established coercive structures—such as the judicial system—to ensure the submission of others.[12] When "confronted by a power that is law" submission and obedience are the expected responses. This seems to reflect the proverb "he who has the stick has the control" used by the medical professional Zafira when talking of influence. Thus, it could be understood that because monitoring others' behavior in KP is a norm, linked to societal codes and expectations as well as to patriarchal and hierarchical values, the province's minorities will automatically comply with the dictates of the majority. Not least, they are positioned by their place in society as juniors and clients, where the majority takes the place of the senior leader and patron. Within this frame, positivity, devotion to duty, and personal integrity cease to be channels of influence or resistance. They operate

11. Turner, *Social Influence*, 99.
12. Foucault, *Discipline and Punish*.

simply as women's compliance to what is expected of them. In such a scenario, the reason why Maryam ceased to blog would be one of compliance, done purely to make life easier for her. In the same way, Samira complied with the decision that the sports teacher should become vice-principal because it was what the majority wanted. As acts of compliance, these responses could indicate a failure to influence. Or they could be seen as decisions not to try to influence for change *at that point in time.* This is what some of the respondents called a necessary compromise.

Therefore, it may be better to view the mechanisms of positivity, devotion, and integrity, as exercised by non-Muslim women in KP, as reflections of a peaceful revolution as used by protestors in Bahrain. Hasso described the non-violent strategy used by activists who "resignified the front stoop as a site of collective politics."[13] That is, they "occupied spaces" in front of their homes during Bahrain's Pearl Revolution when other forms of protest were considered too dangerous. One criticism of this approach is that it happened outside the public space of media visibility and thus lacked major effectiveness. In the same way, the peaceful positivity, hard work, and personal and professional integrity described by the non-Muslim respondents in this study could include a recognition that overt religious protest against marginalization is a sensitive issue in Pakistan.[14] Therefore, they chose to influence quietly, at times and in places where this was appropriate. Yet even this form of quiet activism aimed at changing mindsets does not fit comfortably with the influence exercised by non-Muslim women in their professional capacities as they daily encounter the complex realities of their presence in KP's public sphere.

Consequently, I also considered the defense of identity in the face of opposition as a means of understanding the influence tactics of positivity, devotion to duty, and honor and hard work used by the thirteen non-Muslim respondents. Haeri, for example, in her study of working women in Pakistan, tracked the defense of personal identity, refined through suffering and resistance, as told to her by one of her respondents.[15] Yet, the non-Muslim respondents in my research were not simply *defending* their identities as Christian, Baha'i, or Sikh, although this was a factor; and several of them referred to the pressure put on them to convert to Islam. Rather, their *influence* goal was to *overcome* negative, socialized mindsets about their faith communities encountered in their places of

13. Hasso, "The Sect-Sex-Police Nexus," 118.
14. Fuchs, "Reclaiming the Citizen."
15. Haeri, *No Shame,* chap. 2.

work. Therefore, I turned to the social influence theories of minority self-categorization and minority influence as the lenses by which to evaluate the effectiveness of positivity, devotion and integrity as influence strategies in the hands of non-Muslim respondents in their interaction with the Muslim majority.[16]

The social influence theory of self-categorization provided a lens through which to explore the suggestion that the influence mechanisms being used by these non-Muslim women were shaped by their different-from-same, them-us interaction with the Muslim majority. That is, those influencing from this minority position are required to see themselves in relation to others—the Muslim majority—as well as from the perspective of those others. This is what Kora was doing when she answered questions about her faith community coming from the students at the Muslim-majority school where she worked. However, Kora's action was more than someone from the least privileged in society defending a space she considered to be indispensable to her existence, her job, against the power of the majority who sat in judgement against her. Her use of the possessive adjectives "our" and "we" demonstrated that she was contesting and resisting the identity ascribed to her by the majority, and yet at the same time was consolidating a sense of her own, and her community's, identity in relation to them.

Nevertheless, as D'Souza observed in her critique of academic approaches to "normative" and "alternative" Islam, "it is the dynamics of hierarchy, power, and control, . . . that determine whose views are privileged in a given society."[17] Those in minority positions can resist or even challenge the views held by the majority, but they *cannot compel* change. Thus, the persuasive element of a pro-normative character is essential if influence is to succeed. The suggestion coming from those respondents in my study who belong to ethno-religious minorities is that they are using their pro-normative characters as a positive demonstration of their corporate and personal integrity—expressions, possibly, of a quiet revolution from people judged to be different. They used visible personal and professional integrity—the influence mechanisms of positivity, devotion to duty, and personal integrity—to at least sow doubt regarding the negative portrayals of their communities. Ribca and Kora, for example, were using lifestyle as well as their skills to exercise positive influence aimed

16. Moscovici and Personnaz, "Social Influence"; Turner et al., "Self and Collective."

17. D'Souza, *Partners of Zaynab*, 5.

at changing any negative preconceptions held by young Muslim students towards their religious community.

It was also clear from Kora's responses that she did not think of herself solely as someone discriminated against because of her Christian ethnicity. She also viewed herself as a woman with something to offer the people she worked amongst. In the immediate, one goal of her positivity and devotion may have been to make the workplace a more comfortable environment. However, in the wider frame, her emphasis on similarities, such as an honorable character, sincerity, and devotion, decreased the differences between her and her audience. As social influence from a minority position, any decrease in the gap between her, as the outgroup, and them, the ingroup, increased the possible effectiveness of her influence among the staff, and her students and their parents. They became more likely to let go of any negative preconceptions about Christians.

SIMILAR BUT DIFFERENT

The other grouping of *different* women in my sample group were those who identified as non-Pukhtun Muslims, including Fauzia as an Ismaili. Fauzia was vocal about the discrimination she, her family, and her community experienced. She placed the blame on inaccurate stereotyping. For example, she told me of a conversation she had overheard in which two young men talked of going to Chitral, because they had heard that the Ismaili people living there, who they called *kuffar*, sell their daughters, or will give a daughter and money to anyone who converts. Fauzia's approach was one of direct confrontation; asking them if they had eyewitness evidence to the truth of what they declared. Her goal was to make them ashamed of what they had believed, using shame as an instrument to change their minds.

There was no sense that any of the other women in this grouping of non-Pukhtun Muslim women used confrontation and shame to bring about a change of mindset. Instead, there was an acceptance of the prejudice against their different-to-norm identities. Rather than confrontation they used positivity, devotion, and personal integrity to break down barriers. The goal was to win personal acceptance in the spaces they occupied. It did not seem that any of these women, with the exception of Fauzia, were seeking to influence for a change of mind regarding their people group. At the same time, Fauzia's main avenue to influence was her membership of a group of Sunni Muslim women, who accepted her for who she is, and were willing to use their connections to deal with injustices she identified.

EXCLUSION

Although Fauzia found acceptance in a group of women who were similar but different to her, many of the non-Muslim, minority-Muslim, and non-Pukhtun women in this study had to deal with issues of exclusion linked to their different-to-norm identities. This formed part of their interaction with KP's public sphere and had to be negotiated. This exclusion was not, primarily, a punitive measure, and it was not referred to in those terms by the respondents. Their exclusion was from tribal and Sunni Muslim privilege. Pukhtun pride in their identity, for example, operated as an exclusion filter for those women who sought to influence as non-Pukhtuns in KP, and they acknowledged that it lessened their ability to influence in public-sphere settings.

In my research, for example, Eleesha explained that her non-Pukhtun identity had severely hampered her ability to influence, even though she was married into a Pukhtun family. Operating from a minority position, she had worked—seemingly over decades—to prove that her opinions could be trusted. The issues of exclusionary and discriminatory practices against ethno-religious minorities in Pakistan and growing Muslim nationalism were recorded by Ispahani.[18] She called it the gradual exclusion of ethno-religious minorities from Pakistani life. Respondents in my study identified the micro-events of *ta'sub* (bigotry) that included, for example, items non-Muslims were forbidden to touch, and friendships they were forbidden to develop. A socio-religious belief of pollution associated with non-Muslims, that operates as a barrier to social interaction, was recorded by Keddie and Afary in their research of Shiʻi practices.[19] Fauzia, also referenced this, as she recorded the designation of *kuffar* given to her Ismaili community.

Samira's failure to become the principal of a village school despite her seniority also fits into this frame; something she directly attributed to her Christian identity. Applying Samira's experience to my expansion

18. Ispahani, *Purifying the Land*, 122–25.

19. Keddie, "The Minorities Question," Jews section, para. 1; Afary, *Sexual Politics*, 236.

of the kite structure of influence (figure 6), she was placed in the tail of the kite, unable to exercise influence. Her identity as an ethnic Punjabi Christian marginalized her as person I or J in the network, whereas real power lay in the the external network of Pukhtun identity as it asserted its influence over that of the school's organizational structure.[20]

A second type of exclusion is self-exclusion from the public sphere and peer networks. This is the result of suspicion that flows from minority to majority. S. W. Fuchs and Schaflechner, for example, suggested that minority communities have their own stereotypical views of Muslims that shape their interaction with a majority that is deemed to be dangerous.[21] In my research, the non-Muslim activist, Bushra, referenced the cost of such exclusion for Hindu and Sikh girls and women who were shut out from education and employment. This is mirrored to some degree in Shanneik's study of the effects of self-ghettoization on Algerian Salafi women and their children as a minority Muslim community living in Dublin, for whom the world was polarized into them and us.[22] Religious identity and values were preserved by self-ghettoization; excluding from their space any other forms of teaching and behavior that could confuse their children. However, for these women, and for ethno-religious minority women in KP, while self-ghettoization preserves identity it removes their interactive voice from the public sphere. It is not possible for me to determine, from what was told to me by the ethno-religious minority women in my study, if such community barriers could be individually overcome by the use of social media or other platforms. Certainly, for some, the desire to do so was evident.

A suggestion that did emerge from the interviews was that a suspicion of others, and the defense of religious identity, resulted in a resistance to collaborative networking by non-Muslim communities with each other. This resulted in the loss of influence made possible when people unite around a common cause. This was identified by the respondent Bushra who had encountered resistance to her plan to bring young people from minority communities together. This underscored the ways in which different minority communities held to an "implicit theology

20. I have made no attempt to analyze the impact of a village setting on experiences such as Samira's, nor to draw comparisons between the urban and rural as it affected the respondents in my study.

21. Fuchs, "Reclaiming the Citizen"; Schaflechner, "Betwixt and Between."

22. Shanneik, "Religion."

around impurity and exclusion"[23] that separated them not only from the majority but also other minority communities. Thus, the separation of that which is deemed to be pure from that which is deemed to be different and consequently impure, is also seemingly at work in the relationships of minority communities with each other. Again, referring to the minority Algerian community in Ireland, the Salafi community chose not to send their children to schools run by different Muslim traditions, but instead sent them to a Catholic school where the distinction between them and us remained clear, and a purity of faith could be maintained.[24] In this way the honorable identity of their community was maintained, but their opportunities to influence were curtailed on multiple levels. Self-ghettoization stands outside the category of failed influence. It operates as a collective choice to effectively remove a community from available opportunities to influence for societal change.

23. D'Souza, *Partners of Zaynab*, 159.
24. Shanneik, "Religion," 89.

14

Status and the Challenge
to Social Control

THE ACCOUNTS OF SUCCESSFUL, and failed, public sphere influence coming from the women in my sample group have highlighted the importance of status and position if women are to take their place in Khyber Pakhtunkhwa's proverbial melon field as those able to pass color to other melons. The women who took part in my research talked of social and professional status, personal maturity, and the importance of education. They also spoke about patriarchy as a system of male dominance that shapes the culture of KP. No one in the sample group was asked to identify or define patriarchy, or male domination, as a pre-determined theme. At the same time, there was no sense of reluctance to approach the issue by those who chose to talk about it; and male domination was mentioned by over 80 percent of the respondents.

Eleven of these women proposed that *Pukhto*, as a religio-cultural system, is responsible for male domination in KP. However, as I compared the interviews of the non-Muslim and non-Pukhtun women with those of the Pukhtun respondents, it became clear that patriarchy is a pervasive force for all of the religious traditions represented in this study. Although my sample group was limited, and background information in English about non-Muslim cultural practices in KP was hard to find, it is possible to suggest that the experiences of the majority of respondents in my sample group reflect, to some degree, the lived experiences of many women in KP.

I decided not to independently analyze and evaluate every aspect of every influence mechanism used by women from positions of authority because they are all intertwined with patriarchy in the metaphorical ball of cultural threads. Instead, I have focused my analysis on patriarchy and *Pukhto* as the place where status, as an influence technique, intersects with the cultural norm of compliance. According to my respondents, status, patriarchy and *Pukhto* are the core components of KP's public sphere. As religio-cultural systems, patriarchy and *Pukhto* ascribe honor and status to women, but it is the position of the lesser, the junior to the senior. This is where understanding what women are saying about patriarchy is key to understanding the societal changes taking place in KP at this time.

APPROACHING PATRIARCHY WITHIN THE FRAME OF INFLUENCE

When the women in my study chose to use the English term male domination to talk about patriarchy, I understood it to be more than simple language-mixing. I interpreted it to represent their desire to underscore a social reality that reduces their status and undermines their influence. As an underscore, the use of English communicated the women's resistance to an ideology in which they have certain attributes assigned to them that are believed to be representative of their gender. The term domination, therefore, was not simply how women refer to patriarchy in Pakistan. It was being used to communicate to me, as a Western researcher, the idea of normal, male behavior in a patriarchal society, where "religious and social principles . . . [are] used as grounds to justify different rights, responsibilities and rewards to each gender."[1] The term male domination thus served to highlight female victimhood within a binary social system that characterizes women as lesser than men.[2]

Patriarchy, as presented through the sample group's voices, appears as a deeply rooted societal system founded on a religio-cultural premise that women occupy a place of *sharm*. As already established, *sharm* functions as a form of inverted honor within *Pukhto*. It is seated in modesty and subservience for men as well as women, but for women is also linked to their moral and physical weakness, as something both symbolic and actual. Patriarchy as practiced in KP, and as described by the respondents,

1. Hussein, "Femininity in African Proverbs," 59.
2. Siddiqui, *Language*, 33.

is an expression of classic patriarchy in which women in the private and public spheres are expected to comply with socio-religious rules. These rules work to advantage men; and disadvantage women, especially in issues of access to the world outside their homes. Within a system of classic patriarchy, women can be perceived as lesser: those who simply produce products for the family's benefit.[3]

This was graphically portrayed in the interview with the medical professional Zafira when she asserted that *Pukhto*, as a religio-cultural system, had relegated women's status to that of a domestic animal, a cow. Walby argued that this type of thinking was decreasing.[4] Her research had led her to conclude that the association of women with domestic production was slowly changing in the face of economic considerations and feminism, resulting in the collapse of classic patriarchy. In KP however, classic patriarchy continues as an acceptable societal norm for many women in KP, including Yasmin and her daughters. As Yasmin explained to me, she has always worked from home, doing handicrafts to supplement her husband's income, and continuing this practice after she became a widow. She subscribes to the traditional belief that women are *sinf-e-nazuk*, the weaker sex, whose honor is found only in the home. She explained to me that male honor is greater. This is why "men go outside, and women must not!" She summed this up in just a few words, "Women are good at home."

Kandiyoti in her exploration of conservative patriarchy in sub-Saharan Africa had observed that some women, rather than pushing for greater freedoms and the end of patriarchal attitudes, negotiated for a return to classic patriarchy.[5] This is the type of restrictive patriarchy that Yasmin, in my study, held as an essential for Pukhtun women. The women of Kandiyoti's research put pressure on the men in their families to "live up to their obligations" as a means of retaining or restoring the known of traditional patriarchal norms, even if this included increasing restrictions for themselves. This was a patriarchal bargain in which women accept restrictions in return for greater security and respect. What Kandiyoti did not discuss is whether the push for greater patriarchal security could result in a return to those extremes in which a woman's status becomes comparable to that of a domestic animal.

3. Kandiyoti, "Bargaining with Patriarchy," 278–81; Moghadam, *Modernizing Women*, 119; Walby, *Theorizing Patriarchy*, 178.

4. Walby, *Theorizing Patriarchy*, 61.

5. Kandiyoti, "Bargaining with Patriarchy," 283.

Yet within the realm of patriarchy, some women were unlikely to simply accept restrictions, and the expected response of compliance, without some form of resistance. In rural Greece in the 1980s, women could use the sense of obligation created by their submission to male authority, as a bargaining tool, an influence mechanism used to gain male compliance to their own demands. This obligation was the reminder that male honor is dependent on female behavior, and that women hold the power to disrupt that honor by bringing shame on the family.[6] Kandiyoti had seen this in action in a rural setting, where women resisted male appropriation of the benefits of their labor.[7] In the examples she gave to illustrate this argument, she showed how women chose as a platform for resistance that place within culture where they enjoyed a measure of autonomy—their labor.

It was individual and collective resistance, in this case to a state that demands submission, that caused Foucault to adjust his analysis of power as a system that makes compliance essential, and resistance almost impossible.[8] As noted by Afary and Anderson, Foucault's study of sexuality, and his interaction with the Islamist movement and revolution in Iran, had exposed him to active and successful resistance operating at those points in which hegemonic power intersects with daily life.[9] As Moscovici had proposed, societies do not like conflict and so will work towards a resolution rather than allow the conflict to continue.[10] This is the power that minorities hold: their ability to disrupt the comfortable norm. This can be at home, as in the African example, or in a nation. It is also a matter of status. Conflicts are resolved because there is some recognition of the other's value, be it that of producer to patriarchal beneficiary, junior to senior, minority to majority.

However, resistance to patriarchal practices among the respondents in my research was not a strategy mentioned by many of the women in the sample group. Although one of the respondents mentioned that, as a teenager, she went on hunger strike in order to persuade her father to allow her to go to college. All of the respondents were aware that disrupting a family's honor can have serious repercussions for women in KP-Pakistan. In addition, for these women the strong link between

6. Friedl, "The Position of Women," 51–52.

7. Kandiyoti, "Bargaining with Patriarchy," 276.

8. Foucault, *History of Sexuality*, vol. 1; Foucault, *Discipline and Punish*.

9. Afary and Anderson, *Foucault*.

10. Moscovici, "Conversion Behavior," 213.

patriarchy and female labor was from the perspective of gaining the right to work, not that of threatening to withhold their labor.

In my research, the women talked of male "domination" as men's exclusive religio-cultural right to influence in the public sphere. Hegland called this a challenge to "the hierarchies."[11] Her emphasis was the hierarchies in families, whose authority—male and female—girls were challenging, aided in part by urbanization and the transfer from extended to nuclear families. In addition, education, access to mixed company, and exposure to social media were enabling young women to advocate, disagree, to make demands, be assertive, and to negotiate. However, the tension for the women in my study was that they wanted to use the tactics of advocacy, disagreement, negotiation, and assertiveness that men use, and yet retain their female identity. They did not want to become *as a man*, an honorary male, in order for others to listen to them and/or follow their instructions and advice.

This was illustrated in my study by the challenge that the entrepreneur Daania presented to the patriarchal norms of KP. She resisted male dominance by claiming for herself the right to exercise power and influence in the public sphere, a traditionally male privilege. The limits on her influence were not the mechanisms or strategies she used, but the strength of society's counter-resistance to the weakening of its social control. This counter-resistance is illustrated by Zainab's account of her attempt to use her influence to have a man dismissed for obstructionism and non-compliance. Zainab used the illustration to underscore women's inability to influence in the face of strong patriarchal norms—the man used his connections to regain his job. However, that he was fired at all shows how women's resistance to male dominance is changing the status quo of women's position, and their right to influence in KP. Yet, at the same time, the hierarchical nature of society in KP suggests that women with less societal status and education than Zainab and Daania may not have access to this type of resistance.

Missing from the examples of African and Greek women but found in studies of the women's movement in Pakistan, and illustrated here by Zainab's story, is the counter-response by *men* to women's acts of resistance. This type of resistance can be seen within the frame of Foucault's understanding of "counter-power."[12] That is, a resistance to the power that

---

11. Hegland, "Marriage Modifications," para. 2.
12. Foucault, *Discipline and Punish*, 219.

seeks to dominate. In this study, counter-power is exercised by men, as a powerful majority, in response to female resistance to their hegemony. It is present in the obstacles that are placed in women's paths as men push back against a perceived loss of honor, including an expectation that they comply with female orders. They also resist perceived attempts to usurp their (men's) socio-religious authority and privilege. The suggestion is that male counter-power resistance is built on the premise that women do not have the ability, the strength, or position of ultimate authority that would enable them to fight back. This opposition to female influence can also be viewed as part of a societal move to restore order and discipline, and to end the confusion or disruption brought in by those who want to establish female dominance.

However, as has been observed, women can also subjugate other women using the "privileges of class, race, ethnicity, and seniority associated with the patriarchal order."[13] Additionally, women can advocate for the restrictive norms of classic patriarchy, "because they see the old normative order slipping away from them without any empowering alternatives."[14] It has been argued that unveiled women are more likely to be criticized by women in full covering than by men, but this was not something that emerged from my own interviews. No one spoke of being criticized by other women, although some of the respondents commented that it had been hard to change the traditional mindsets of their mothers. These women were focused on marriage and grandchildren, rather than higher education and a career for their daughters.

However, for two respondents, Fahima and Shazmina, the traditional division of male-female roles had a socio-religious rightness they wished to see re-established in KP. Their comments pointed to the strong conservative/traditionalist religious voice among women in the province. It is possible that their views reflect a modern, pious Islamic middle-class identity. However, it may also be possible to suggest that cognitive dissonance was a factor in their experiences as conservative women working in the public sphere.[15] Fahima, for example, worked in a leadership position in a majority male context even as she expressed support for a

13. Afary and Anderson, *Foucault*, 27.

14. Kandiyoti, "Bargaining with Patriarchy," 282.

15. The subtleties of cognitive dissonance experienced by women in KP's public sphere, including the impact of social status and religious affiliation, fall outside the scope of this research but require further study.

restored patriarchal system, and opposed feminist activism as a wrong interpretation of male domination.

This type of dissonance, experienced by religiously conservative women engaging with modernity, was illustrated in Jamal's study of the women's wing of the Jamaat-e-Islami.[16] Jamal highlighted the case of one JI supporter working through the issue of women in the workplace. She was balancing her desire to see women stay at home supported by men, against the reality that Pakistan's economic situation requires some women to work which necessitates the provision of safe working environments that protect their dignity. In addition, Al-Huda and the wider piety movement in Pakistan are representative of an influential female counter-response that advocates a return to conservative values for the sake of female dignity.

THE RECASTING OF PATRIARCHY AND *PUKHTO*

Moghadam, writing of the destabilizing impact of the modern world on conservative societies, observed the tension caused when values and behaviors are changed in ways that are seemingly at "odds with religion or moral beliefs."[17] Applied to KP, women's visible presence in the public sphere can be viewed as a movement for change that challenges societal perceptions of patriarchy and *Pukhto* as socio-religious belief systems. Foucault, in his analysis of crime, punishment, and the penal system, separated "the permitted and the forbidden" from the "crime."[18] He argued that the permitted-forbidden remained consistent through the centuries, while the crime could be profoundly altered. He concluded that judgement based on the code of permitted-forbidden, true-false, was directed not at the crime, but at what he called "the 'soul' of the criminal," that "element" upon which power is affected.[19] Within this frame, the aspect of permitted-forbidden that underpins the codes of *Pukhto* can be understood as a constant. Therefore, following Foucault's arguments, the right-wrong division is not applied to women's crime, such as breaking *Pukhto*'s patriarchal rules to work alongside men in the public sphere. Instead, society's judgement, both positive and negative, is being exercised

16. Jamal, *Jamaat-e-Islami Women*, 187.

17. Moghadam, *Modernizing Women*, 152.

18. Foucault, *Discipline and Punish*, 17.

19. Foucault, *Discipline and Punish*, 19, 29.

against what these women might become, as their future in the public sphere develops.[20] There could be a future loss of family honor caused by a daughter or daughter-in-law, sister or niece entering the male spaces of graduate studies or the wider workplace. For some, this was seen as a threat to societal norms. Viewed this way, there is a wrongness, a danger, even a madness, about women's presence in the public sphere that requires them to be contained.[21]

Yet, as this study underscores, women *are being granted* permission to be in the public sphere, and in that space *endorsed* as someone of worth. Among the forty-eight women who participated in my study, thirty-one were engaged in their careers with the permission of the men in their households and/or the support of their families. Only two of these women spoke of opposition coming from the senior men in their extended families because of their public visibility; they were involved in activism and politics. This suggests that societal legitimization—including an endorsement by at least one senior male in a woman's close family—is central to both male and female honor in the KP setting. The importance attributed to male support by the respondents in my study cannot be minimized, because it indicates that these households have established a new way of viewing, judging, and justifying their wives/daughters/sisters presence in the public sphere. It suggests that the knowledge base against which such decisions are made is being changed by a new understanding. This new understanding could be viewed as the establishment of types of *nikokyrio*[22]—places where men and women share responsibility—that will be available for future generations. Although in the KP setting, these places would be fully in the public sphere, rather than attached to the domestic realm.

This is seemingly the breakdown of classic patriarchy and a move to public patriarchy within the public spaces of KP. Within public patriarchy women have access to the public sphere, but the practice of male subordination of women continues within those spaces. Access to the public sphere has enabled women to visibly and successfully gain positions of influence. In these places, they act as catalysts for ongoing changes, not least that of male submission to female authority. The depth and breadth of these changes cannot be understated. As a result of women's presence and influence in KP's public sphere the patriarchal opinions and

20. Foucault, *Discipline and Punish*, 18.
21. Foucault, *Discipline and Punish*, 20.
22. Salamone and Stanton, "The *Nikokyra*."

processes by which societal judgement is made are being (re-)shaped to make the formerly prohibited a possibility. This demonstrates a power at work, even if this power is not socially acknowledged.

The lack of acknowledgement may be attributable, in part, to an under-reporting of the roles women play in societal change, not least because scholarship tends to emphasize the political over the social and cultural. This gap in scholarship is being addressed in Pakistan by the studies of women involved in activism, feminism, the piety movement, and religio-political Islam. However, in many of these studies, the actors are drawn from the middle, upper and elite classes with less attention given to influence coming from less privileged women; something I am seeking to address in this book.

ISSUES OF GENDER FALL AWAY

Patriarchy automatically positions men as those with senior status. As Yasmin and Tamina pointed out, male honor is more, and so is male influence. However, this study has shown that women with senior social and professional status are able to exert influence because compliance from their societal juniors (male and female) should be an automatic response. Within the frame of hierarchical patriarchy, the mechanism of expected/required compliance works because the structures of superordinate (patron, department head, senior leader) and subordinate (client, junior staff) are at the core of KP's hierarchical societal structures, found in professional and social relationships. As Gill and Brah identified, failure to comply brings with it a loss of honor and ostracism, just as compliance affirms honorable identity and inclusion, for Hindus, Sikhs, and other communities, not just for Muslims.[23] The pressure to comply with instructions from societal seniors, interwoven as it is into socio-religious codes, is, therefore, strong on multiple levels.

As the psychologist Wren noted, writing of obedience within the frame of social influence, an authority figure is someone who is obeyed simply because he/she holds a position of authority.[24] In the examples Wren provided, the authority figure is a soldier, teacher, or from the police, suggesting that compliance is linked to higher-level professional status. In contrast, the results in my research show that the authority

23. Gill and Brah, "'Honour'-Based Violence," 74.
24. Wren, *Social Influences*, 5, 7.

figure need not have high professional status in order to demand compliance. Rather, this mechanism can be exercised by women in the humblest of roles because it is the authority of the post that makes them *senior*. They influence with the power the institution has invested into that role. Therefore, Humaira the hospital security checker and Zafira the department head can both expect compliance from those placed as junior to them. They influence because of their ability to reward or punish those who are dependent on them. This type of influence is underpinned by the cultural norm of senior-junior compliance.

Wren, however, also noted that obedience is not absolute; disobedience is possible depending on the situation. The factors he cited included disobedient others who exercise group pressure, and disobedience during the absence of the one to whom obedience is due.[25] However, in this study, the factors that lessen compliance in KP's public sphere are hierarchical. They are linked to the social status of the authority figure especially when she is seeking to influence others outside her normal professional context. Therefore, Alishba, as someone newly entering the middle class, spoke of the struggle to get paperwork completed by a government department, whereas Zainab could use her family's name to coerce the local authorities into doing what she wanted.

In addition, as Zafira noted, when influence *is* a post, issues of gender fall away. In social influence terms, the credit of earned professional status or superior rank can offset the deficit of the counter-cultural activity of a woman exercising influence in a highly patriarchal society. Du Boulay suggested, within the context of rural Greece, that the recognition of another, in this case religious, nature within women works to offset her ontology as weak and shameful.[26] In the similar but different situation of KP's patriarchal public sphere, it is the recognition of the *nature of a woman's post* that offsets the deficit of any religio-cultural weakness associated with her gender. However, this offset, for my sample group, occurred for them within the limited scope of an organization. Recognition is more likely to be an expression of public compliance in the workplace rather than any deep-seated alteration of mindset that could result in societal change.

25. Wren, *Social Influences*, 6, 7.

26. Du Boulay, "Women," 141.

INFLUENCE OR POWER

Using Humaira's example, her post enables her to reward people with entrance to the hospital or punish them with a denial of entrance. This suggests that the mechanism of required compliance operates as a mechanism of *power* rather than influence. Nevertheless, seventeen of the women in the sample group used this power language to explain their *influence*. This shrinks the gap between power and influence in contrast to (Western) definitions that seek to separate these terms. Power is understood to encompass (authoritarian) command and the expectation of obedience. It is getting people to do those things that facilitate one's goals. In a sense, a mutually acknowledged contract has been formed in which some in society are given the power to demand and expect obedience.[27] Obedience occurs, even without coercion, because those in the place of authority assert that they have the right to exercise control, and this right is ascribed to by the subjects of that control.[28]

Yet, these *power* definitions parallel the description of *influence* as the mechanism of required/expected compliance made in this study. There was even the suggestion that some form of coercion, the controlling stick or the forceful club, could be used to bolster the exercise of influence. Whether or not force was used, there was an intentionality in the use of the influence mechanism of status-based compliance that reflects the language of power. One possible reason for this may be that the mechanism drew some of its strength from pre-existing societal structures that expected compliance from those within its scope. Not least, hierarchical patriarchy expects juniors to automatically submit to their seniors.

These findings challenge Klein's proposal that influence is the "weakest form of public power."[29] In the KP context, the influence mechanism of status-based compliance, exercised by women who hold societal positions of rank or status, is an expression of real power. However, a paradox arises at this point. Although the mechanism of required compliance offsets gender-based marginalization, the women in my study had to use this mechanism *because they were marginalized by their gender*. They needed the power contained in the normative response of compliance to their post, and access to stick or club, if their words were to be taken seriously.

27. Foucault, "Questions of Method," 98.

28. Milgram, *Obedience to Authority*, para. 7.

29. Klein, *Women and Men*, 192.

An additional element identified from the interviews is that gendered marginalization in the public sphere requires some respondents to use the tactic of personal assertiveness alongside the mechanism of expected compliance. Assertiveness in this context is not simply strength of character. It encompasses a woman's right to influence, and expect compliance, based on her professional status. It implies a move into the place of strength traditionally seen as belonging to men. That is, assertive women influence *like a man* rather than like a woman. It challenges and interacts with the norm that influence is a male characteristic not a female one—as conveyed in the melon proverb. In the Bahrain context, the female activists did not stop being women. They worried, for example, about the care of their children, even as they engaged in acts of civil disobedience—like a man—and took men's places when they were imprisoned. The women in my study were doing the same thing. As working women, they were concerned to find adequate day-care provision for their younger children, even as they took up the responsibilities of their employment. As in Bahrain, these KP women had to deal with male responses that included "competitiveness and 'envy,'" admiration and protectiveness, and a call from conservatives to return to their homes.[30]

BRINGING THE DOMESTIC INTO THE PUBLIC SPHERE

The polar opposite of influencing as a man, is for women to influence as they do at home—bringing the domestic into the public sphere. In KP, there is a strongly developed system of female power, authority, and even dominance within the home that is familiar to women and men. Grima had observed a jocular stereotyping of older women by Pukhtun society as "cunning, powerful, and dangerous" because of their age and experience, the respect they had acquired, and the deference they expected.[31] This had led me to expect that some reflection of women's domestic power would appear as an influence mechanism in the public sphere, especially when exercised by older women. The most obvious expression of this power is that of mother/mother-in-law, although the authority of an eldest sister in Pukhtun families has also been identified. Yet only four respondents spoke of the figurative mother/sister role in the public

30. Hasso, "The Sect-Sex-Police Nexus," 124–25.
31. Grima, *Performance of Emotion*, 96.

sphere, which they used to enhance their professional position in mixed as well as all-female environments.

Two reasons for the low percentage of references to mother/sister influence might be in play. First, the move from classic to public patriarchy in the face of societal change. The move to nuclear households may have removed the "power and respectability" of the mother-in-law role for most of the respondents.[32] Secondly, the lack of reference to the relational influence of the home may indicate that it is not possible to effectively transition domestic influence into the public sphere, except in majority female settings. This is because of the cultural weaknesses in the roles of mother and eldest sister. All of the respondents in my study would have been aware that, in the patriarchal context of KP, women occupy a lesser role in the family structure, they are expected to be obedient and subservient, and they can be punished for making a mistake.[33] As Zainab and Nadia were aware, there is no space for error, either professionally or personally. At the very least, mistakes damage a woman's public identity and marginalize her influence.

Yet, although the smaller percentage of responses seems to indicate less use of mother/sister as an influence tactic, there was no indication of a hierarchy of mechanisms coming from the respondents. Rather, the women simply identified the different types of influence strategies that work for them in the situations in which they find themselves, be it honor, status, or persuasion.

32. Hegland, "Marriage Modifications," para. 1; Kandiyoti, "Bargaining with Patriarchy," 282.

33. Grima, *Performance of Emotion*; Lindholm, *Generosity and Jealousy*, 173.

15

Female Persuasion

PERSUASIVE ARGUMENT—PUTTING KNOWLEDGE AND experience to use—is an influence technique used by a cross-section of the women in my sample group, from an uneducated security checker to elite politicians. With the exception of those who worked in majority-female environments, these women were often in the minority within their places of study or employment in KP. They used informed argument to persuade others to do something, or to advocate on behalf of others, or to negotiate for a change of mindset. This persuasion was not always verbal; they also used their visibly honorable lifestyles, as role model exemplars, to challenge traditional attitudes. On this level, the goal of their persuasion was to influence people to accept the new and leave behind their old ways of thinking as no longer valid. They were looking for a deep level change of mindset that would create new spaces for women, in effect, giving them a new identity within the public spaces of a religiously conservative society.

In addition, my study has shown that although positioned socially or professionally as a minority, a number of the respondents were able to use persuasion and advocacy, *because* of their social or professional status. Status took them, as it were, out of the minority and placed them among the majority. For example, they belonged to the Pukhtun majority, or were part of the majority of Sunni Muslims, or were seated among their social equals. Persuasion was needed simply because they held different opinions to their peers, or because their gender was an obstacle that others needed to overcome. In social influence terms, they were simply working to change the attitudes of those with whom they were already in relationship.

NETWORKED INFLUENCE

Peer-to-peer influence is the model that Contractor and DeChurch drew upon, as they investigated how a medical innovation designed to radically reduce the number of neonatal deaths could gain acceptance among those it was intended for in India.[1] To do this, they explored the communication of information through pre-existing networked relationships within one community. They first identified the opinion leaders as those who need to be influenced if societal norms are to be changed. Then they identified which peers were relationally best positioned to influence these leaders. The third step was to provide the peer influencers with the information, packaged in such a way that it would enable them to persuade the leaders to consider it as something they could accept for themselves and the community.

Contractor and DeChurch's study is of great value to my own research because it took a Western theory and applied it to a non-Western situation. My conversations with women in KP have worked to highlight what is implicit but unstated in Contractor and DeChurch's study: that other active societal networks can hinder or advance persuasive argument (see figure 8). In KP, these networks include the peer-to-peer relationships of religion, gender, societal status, kinship, and patronage. Women, as well as men, can turn to these external networks to provide additional persuasive influence, or to circumvent other influences. The networks they use are organizational and relational. They operate between peers, but also between patrons and clients. They include *birādari* and women's use of lineage; that is, familial relationships within a tribe or extended family. In addition, there are the relational links of a social movement, where women are linked together because of their connection to a cause. There is, also, the much used, but little talked of, system of *sifārish* that taps, often unethically, into relational networks.

1. Contractor and DeChurch, "Integrating Social Networks."

Societal Networks

Pukhto operates as the major societal framework in KP. Importantly for female influence, its organizational structure is centered around the separation of men from women, and collective decision making, sometimes by a council of male elders. Sunni Islam is also central to *Pukhto* because of its function in defining Pukhtun identity. Parallel societal groups in KP-Pakistan, Muslim and non-Muslim, are also centered around religious, ethnic, and linguistic identity. These closely interconnected ethnoreligious societal groups operate as organic networks through which influence flows.

In my research, these organic networks seemed to work best for women with elite and upper-class status who could use their connections with high-level (male) decision-makers through prestige centrality. Their prestige was measured by the quality of their relationship with the one whose thinking they wished to change, not simply the number of ties they had with him/her. As in the example of the influence exercised by the USA's First Lady, not only were these respondents positioned as those with the best (i.e., prestige) connections to high-level decision-makers, but they also had the influence of their prestigious family names. Thus, Zainab recalled how she was able to establish a project based solely on her elite family background. She connected horizontally within her class and social networks to draw on the hierarchical power these groupings contained.

At the same time, *birādari*—the network of male friendship relationships that operates within a family, tribe, or religious grouping—was available for all classes to use in horizontal, peer networked connections. Nagina could expect to receive preferential treatment and have her voice heard above the opinions of others, simply because of her lineage connections to the school principal, her cousin. Sookhdeo's references to the use and abuse of *birādari* within the Christian community suggests that such connections work in other ethno-religious groupings within KP-Pakistan, and at all social and professional levels.[2] However, from the interviews given by the non-Muslim respondents in my study, it was not possible to qualitatively determine whether networked female lineage worked for them as it did for the men of Sookhdeo's research, and for the Pukhtun respondents Zainab and Nagina. I could only assume that it did because of my own observations of life in KP-Pakistan.

2. Sookhdeo, *A People Betrayed*, 308.

The importance of networks for ethno-religious minority communities was described by four respondents. Three of these women, non-Muslims with upper-class status and professional prestige, were positioned to network organizationally with senior male decision-makers. Yet, the capacity of pre-existing societal networks to reduce non-Muslim women's influence was also identified by the respondents. For example, the Christian Samira's failure to attain the promised principal's job, as recounted earlier in this book, demonstrated that the stronger societal network of Muslim identity could overrule any decisions made by organizational heads. The SI framework I developed was designed to present in graph format aspects of stories coming from the sample group: that some forms of external networks could exercise influence over an organization even though they had no legal authority to do so.

Other societal groupings based on feminism and activism, piety, religio-political Islam, and middle-class Islamic identity were also identified in my study as powerful networks operating in KP-Pakistan, although primarily among the middle and upper classes. This suggests that some element of their status-based prestige enabled them to influence diplomatically behind the scenes. However, my research has also suggested that networking is an equally important influence strategy for women who have *no* social or professional status. Positioned societally as juniors, these women, with little personal or public authority, require powerful allies in order to influence. For example, Fauzia described how she represented her Ismaili community in a predominantly Sunni Muslim feminist network working to improve conditions for women in KP. For her, as a woman without professional or social status, her networked connections to key opinion leaders *was* her influence. Being networked changed her vertical relationship based on status (junior-senior, lower class-upper class) to a horizontal peer relationship. Positioned now as a peer influencer, a fellow activist, she was able to motivate other activists to engage with specific social issues.

This challenges the proposition that influence is achieved through networks of societal peers. Clark had observed this in her research into social movement theory and patron-clientelism in the Middle East, concluding that the strength of a network is in its horizontal connections among social peers.[3] Fauzia's experience suggests that urbanization, education, feminism, and activism challenge rigid social structures,

---

3. Clark, "Social Movement Theory," 943.

enabling at least some women to break into groups that are largely structured around class. Yet, as Fauzia had observed, those with real influence within the group she had joined, were women who carried the power of social status. Fauzia's strength was that she understood how the network operated, and who held what kinds of power. She was then able to use this knowledge as her influence strategy. At the same time, Fauzia's experience may have been an exception: an example of the vertical recruitment of someone of lower status into a higher-class network.

The stories coming from the ladies in my sample group showed that women in KP are using networks to promote a unified voice. This is the influence of a group of like-minded individuals. These networks, however, were for women from the elite and upper classes; their advocacy had the potential to impact legislation. Or they were for women who, through the power of their senior posts, had garnered many influential people around them. The strength of their networks came from the breadth of their peer relationships. Those from the upper and elite classes were also able to draw on family and friends of a similar social status. When called upon by someone in an organization, they could enable that individual or institution to reach further and achieve more than would have been possible without their assistance. Not least, the voice of the networks spoke louder and further than any individual acting on her own. This was why, when talking of influence, Qamar referenced her place in a network of senior, well-connected women, in touch with men who supported their views. It was the support of these men that enabled their message to reach the men in government who determine policy.

Patronage

In contrast to the potential equality of some of the networks the respondents were involved in, patronage functions as a vertical, unequal social network of hierarchical relationships between patron and client and/or client and patron.[4] Lyon proposed that patronage was a cultural expression of power present within Pakistani society, manipulated by its user for his/her own advantage.[5] Although Lyon's research was among male patrons only, the frame he identified fits the language used by eight of the women in my study. As women with senior social and/or professional

4. Clark, "Social Movement Theory," 946.
5. Lyon, "Power and Patronage," 2.

status, they extended patronage through social work, interacted with the expectation of their clients, and used success to enhance their own reputations. Hine, from her research in Pakistan, had also noted that female activists, as women of status, were acting on behalf of lower-class victims in the role of patrons.[6] Their clients were women who had been involved in such critical incidents as gender violence and rape. Her study demonstrates that in Pakistan patronage is available to women and men, hence its usefulness as an influence mechanism.

Hine identified the core components of patronage as "inequality of power, status and wealth."[7] She documented the ways in which activists operate as the patrons of "less privileged women, enabling them to access the legal, political and social system."[8] The activists/patrons saw the incidents in which their clients were involved as opportunities that would enable them to mobilize for collective action, exert influence and expect changes to the societal systems that allowed such incidents to occur. Hine proposed that their strategy failed because the elite status of most patrons prevented them from viewing and handling the issue of gender violence in a way that could bring about permanent societal change. In addition, "for the client, the relationship establishes and maintains limitations on both access to and control of resources, and access to the centres of power, because these are part of the status of the patron. Without access to resources, the client lacks the ability to influence the centre of power."[9] Hine's observations are mirrored in my study. Eight of the women Mariya and I spoke with identified as having patron influence; they all came from the elite or upper classes. Among them, women like Aafiya and Zainab influenced through the social outreach programs they had established for those less privileged than themselves. In the example Aafiya gave, she even chose the critical incident she wished to act upon: the lack of literacy among the women in her village.

Within this frame of elite patron-lower status client, it is possible to interpret Fauzia's place as a working-class Ismaili woman in a Sunni activist organization as one of client to patron, rather than that of a peer, as argued above. Viewed through this lens, she was required by her lower class and religious status to make requests of women with privileged status and connections to powerful families. At the same time, even the

6. Hine, "The Hard Knot," 342.

7. Hine, "The Hard Knot," 23.

8. Hine, "The Hard Knot," ii.

9. Hine, "The Hard Knot," 331.

elite respondents and organizational leaders spoke in their interviews of how they were marginalized by their gender and required help from powerful male allies. These upper-class activists were clients of the state as patron—the one they were required to approach to get things done. Sadly, the information that emerged from the interviews was not enough for me to adequately explore the other side of the relationship: the power that clients extend over their patrons. Nor could I test Hine's suggestion that patronage, as a system, worked to maintain the gap of inequality it seemed to be inviting the client to cross.[10] However, it is clear from my respondents' interviews that patronage is an influence mechanism that women in KP's public sphere are able to use both as clients and as patrons.

Sifārish

It is also possible to view the practice of *sifārish* as a type of patronage. It involves patrons and clients, rescue and deliverance, and is part of influence at work for men and women in KP-Pakistan. The normalcy of *sifārish*—the act of using one's connections to a person in authority to recommend another person as being worthy of a favor—may be the reason why most respondents did not mention it as an influence mechanism. It may also be the reason why two respondents *equated* influence with *sifārish*. However, unlike patronage, which is built upon the vertical relationships of a hierarchical society, *sifārish* can also operate on a horizontal, peer to peer level. Ribca, for example, received the recommendation of her peer, a work colleague, and agreed to grant a favor to an elderly woman.

There are, however, two other possible reasons why *sifārish* was not widely identified as an influence mechanism by the women in my study. First, its association with corrupt practices could make it a thing of shame. Secondly, its links to reward power could make *sifārish* a power mechanism rather than an expression of influence. It is my belief that both reasons, unethical favoritism and the use of power, were in play in the minds of the women in the sample group. However, as an influence mechanism, *sifārish* seemingly held the power, as did lineage and patronage, to undermine influence being extended in other ways. It did not involve honor and hard work, or the cultivation of an authentic name.

10. Hine, "The Hard Knot," 332.

It was solely based on the petitioner's ability to have the one being asked to agree to implement the favor. Issues of status—that of the petitioner and the one petitioned—were interwoven into this cultural influence mechanism.

DISASSOCIATION AND ASSOCIATION

The roles played by personality, especially strength of character and assertiveness, personal experience, and the cultivation of maturity, were also seen in the interviews to enhance a woman's ability to persuade others to share her point of view. The women highlighted three core factors linked to personality: self-perception, self-projection, and audience perception. Audience perception refers to the ways in which society views, interprets and responds to what they are seeing, as women enter KP's public sphere. Their responses are shaped by their own personal experiences, the collective cultural background of the ethno-religious community they are part of, and the context of their exposure. The first factor, self-perception or self-categorization, has already been explored when looking at honor. The second factor linked to personality is self-projection: the cultivation of confidence and assertiveness. One part of this confidence, still to be discussed, is strength of character.

Significantly, strength of character has the ability to transition women from their traditional place of weakness, submission, and *sharm* to occupy the space of strength—traditionally occupied by men. "Femaleness" in this context is not about sexual orientation. Nor is it about women behaving more like men. As Khadijah observed, when she spoke to Mariya, it is possible for women in KP to have both a strong character and retain their *i'zət-e nafs*, their female dignity.

The recasting of femaleness is about societal *disassociation* and *association*. It concerns the disassociation of female identity from traditional, negative stereotypes such as female deviousness and weakness. As disassociation takes place, society is then able to *associate* women with decision-making capacity and strength. Disassociation and association occur in those spaces where norms have been disrupted by change. For example, one result of Bahrain's Pearl Revolution, as observed by Hasso, was the loosening of gendered restrictions.[11] This enabled the creation of new spaces in which it was possible to imagine a different type of social

11. Hasso, "The Sect-Sex-Police Nexus," 129.

whole, with changed values, laws, institutions, and symbols. In the KP context, ladies in authority within these new spaces, facilitated the disassociation of women from the concept of *sınf-e-nāzuk*, the weaker—that is, societally marginalized—sex.[12] Not least, as Zafira's affirmed, the women in KP's workplace were strong on multiple levels, otherwise they could not be there. Experience and knowledge brought a personal maturity that created a new space, effectively weakening former cultural boundaries and societal labelling.

At the same time as causing a public sphere disruption by appearing in the public sphere, the women in my sample group were clear that knowledge and experience *had to be knitted into* demonstrable personal honor and dignity if it was to be effective. This relates to audience perception. Safia emphasized that first people decide whether a woman has good moral values, and after that, they consider whether she has the professional capacity to do the job. The attribution of worth in the public sphere enabled women both to influence in their places of work, and influence as exemplars that other women can imitate.

EXEMPLAR AND CELEBRITY

There was contained within the respondents' comments the sense of an idealized woman—that perfect role model that others could imitate. These role models were those women who were visibly successful in the public sphere and yet had retained their authenticity as those who could be respected and trusted. This was clearly presented by Zainab, who was well aware of her responsibilities as a role model. She described the vulnerability contained in being that ideal woman that others want to emulate. It gave no margin for error.

Ruffle explored the cultivation of a higher or idealized self through her hagiographical research within Shi'i Islam.[13] She proposed that stories and ritual performances about Imam Husain's family transformed these historically significant heroes and heroines into "socially, culturally,

12. A 2021–2022 television drama directed by Nadeem Baig coined the name Sinf E Aahan, translated as Women of Steel (literally iron), to directly counter the term *sınf-e-nāzuk*. It presented the lives of seven young women who joined the Pakistani army, including one woman from KP. The series was produced in collaboration with the Inter-Services Public Relations wing of the Pakistan Armed Forces. The military's engagement in the modern debate about women's rights lies outside the scope of this research, but it is part of a wider conversation taking place in Pakistan at this time.

13. Ruffle, *South Asian Shi'ism*.

and morally relevant figures through whom one can cultivate an idealized self."[14] Their lives and identities, interpreted through local cultural, social and political norms, re-shaped them into those who, as "socio-ethical exemplars" represented an ideal yet real person in Shi'a society.[15] This concept was challenged by D'Souza who observed that Bibi Fatima's elevation placed her "beyond the realm of ordinary women," causing her to be loved and revered as holy rather than emulated as a role model.[16]

The idea of a religious and sociological ideal for women to imitate was promoted in Pakistan by the Jamaat-e-Islami, often through the use of *dars*, and also by Al-Huda as a piety movement.

> When women who already possess faith encounter an institute that heightens their love for Allah and tells them that Allah wants them to live their lives via a particular framework . . . and presents them with a concrete picture of who a pious Muslim is in accordance with it, women do alter their ideology, behaviour and lifestyle in an attempt to match that model of piety.[17]

However, in this research, the respondents pointed to role model exemplars drawn from family, history and politics rather than heroes and heroines from the scriptures. Bushra recounted how she was inspired by the life of Tahirih Qurratu'l-'Ayn, who gave her life for women's rights in nineteenth century Iran. Similarly, Roshni referenced Bhagat Singh, a twentieth century activist against colonialism. Maryam's heroine was a well-known twenty-first century female Pakistani blogger. At the same time, Maryam was aware that a part of this social influencer's success what that she lived outside of KP. The ability to influence online for social change was not possible, in Maryam's view, for women living in the province.

Bushra and Roshni were among the twenty-six women in my study who spoke of the influence of role models, celebrities and/or mentors on their own lives, or spoke of themselves as occupying one or more of these roles. They identified women who had visibly succeeded in a male-dominated public sphere. These were people who had earned the right to be listened to because they had demonstrated that their opinions could be trusted. As exemplars, they acted as role models for others to emulate, and as celebrities, they endorsed previously male-only professions as now

---

14. Ruffle, *South Asian Shi'ism*, Teaching Shi'ism section, paras. 6, 7.

15. Ruffle, *South Asian Shi'ism*, Saints section, para. 1.

16. D'Souza, *Partners of Zaynab*, 30.

17. Ahmad, "Identity Matters," 70.

viable for women. In addition, they were providing reproducible alternatives to Western models of personal behavior and professional practice because of the emphasis given to female dignity and modesty.

As role models, these women influenced through a combination of visibility, status, authority, legitimacy, personal charisma, and their observable retention of *i'zət*. However, there was the sense that being a role model was less about personal choice and more about an inescapable responsibility. As Zainab had observed in her interview, it was public sphere visibility that turned successful women into role models. This echoes Hasso's observation that women who suffered for their visible participation in revolution became "national figures in their own right," and role models for others to copy.[18] Shaheed, writing in 1995, had noted that female role models were rare in Pakistan—including in literature—which she attributed to the dominance of patriarchy in society.[19] Twenty-five years later, the thirteen women in my research who identified as visibly effective leaders and role models also viewed themselves as being marginalized by patriarchy. Yet, influencing from the vanguard of successful women in the public sphere, their message to other women was that this is possible for you, too.

The ability to move beyond the influence of a role model exemplar to that of a celebrity endorser has increased in recent years in Pakistan with the introduction of micro-celebrities, or non-traditional celebrities, who have become famous through online media usage.[20] In her blog, for example, Shireen Hall featured 12 influential Pakistani women who were celebrities as well as role models because of their mainstream and social media presence.[21] However, studies of celebrity influence in Pakistan have concentrated on product endorsement by personalities from film and sport. Hassan and Jamil, for example, looked at the influence of celebrity endorsement on consumer purchasing.[22] Such studies have added little to understanding the influence exercised by female micro-celebrities in KP.

For the women in my study, a woman moved from a simple role model to a person with celebrity status when she appeared in mainstream and online media. For example, among those interviewed, Roshni spoke about herself as someone that others followed because of her appearances

18. Hasso, "The Sect-Sex-Police Nexus," 121.

19. Shaheed, "Networking for Change," 90.

20. Nouri, "The Power of Influence," 2; Dad and Khan, "#MeToo."

21. Hall, "12 Influential Women."

22. Hassan and Jamil, "Celebrity Endorsement."

on mainstream and social media. In that place of celebrity visibility she could demonstrate that women can be successful in the field of litigation. Her celebrity endorsement was not that of a famous person endorsing a product or a political party. She was endorsing an honorable profession against the background of women's recent emergence into the public sphere. Her endorsement worked because of the consumers' admiration for her as a woman proven to be trustworthy in the public eye. In this case, the consumers were young women and their families.

MENTOR

Alongside the influence of role models, a quarter of the women in my study talked of mentoring or grooming. The banker Gohar used her experiences of mentoring as the best way to describe the term influence. As a scholar of management and leadership, Gary Yukl described mentoring as a relationship in which someone who is more experienced helps a protégé with less experience.[23] It is a professional relationship that enables the junior to develop in confidence and skills. This type of mentoring was referenced by senior women in my sample group, as they helped advance the careers of younger women. Romika's comments about the use of vanguard mentors in the engineering field is just one example of professional grooming in KP.

However, for the majority, mentoring was something they had encountered in a less formal way at school or work. Their mentors did not necessarily have visible profiles in the public sphere and were often schoolteachers. What made them mentors in the respondents' understanding was the long-term impact of their influence. Additionally, in Pakistan, male and female teachers, especially those who teach religion, can have celebrity mentoring status attributed to them, like Farhad Hashmi. What has made Hashmi successful as a mentor is not simply her piety and personal charisma; it is her knowledge of Islam backed-up by education. She holds a PhD in Islamic Studies from the University of Glasgow and an MA in Arabic from the University of the Punjab. This knowledge marks her out "as an authoritative figure in a context where knowledge has a privileged position."[24] Knowledge and position thus validate her as a mentor and validate her authority in the eyes of those who sit under

23. Yukl, *Leadership*, 391.
24. Ahmad, "Al-Huda," 367–68.

her teaching. In addition, she seemingly exercises influence not only as an expert, but as a matriarch and sister. She is someone that teachers and students within the Al Huda movement can copy as they seek to mentor and influence other women.

16

Influence can be Female Too

THIS BOOK BEGAN WITH a proverb about influence that is normal for men and alien for women: "A melon gains its color by sitting with melons." A person is influenced by the company he keeps. As a proverb, it points to the awkwardness of female influence as a concept, and to women's struggle to find cultural and religious appropriateness in the public sphere of Khyber Pakhtunkhwa. My research is in part, therefore, a test of the premise that influence is male because KP's public sphere is male. This test has shown that men's control of the public sphere, expressed as patriarchy, *Pukhto*, patrilineage and socio-religious practice, affects the how, who, when, and where of all influence exercised within that space.

The stories coming from the women in my study group operate as a critique not just of the public sphere, but of society in KP: will the inclusion of women in KP's public sphere result in a societal acceptance that influence can also be female? They have shown that the nature of KP's public sphere is being challenged and changed as patriarchy and *Pukhto* change, enabling female influence to be exercised alongside that of men. This is the reality that dawned on Aafiya as a result of her interview. All her life she had been influencing people but until that moment had never thought of her actions as influence, because influence is something that men do. This pattern of thinking had now changed for her.

The goal of my research has been to increase understanding of Muslim and non-Muslim female influence in the patriarchal, hierarchical Muslim-majority setting of KP where women have only recently become a visible part of a space that is traditionally male. I had asked two core questions. First, what are the mechanisms by which Muslim and non-Muslim women exercise influence in the public spaces of Muslim-majority Khyber Pakhtunkhwa? And, secondly, how does the ethno-religious background and/or societal status of the women affect these mechanisms? In answer to the first question, I was able to identify the three meta-themes of honor, status, and persuasion as the over-arching strategies of influence identified by the respondents. These meta-themes brought together twelve major influence mechanisms: honor and hard work, personal integrity, devotion to duty, positivity, expected/required compliance, patronage, persuasive argument and advocacy, networking, *sifārish*, role model exemplar, celebrity endorser, and mentor. These were the mechanisms the respondents identified as being available for women seeking to influence or be influential in KP.

Not unexpectedly, all of the influence mechanisms were shown to have the capacity to function simultaneously in the lives of the respondents, as women living in the multiple publics of KP-Pakistan. Although their definitions of influence were divided between status-based compulsion and persuasion, the interviews demonstrated that there was no one influence tactic favored by the respondents. The women in my sample group simply turned to the tactic that best fit their current situation. Khadijah, for example, believed *sifārish* influence to be inappropriate for her work environment, but was happy to employ it in a personal setting. This, and the many other conversations that make up this research, led me to conclude that, at least for these forty-eight women, *all* the influence mechanisms were available for everyone to use.

It was also clear that while these mechanisms were available to all, social and professional status were factors that limited or enhanced the reach of the influencer. Access to and use of the different influence mechanisms was not impacted by minority ethno-religious identity, with one small exception. Positivity, devotion to duty, and personal integrity were used by Muslim and non-Muslim respondents alike. However, for those women from ethno-religious minorities who wished to counter marginalization by presenting their community in a positive light, and for those simply seeking a place of acceptance within the Muslim-majority context of their workplaces, positivity, devotion to duty, and personal integrity became key influence tactics in a way that they were not for women from the majority.

To borrow from Foucault's approach to power,[1] the mechanisms, the nuts-and-bolts of influence that I identified, are those factors that had remained unanalyzed even as the concept of influence was discussed within the field of societal change. This serves to underscore the importance of my study to our understanding of female influence in a conservative and patriarchal society. In addition to mechanisms, my study has captured the processes, the social proofs and the societal power that facilitates the exercise of influence. These processes function as subthemes, and include the authority contained in a recognized post, the ethical nature of honor, the familiar roles of mother and eldest sister, age, maturity, and experience, confidence, and positivity. A sense of indebtedness, and an unwillingness to accept failure as final, also worked to provide additional motivation for the influencer. In the complexity of the metaphorical ball of societal threads, some of these proofs also operate as additional influence mechanisms for women in KP's public sphere. The three broad meta-themes enabled my exploration of the key role played by identity, as well as the importance of *i'zət*, ethnicity, societal status, and power to female influence.

My analysis of how women are able to be in and influence in KP's public sphere enabled me to unravel the complex concept of honor as a lived reality for women in KP. *i'zət*, was shown to include the practices of respect, worth, dignity, prestige, reputation, esteem, status, and trust. As an influence tactic and proof, *i'zət* is available to all women working in KP's male-majority public sphere. However, *i'zət* can also be used in all-female spaces, because it is an expression of personal integrity, respect, dignity, and trustworthiness. It is also a tactic that ethno-religious minority women can use to challenge those who carry negative preconceptions about their communities. Thus, *i'zət* becomes a demonstration of a similar-to-norm presentation of an ideal woman. As an influence tool, it works to change mindsets by creating a positive assessment of women aimed at ending female marginalization in KP's society. In the hands of ethno-religious minority women, *i'zət* is also a tool that proves a similarity-to-norm that is aimed at breaking down stereotypical assessments of the influencer's minority community.

1. Rabinow, *The Foucault Reader*, 57.

ATTAIN AND MAINTAIN A PLACE
IN THE PUBLIC SPHERE

In *Voices of Change*, I have focused on the lived reality of women as they exercise influence within the public spaces of a Muslim-majority society, using Khyber Pakhtunkhwa as the frame. The data that emerged from the interviews deepened my own understanding of how female influence works in a context where women are often not required to be, or expected to be, influential. It became clear from the women's stories that the effectiveness of their influence is centered around an honorable identity.

In an attempt to bring my thoughts together as I continued unravelling the metaphorical threads of culture that surround and entangle female influence in KP, I grouped the three meta-themes of honor, status, and persuasion into two broad approaches to influence. The first approach contains the influence mechanisms that enable women to obtain and maintain a position in KP's public sphere. The second brings together the themes of status and persuasion: the key ways in which women exercise influence from the positions they occupy in that public space.

Honor and Hard Work

Many of the women in my sample group identified honor and dignity, their *i'zət-e nafs*, as central to their ability to influence. This was an expected finding because of the role played by *i'zət* and *ghe'rət* in Pukhtun society. As a deeply embedded cultural norm, honor, like *Pukhto* is not something one simply appropriates by obeying the rules of right behavior, although compliance to the rules is expected. Honor is something one has and does. It is both a state of being and an ethical behavior. These same principles of honor, modesty and compliance to cultural rules were seen to extend to all of the ethno-religious groupings in the sample group. Yet, this analysis of identity-based honor was somewhat idealistic. At least one of the respondents demonstrated that it maybe possible for a woman to create an honorable persona that did not, necessarily, reflect actual ethical being or even doing. This honorable persona was based solely on a reputation obtained because of *successful* influence. However, for the majority of those interviewed, demonstrable personal *i'zət* was a vital part of their identities, not least because it functioned as a bulwark against allegations that their *i'zət* was lost because they were in the public sphere.

Hard work was used by the respondents to overcome cultural prejudices and establish personal honor, not just professional capacity. Together, honor and hard work operate as two sides of a single influence mechanism. Stories from the sample group revealed that, as women, they were required to demonstrate a dignity and purity of being that met the expectations of their audience *before* their professional capacity was considered. In this way, honor and hard work, in addition to being an influence mechanism, function as a social proof of women's right and ability to be in the public sphere. Influence occurs through the demonstration—the proof—of personal integrity and trustworthiness, which, together with professional ability, are established and underpinned by a woman's hard work. This is the influence that gains her entrance into the public sphere and enables her to retain her place there. As a result of publicly acknowledged honor and visible professional success, women are taking on the roles of public-sphere influencer and decision-maker that had previously belonged to men.

In social influence terms, the success of honor and hard work as one double-sided influence mechanism is shown in the legitimization of the respondents' worth in the public sphere. True influence has occurred because there has been an acceptance, and seemingly permanent attitude change, among some in society. This change in attitude has occurred because of the challenge a successful and honorable woman is to the expectations of KP society. As an influence mechanism, honor and hard work are being exercised by women who are acutely aware of how society views and evaluates them. It is a tactic women use to counter male expectations that they should adopt positions of *sharm* in public—to be subservient and silent in the presence of men. In the same way, they use this tactic to challenge and change the attribution of moral weakness that is attached to their gender. Although there has been a suggestion that female purity in Pakistan is symbolic, for the respondents in my study, the demonstration of personal purity is an everyday necessity to be underpinned by hard work. The importance of purity is such that there is no margin for personal error, especially for those women in visible positions of successful leadership.

In a process of self-categorization, these women are choosing to accept or reject external judgements about them and their presence in the public sphere. The judgements come from their families, their socio-religious communities, and from the male-majority melon field of KP's society. The seeming different-to-norm inappropriateness of their behavior can cause a reaction sometimes couched in negative language. These judgements, positive as well as negative, worked to shape how the respondents in my study viewed themselves, especially when working in spaces where men are in the majority. Unconsciously as well as consciously, they used self appraisal, an awareness of their difference to what is considered normal or right for a woman, to shape their own beliefs about themselves, and about their behavior as they interact with others. For a number of the respondents, this self-awareness helped them in their choice of influence mechanisms as they encountered different situations and challenges.

One of the beliefs that came out of the process of self-categorization was confidence. Women in my study were tapping into the deep-down certainty in themselves as having the abilities and skills required to be a person whom KP's patriarchal society could trust. It worked to enhance their ability to influence. On one level, confidence simply gave timid women the courage not to be scaredy-cats but to engage in the public sphere. On another level, confidence operated as an expression of resistance to traditional norms, creating a conflict which also worked to women's advantage as a marginalized minority in society. Female, public sphere confidence was a new phenomenon. It created uncertainty and disquiet among the majority that required a shift in thinking. As a result, for some among the male majority of KP's public sphere, there was a change to the norms of their beliefs and a new acceptance of women's honorable presence in the public sphere.

Honor and hard work, underpinned by confidence, thus worked to legitimize women's right to be in, and influence in, the public sphere. Such legitimization occurs when (a section of) society affirms that women have the right, social as well as legal, to be active participants in the province's institutions and organizations. This supports the suggestion I made at the start of this book: that women's ability to provide recognized social proof may be the most vital aspect of female influence in KP's public spaces. The social proof was the same *i'zət* they used to influence. This explains why some of the respondents claimed that *i'zət is* influence.

Space in the Melon Field

KP's proverbial melon field is not a new public sphere created, for example, by revolution, in which men and women together enter and share a newly formed gender-neutral space. There are such spaces, in Pakistan, on social media, where the old social boundaries are no longer enforced. However, the physical public sphere in KP is an established male space. It is this sphere that women are intruding into, to take to themselves tasks that are usually associated with male influence and control. Society is more comfortable with the system of gendered space, *parda*, that provides for an ordered, physical separation of women from men and men from women. For men, *parda* operates as a system of power by which women can be controlled. Yet, behind the power are the cultural mores and the socialized messages that perpetuate a patriarchal social system that privileges men and marginalizes women; a system that women themselves perpetuate.

One of the many complexities unraveled during my research was the discomfort or awkwardness faced by women who were breaking the norms of gendered space to work in the public sphere. One of the topics they talked about was their need to demonstrate strength, when they were more comfortable with softness. They found that in order to maintain their role, and their influence, they were required to be strong or assertive—like a man. This was not an issue of sexual orientation but of the attributes culturally recognized as belonging to gender. For them, strength is a male characteristic, not a female one. Cultural dissonance occurred for some of those interviewed because, although assertiveness and strength were necessary for influence, they felt uncomfortable, even wrong, as influence strategies for women. This inappropriateness was also felt by those they sought to influence, which is why men refused to hear women's voices in meetings or walked out of committee meetings if they were to be chaired by a woman.

However, the use of a softer, domestic style influence, that took advantage of the prestige of matriarchal mother(-in-law) or eldest sister, was not a tactic that the respondents in my study employed in the public sphere, except to enhance positions of established authority. Although not verbalized directly, the message was that the norm of female marginalization in the domestic sphere made it an unsuitable technique for influence. Yet, in the right setting, the authority of a mother, or the trust relationship implicit in eldest sister status, could be effectively used as social proofs that enabled women to assert their influence and change male attitudes and opinions. For Kiran, as a young, unmarried lecturer, being as a mother to her male students operated as a protection against verbal and physical abuse. It reshaped male attitudes, at least towards her in that situation.

Even where the opportunity exists in KP for women to work side-by-side with men, some women still prefer the familiarity and safety of a segregated all-female space where they feel more comfortable and culturally at ease. In these gynesocial spaces they are able to exercise all of the influence mechanisms identified in this research. However, their influence has a different scope and impact because of gender separation. For those women working in female schools and colleges, or who are part of Al-Huda, or involved in the Woman's Wing of the Jamaat-e-Islami, their direct influence is directed solely at other women. Indirectly, however, through their students and female programs, their influence is felt in the wider community. This, for example, enables women involved in the piety movement to influence for societal change: the restoration of conservative Islamic practices in Pakistan.

Gynesocial workplaces thus facilitate the exercise of influence that parallels, yet is different to, the influence exercised by women working in male-majority spaces. It was clear from the respondents that confidence and positivity operate in both spheres as an influence strategy. It is there to assist senior staff dealing with bureaucracy in all-female schools and colleges just as it helps female politicians seeking to influence male government decision-makers. Juniors in majority-female settings are still expected to respect and obey their seniors, as in mixed settings, and obstructionism and resistance are factors in hierarchical organizations across the board. However, the interviews seemed to indicate that obstructionism takes on an extra level of resistance when it occurs in those spaces that women share with men. The respondents in majority female workplaces spoke of *tang*, obstructionism, in terms of organizational bureaucracy and lazy staff, or the hindrances put in their paths by jealous colleagues. However, for women working in majority-male spaces, *tang* also included patriarchal resistance to women's presence and authority. This could be expressed as negative behavior, verbal abuse, or even a total refusal to do the job they have been tasked to complete. I have sat in the office of a senior, female government officer and experienced the obvious obstructive behavior of male staff tasked to serve tea to her guests. They were using *tang* to shame her in public.

There was, however, one exception to the finding that women in all-female workplaces use the same influence mechanisms as women in majority-male spaces, which echoes the exception already identified regarding the use of positivity, devotion, and integrity by women from ethno-religious minority communities. The non-Muslim respondents described in their interviews how they used the tactics of demonstrable personal integrity and devotion to duty to gain acceptance in Muslim-majority gynesocial environments as well as in traditionally male spaces. In contrast, there is no indication in my research that Muslim staff are required to prove their moral and professional capacity in all-female settings. This is presumably because honor and ability are already attributed to them, in such settings, by their religious identity.

It was not possible to determine from the interviews if women from Muslim minority communities, working in all female settings, use positivity, devotion, and integrity in the same way as their non-Muslim counterparts. This would require further investigation. Similarly, I did not include in my research a separate analysis of the influence mechanisms used by Muslims working in majority non-Muslim contexts in KP. Only two of my respondents were working in such settings, as part of Christian institutions. However, it could be a helpful study especially in nations where the ratio of Muslims to non-Muslims is not as large as in KP-Pakistan.

Forty-eight per cent of the women in my study, including ten non-Muslims, were working alongside men, shoulder-to-shoulder, in shared spaces. However, only two respondents described how women make a physical space for themselves within a shared public sphere. Their examples were the separate place of little influence that women parliamentarians had created within the KP Assembly, and the use of veiling as a means of protection from male jeering and abuse. This lack of focus on safe physical spaces by the sample group suggests that women in KP automatically create the space they need for their interaction with the public sphere. Where the subject of female spaces occurred in conversation, the women most often talked of access to washrooms, staff or rest rooms, and areas set aside for their prayers. Further research using a larger sample group and a wider spectrum of industries would be required to find out how close proximity with men is physically negotiated, given its counter-cultural dissonance, and what this means for female influence in KP-Pakistan and comparable settings.

In addition, further research is needed to investigate just one respondent's claim that religious conservatism is shrinking the spaces available for female voices speaking in opposition to accepted norms. In 2011, the Pakistani activist Shaheed had argued that the use of derogatory language against activists was removing women's right to disagree and shrinking the space available for secular argument.[2] The lone voice in my research has seemingly confirmed this proposal, made a decade earlier. Further study is required to establish whether this shrinking space is a growing obstacle for all women, or only for those who speak out for women's rights. If proven to affect all women, then its impact on current and future female influence requires investigation. It may represent the power of conservative and religious voices to effectively oppose women's presence in the public sphere as part of the continuing process of Islamization.

Lastly, it could be presumed that employment in a female-only space, and the comfortable similarity of such spaces to the domestic sphere, would lower the status of the women who worked there in the eyes of the public. A lower status would reduce their ability to influence outside their places of employment once the nature of their work was known. However, those respondents employed in gynesocial spaces did not talk about their ability to influence in these terms. There is no suggestion that working, for example, in the gendered space of an all-girls school or college reduces a woman's professional status as compared to that of women who work alongside men. What it may have done, however, is separate her from being influenced by, or speaking into, issues that women in shared spaces can engage with.

Ethno-Religious Minority Influence

My research questions asked what mechanisms are used by non-Muslim, as well as Muslim women, in their exercise of influence in KP's public sphere, and what impact does ethno-religious identity have on female influence. These questions addressed a gap in knowledge; that not enough is known by national and international decision-makers regarding the country's Christian, Hindu, Shi'a, and other communities outside the context of marginalization. In KP-Pakistan, racialization, sectarianism, and discrimination are seen to emphasize religious difference, as they do in comparable contexts.[3]

An awareness of religious difference was in many ways the context in which the ethno-religious minority respondents in my research shaped their influence. It often was responsible for the type of tactic they

2. Shaheed, *Great Ancestors*, xiii, xxiii.
3. For example, see Hasso, "The Sect-Sex-Police Nexus"; Shanneik, *Art of Resistance*.

adopted, especially if influence was being use to forge a greater level of acceptance among KP's Sunni Muslim, Pukhtun majority.[4] As has already been noted, the mechanisms of positivity, devotion, and integrity became significant tactics used to influence a Muslim-majority audience where mindsets had been shaped by socialized negative stereotypical ideas of the influencer's minority community. To attain and maintain places of influence in KP's majority Muslim public sphere, non-Muslim respondents are likely to use positivity, devotion to duty, and personal integrity to demonstrate areas of similarity as a pro-normative social influence strategy. These tactics demonstrate a consciousness of Islam and *Pukhto*'s dominant roles in society. Influence is mediated through both the respondents' understanding of the majority and of self in relation to that majority. Self, in this case, is not simply an expression of personal identity; it has a collective nature. As the non-Muslim respondents talked of changing preconceptions about their identity, they were influencing for change to the majority's ideas regarding their community. Similar approaches were used, but in a less pronounced way, by the respondents in my study who came from Muslim communities that were either not *Pukhtun* or not Sunni.

In addition, positivity, devotion to duty, and personal integrity were influence tactics used by the non-Muslim respondents in gynesocial environments as well as the spaces where they worked with men. The key issue was the preconceptions that their majority colleagues held about them, as representatives of their different-to-norm communities. The social categorization, marginalization, and to some degree punitive exclusion of those who are different to self, generated a sense that these people were not those that the majority could trust nor expect to be influenced by. Women from these communities had to demonstrate that they were equal to their Muslim counterparts, especially morally. Their morality, presented as positivity, devotion and integrity, would then operate as a social proof of their honorable, and thereby trustworthy status. In this context, the social proof of what at times seemed like *better than* statements from the respondents was simply a means to establish an *equal to* status for them as non-Muslims. As such, these mechanisms functioned in a similar way to those used by the women who, required to prove their

---

4. Socio-religious difference and exclusion were also mentioned by non-Pukhtun Muslim respondents but, with the exception of the Ismaili respondent, they did not develop the use of positivity, devotion to duty, and personal integrity as did the non-Muslim respondents.

professional capacity, had to show that they were *better than* their male counterparts.

Although positivity, devotion to duty, and personal integrity were individual proofs, given in the exercise of influence by marginalized respondents, they were also apologetic in nature. In the hands of ethno-religious minority women, they were tactics to be used in gentle defense of their religious community's identity. By women marginalized by their gender, they were a defense of their right to be in the public sphere. At the same time, for both groupings, they were influence tactics aimed at securing a more comfortable space for a woman within her place of study or employment.

The degree to which non-Muslim women share in the broader apologetics of community loyalty to the nation, as a means of reclaiming citizenship and countering Muslim majoritarianism, was unclear from the interviews. The studies by S. W. Fuchs and M. M. Fuchs and Fuchs of religious minorities in Pakistan are of communities in general, with less reference to individual responses.[5] This type of collective support of the nation was not something the women in my research talked about, with one exception. However, a well-connected, well-educated non-Muslim respondent was active in advocating for the nation and the women of Pakistan.

Although Muslim majoritarianism could result in the exclusion of minorities from positions of influence, exclusion was also something practiced by KP's minorities, according to one of the ethno-religious minority respondents in my sample group. She referenced the steps taken by Hindu and Sikh communities to exclude their girls and women from participation in KP's Muslim-majority public sphere, and Christian leaders' exclusion of their youth from programs run by another religious minority. There are parallels with the self-ghettoization of Algerian women in Dublin, for whom the world was polarized into self and others. Shanneik, writing of this self-ghettoization observed that, "binary oppositions are much easier to construct when it is possible to draw clear lines of distinction between who is who."[6] Exclusion is, thus, not simply a defensive measure to protect identity, but in the KP context, an expression of community power; resistance to the greater power of the majority, and to forces coming from other minority communities. One consequence of

5. Fuchs and Fuchs, "Religious Minorities"; Fuchs, "Reclaiming the Citizen."
6. Shanneik, "Religion," 89.

exclusion and resistance is a further limitation on female access to the public sphere, among communities that may otherwise not have the strict *parda* restrictions as found in *Pukhto*.

Further study is needed to discover if women from these non-Muslim communities subscribe to the limits placed on their access to KP's public sphere. Additional research would show whether lack of access to the public sphere is a new phenomenon removing what was formerly considered to be culturally and religiously appropriate for women, and to what degree these women accept or resist collective decision-making that impacts their individual lives. Shanneik, for example, had identified that Muslim women, living as a minority in a Christian majority context, consciously practiced loyalty to their ethno-religious identity even as alternative—and seemingly less restrictive—options were available to them.[7] In addition, an investigation of the views held by the different ethno-religious minorities in KP-Pakistan would provide a greater understanding as to the depth and breadth of an exclusionary reaction, and suggest solutions other than the further marginalization of women within those communities.

FEMALE INFLUENCE FROM WITHIN THE PUBLIC SPHERE

For the respondents in this study, the binary lines of us-them, majority-minority, cease to be clear cut when moving outside the frame of religion. For example, the elite Pukhtun respondents in my study influence from positions of majority and minority simultaneously. Positioned by their status and by ethno-religious identity among the majority, they can command submission from those junior to them. Positioned as a minority, because of gender, they are required to use persuasive influence in an effort to change patriarchal or discriminatory attitudes, coming even from members of their own social class. Or they might form a networked group, perhaps operating from the counter-public spaces provided by social media, to advocate for a change to societal practices that marginalize or discriminate against all women because of the patriarchal nature of KP's public sphere institutions.

7. Shanneik, "Religion."

Patriarchy and Pukhto

Male dominance, as a societal system that privileges men and marginal-izes women, was presented by, or affirmed by the respondents in my study as the norm in KP. They were acutely aware of its impact on the public spaces where they worked and studied. They also spoke of the value of weaker or lesser than men that is attached to female identity, especially for Pukhtuns. The degree to which a religious understanding of women's weaker nature is part of the socio-religious norms of *all* the religious com-munities represented in this research is something I could not determine from this small sample group. It requires further study. However, there was the suggestion that these other communities have borrowed conservative patriarchal norms from *Pukhto*, especially regarding *parda* and access to education and employment. The ethno-religious minority respondents spoke of being required to negotiate the socio-religious norms of their own communities in addition to any *Pukhto* or Sunni Muslim norms op-erating within their area of interaction with KP's public sphere.

Thus, patriarchy in KP, in the minds of the respondents, operates as a system of male domination and societal inequality in which *all* women are required to be in submission to *all* adult men. Yet, in this same sphere, women are able to exert authority over men. This is *not* "a type of moral authority" exercised by women over some men founded upon female piety in which women demand that men "conform to religious ideals of behavior."[8] This is the power and authority of a post that requires com-pliance no matter what the gender or character of the post-holder. The influence mechanism of status-based compliance overrules the norms of patriarchy within the context of the professional space in which it was exercised. As Fahima clearly stated, her female influence is acceptable because of the position she holds. Whether her staff agree or not, they have to accept it.

Women's authoritative presence in the public sphere has its roots in changes occurring in the domestic realm. All but one of the women in the sample group had obtained their posts and positions in the public sphere with the permission of at least one senior male. The exception had the support of her mother as there was no father or husband for her to refer to. This is a significant change in male attitudes. As one re-spondent noted, men have been given the religio-cultural power of mak-ing decisions for the women in their households. Fathers and husbands

8. Aghaie, "Symbols and Rituals," 54, 55.

traditionally determine every level of female access to the public sphere. Brothers can also decide what their sisters are permitted to participate in, and uncles can put pressure on a household where attitudes to *parda* are felt to be lax.

Thus, the seemingly simple act of male permission for women to work in the public sphere underscores the deep but quiet changes taking place to the structure of KP's patriarchal norms. This includes changes to *Pukhto*. Men are being influenced by the visible success of women in the public sphere to, first, accept and promote previously male-only fields of employment as suitable for their daughters, sisters, and wives, and, secondly, redefine their interpretations of *parda*. That these men have been persuaded in this way is evidence of a female narrative that has effectively contested the norms of women's socio-religious identity. This counter narrative—communicated through the respondents' lifestyles—has persuaded significant male others that their current ideas about women in the public sphere are wrong and that alternative ideas are right, or at least, beneficial to them. This is proof of successful social influence. The alternative idea that men have accepted is that women's presence in the public sphere is no longer one of *sharm*.

This indicates that in some households the knowledge base of *Pukhto* is being changed to incorporate a new understanding of women's presence in the public sphere. *Pukhto* operates as the foundation upon which Pukhtun male gatekeepers base their decisions. The limited nature of my sample group meant that I could not determine the spread and permanency of these changes. There remains the possibility, because of the strength of conservative attitudes in KP, that at some future point, stricter levels of *parda* will be enforced on a regional or even a provincial level. In KP, families are acutely aware of the state imposition of conservative patriarchy in neighboring Afghanistan that has required women to return to their homes.

In addition, in the KP-Pakistan context, the changes to societal codes seem to indicate that Islam is also being challenged, not least because of its integral role in *Pukhto*. Ahmad, Jamal and Weiss are among those who have addressed the tensions between conservative, traditionalist, and modernist forms of Islam regarding female identity in Pakistan.[9] These tensions were not reflected in the interviews given by the sample group. Westernization and modernism, and women's interaction with societal

9. Ahmad, *Transforming Faith*; Jamal, *Jamaat-e-Islami Women*; Weiss, *Interpreting Islam*.

change caused by these forces, were not overtly a part of my study and were given little direct emphasis by the respondents. Yet, this sample group could be understood as representing modernity, in that all but one respondent had broken with conservative practices and were active in the workplace. The one exception, an older woman, had never held a job but was a known and respected influencer in the community where her family lives.

While the tensions between the modern and conservative were not highlighted in the interviews, there was some reflection on personal encounters with religio-cultural practices by a few of the respondents. For example, one respondent noted that her activism brought her into conflict with her family, and with the elders of her religious community. Her counter-cultural presence in the public sphere and her activist message were of concern to them. As Maryam had noted, there are some social, religious, and political issues that KP society deems inappropriate topics for women to discuss. Others in my sample group also spoke of negative reactions to their being in the public sphere coming from religiously conservative men. However, unlike the issues of patriarchy and *Pukhto*, there was not enough data to explore changes to the knowledge base of Islam caused by female influence in KP's public sphere. This is also true of the other religions represented in this study.

Societal Status, Compliance, and Persuasion

As influence tactics that operate in specific situations, successful influence has been shown in this book to be directly impacted by the influencer's professional and/or social status, and also by the strength of the resistance she encounters. The mechanism of status-based compliance, for example, was exercised by those respondents who had the requisite professional or social status to expect obedience from others. Within the frame of social influence, this was not conformity in response to group pressure, although it occurred because of the power of the post to reward or punish. The mechanism of compliance worked for the respondents because it operates in a socialized hierarchical and patriarchal society within which those with junior ranking are expected to submit to their seniors. There is also the suggestion that compliance draws on the strength of other pre-existing religio-cultural norms, such as *taqlid*, Islamization, *Pukhto*, and patriarchy. These norms work together to make compliance something that is desirable and necessary.

The women's stories have also shown that professional status—an organizational post—provides those with low social status the power to influence within the scope of their positions, just as it does for women with high social status. The power of a recognized post ensures that female influence works as if by magic (*kamāl*), because the *positive* of the post offsets the *negative* of female gender or low social status. However, this did not necessarily apply outside an organization, where the social status of the influencer, and her ability to reward/punish, was also considered by those she was seeking to influence. Within organizations, resistance to command was seemingly stronger when the job and social status of the influencer were low in the group's hierarchical scale. Yet, the findings also showed that even women with upper and elite social status sought out the power and authority of senior professional positions, particularly those that were government related, as providing them with greater capacity to demand compliance. This highlights the pervasiveness of patriarchal norms that marginalize women and resist their influence even at an elite level.

Persuasive argument, known as convincing power by one respondent, is the ability to sell an idea, to use informed argument to persuade someone to do something, or to negotiate for a change of mindset. It was exercised by some of my respondents as advocacy: a vital means of moving ideas as well as projects forward. However, the need to use persuasion could underscore the marginalized status of the influencer caused by her gender, her ethno-religious identity, or her low social status. This could require her to reach out to others for their support. As demonstrated in the SI framework presented in figure 8, the networked contacts provided by professional or social status, or familial or tribal relationships, offer external connections that could be utilized in the achievement of one's goals. These networked connections facilitate an indirect influence, although one that can have considerable power. When called upon, they are able to bolster the status of individuals within an organizational network and put pressure on the decision-maker to make the desired change. The use of pre-existing networks demonstrates an appropriation of one aspect of culture by women newly active in KP's public sphere. To what extent they consciously use other parts of culture as mechanisms to facilitate influence requires further investigation.

Networks

The networked connections of patronage, female lineage, *birādari*, and *sifārish* were also available as influence mechanisms for the women in this study. As clients, women in KP can exercise indirect influence when initial attempts at direct influence have failed, or if they are positioned, by professional or social status, in a junior position with little reward power. As patrons, women were able to use their connections and resources, and their own power and influence, on behalf of a weaker client. In my study, patronage was linked to the development of a woman's reputation as someone who can be trusted. Such a patron was believed in and listened to. This is an important point to underscore. Women who achieve an authentic persona have undone the designations of weak, deceitful, and licentious that are traditionally associated with their gender. They have transitioned from being *bura* (evil) for being in the public sphere, to those who can be trusted by men and women alike. Further study is required to understand if and how the processes of patronage differ for women as compared to men. Its use and effectiveness for non-Muslim women also needs to be determined, including situations where non-Muslim women are clients of Muslim patrons, and vice versa.

The use of *birādari* networks was not a theme that emerged directly from my research. Indirectly, however, it appeared in the influence mechanism of *sifārish* that took advantage of patrilineal family connections to obtain a favor. What was more likely to impact the women in my sample group were female or familial lineage networks that enabled them to occupy a privileged position of influence, no matter their professional status. Such external familial networks are potentially available to women from all social classes and religious identities, as influence is linked to the power implicit in a family name. While the example in my research came from a respondent who is part of an elite, Pukhtun family, the implication is that a family name can be used influentially within all the different communities of KP, if it is known to carry power.

Influence is *sifārish* in the opinions of two of the women in my study. They equated this system of recommendation with the influence that enables some to achieve their goals in an unethical manner. It was, therefore, not appropriate in their minds for use in an organizational context. Yet one of these respondents was willing to use *sifārish* personally, outside of work. For her, this was not an unethical use of her influence, even though it was the organizational workplace of those she wanted the help from. In social influence terms, *sifārish* operates as another form of influence that can overlay official organizational networks to give an undeserved advantage to a woman seeking to influence others. However, the positioning of *sifārish* within social influence theories requires additional investigation, with reference to the elements of networked reward-power and patronage found within this system of recommendation.

Exemplar, Endorser, and Mentor

The tactic of persuasion was not necessarily limited to verbal argument. Persuasion could be achieved through a woman's visibly successful lifestyle as observed by others, in which age, maturity, and experience operate as social proofs. The mechanisms of role model exemplar and celebrity endorser are founded on the visible honorable reputation and successful career of the exemplar or endorser. Mentoring draws upon these same visible markers of success. As a mechanism, however, mentoring is mainly directed at equipping women in the skills they will need to safely work and flourish in an environment that is largely alien to women.

Two factors were emphasized by the respondents as key to the mechanisms of role model exemplar, celebrity endorser, and mentor. The first was responsibility, and the second was capacity. Successful women should feel their *responsibility* to become role models and mentors. Their *capacity* to influence from this position was contained in their *i'zət-e nafs*, their visible honor, dignity, and worth. For those who appeared on mainstream and social media, their micro-celebrity status enhanced their influence and widened its scope. As celebrities they could, for example, endorse a profession as a *brand* appropriate for women. Thus, an act of immorality or the loss of character by a visible role model or celebrity endorser had the potential to damage public-sphere opportunities for other women. What was less clear among the societally senior women in the sample group was whether a serious professional mistake would bring the same consequences. This sense of responsibility underscores the newness of women's public-sphere presence in KP where, as the respondents indicated, influence is being exercised by women in the vanguard of social change. The extent to which famous role models have the potential to become idealized in the minds of those they influence was not clear from the interviews. The potential is there, seen in, for example, the respect given to Dr. Farhat Hashmi as an Islamic scholar, founder of a religious school, mentor of many women, and an effective social worker.

FAILURE TO INFLUENCE

No specific mechanisms were identified by the women in my sample group as working less well than others. Where influence failed it was simply because that mechanism had not worked at that time within a certain set of circumstances. A failure to influence was often linked by the women to a lack of recognized legitimacy. She is just a woman, what can she do! Or the lack of a powerful family name. Such attitudes resulted in obstructionism and resistance to influence on multiple levels. There was also the resistance of a culturally stronger male voice, and obstructionism from men angered by women who had disrupted their comfortable norm, or who felt shamed by women's visible success. They also had to deal with cultural or organizational inertia, and the complexity and sensitivity of the terrain in which the women work.

Within this terrain, which includes both digital and physical public spaces, there was also resistance from other women, although the respondents in my study most often referred to obstructionism arising from jealousy regarding another's advancement. Female resistance associated with growing Islamic piety and a push to return to classic patriarchy was also referenced during the interviews, but it was not a strong sub-theme. At the same time, one well-placed respondent noted that the outworking of resistance to the changes in society occurring because of female influence, was the reduction in the space available for women to disagree publicly with societal norms, as discussed above in the context of honor. This could potentially increase failure to influence by women unable to insert their voices into the public domain.

INFLUENCE THAT ADDS TO UNDERSTANDING

Women's visible presence as influencers in KP's public sphere is a relatively new phenomenon, occurring over the past twenty years. Thus, little is known of how their influence works—its mechanics. This book is the fruit of my proposal that the identification of influence mechanisms is a helpful means by which to assess the effect of women's presence in a religiously conservative and patriarchal society, and to better understand the part played by female influence in the obvious societal changes taking place in Khyber Pakhtunkhwa.

The contributions made by this study are to two academic disciplines: women's studies, particularly in the Muslim majority context, and social influence studies. I have also addressed a gap in understanding by using a methodology that brings together Muslim and non-Muslim voices, and the voices of Muslim minority communities, to describe a shared action rather than studying each community separately. In addition, the research in this book has addressed an over-focus on minorities in KP-Pakistan as victims or casualties. At the same time, I recognize that there are issues of discrimination and stereotyping that can separate majority and minority women and their communities from each other.

Female Honor

When I started my research journey, I had expected to find that issues of honor-shame, interwoven into the need to provide social proof, will be impacting female influence in KP in ways not always noted in women's studies literature. Mine is not a study of gender and sexuality, nor an anthropological approach to the practice of honor and *sharm*. It is an exploration of the *how* of female influence. I made this journey by listening to what a group of women had to say on the topic of their influence. One of the contributions made by *Voices of Change* is a recognition of the importance of *I'zət* to women in the public sphere. It is the key tactic by which women obtain and maintain their influence in that space. The respondents were clear that, in KP, regardless of ethnicity, women have to use *I'zət* influentially, to prove personal honor, dignity, respect, and trustworthiness. Then they need some in society to legitimize their *I'zət*. Only after that can they influence like a man. That is, they now have the right to influence from a place of authority. It is conceivable that a woman without recognized honor can use the power of her post to command and expect compliance. Indeed, I was told about women with reputations reportedly linked to corrupt practices and a loss of personal *I'zət* who hold positions of public sphere authority. Yet, overall, it is possible to conclude that for many women in KP, sustained and persuasive influence in the public sphere has to be founded on and maintained by her *I'zət-e nafs*, her dignity, and her demonstrable integrity.

The maintenance of integrity requires hard work, as has been established from the interviews. Socialized or stereotypical views of female honor founded on *sharm* have to be overcome through a redefinition of women's honor that retains socio-religious resonance. My journey of exploration revealed that women are effectively changing patriarchal societal mindsets and socio-religious codes, not through activism or an overt emphasis on feminism, but through their *ı'zət*. This is the simple expedient of consistently proving themselves to be as honorable, and also as capable, as their male counterparts. They labor to preserve the untarnished space that is essential to the ethic of honor as found in the terms *ı'zət, ghe'rət,* and *Pukhto.*

Barth has suggested that where societal change is endorsed by a majority, the basic characteristics of Pukhtun identity can be modified in a manner associated with honor rather than failure, thus maintaining Pukhtun autonomy.[10] The issue of failure is an important one. My research has provided, through its study of opposition to female influence, insights into the male defense of their privileges, even as, paradoxically, men contribute to the challenges they were facing by giving permission for their daughters, sisters, and wives to be in the public sphere as persons whose *ı'zət-e nafs* remains intact.

Kakar and Edwards had observed that when a community is faced with challenges to its patriarchal norms, it is able to change its understanding of the boundaries of *parda* and female honor, and have this change endorsed by society.[11] In *Voices of Change,* I have shown that Pukhtun women's presence in the public sphere is a change to the boundaries of female honor that has been endorsed by some in KP society. This societal endorsement is key to the long-term effectiveness of a change that is happening quietly: the result of and a catalyst for women's honorable status in the public sphere. As part of this catalyst, women who successfully balance their honor with their professional capacity, influence not only other women but also the male patriarchs and gatekeepers of female access to the public sphere. There has also been a societal change from classic to public patriarchy by those in society able to accommodate a new definition of female honor. My interviews with women from Pakistan's ethno-religious minorities have shown that parallel changes are happening among the non-Pukhtun Muslim and the non-Muslim communities

10. Barth, "Pathan Identity," 133.
11. Kakar, "Tribal Law"; Edwards, "Marginality and Migration."

represented in my research. In part, these changes are happening because of the redefinition of honorable female status for Pukhtun women.

In this redefinition of female honor, there was no indication among any of the Pukhtun respondents that their *Pukhto* has changed. None of the Pukhtun women spoke of having lost their *Pukhto* or their *ı'zət* despite the changes to cultural practice that many of them described, and their own counter-cultural places in KP's public sphere. This was partly a lack of reflection on the subject; it was not a focus question in the interviews. There was also a sense of retained normalcy that the women radiated, together with a belief that women's empowerment need not conflict with any religio-cultural values. They were still dealing with issues of male domination, but their settledness, and a sense of their own *ı'zət*, remained. This indicated that the changes to patriarchy and *Pukhto* are occurring organically *within* the culture. Even when some in my sample group were dealing with cognitive dissonance, as they balanced their need to be in the workplace alongside a belief in the ideal of women's place in the home, they were working within culture and religious values. Thus, this research has added to understanding by exposing, on a micro-level, some of the processes by which a society transitions from private to public patriarchy, and the ways in which, once in the public sphere, some women continue to press for new patriarchal norms that fit their professional status.

There is an argument that women in the Middle East are destabilizing the status quo from within—using their own, redefined religious and cultural beliefs, values, and principles to challenge societal norms and bring about change.[12] My research adds to this argument, showing how changes from within to some of the traditions of *Pukhto*, patriarchy, and religious beliefs are visibly disrupting and changing societal norms in KP-Pakistan. These changes are occurring in urban areas where issues of *parda* can be more relaxed, and there is greater access to education and employment. Societal change in KP's rural areas will require additional research.[13]

---

12. Mahmood, *Politics of Piety*; Shanneik, *The Art of Resistance*.

13. Data analysis of the similarities or differences based on urban-rural demographics was not part of my study.

Social Influence Studies

In *Voices of Change*, the frame of social influence has been an additional way for me to explore how influence works. Social influence theories, developed in more individualistic, Western settings, became useful lenses through which to view female minority influence in the complexity of KP's public sphere. As such, my research adds to studies, such as that of Contractor and DeChurch, in the application of a theory or theories to the lived reality of women in a non-Western setting.[14] It is important to note, however, that in the KP context, religion has a greater prominence in society than is attributed to it in the theories I accessed.

In KP's public sphere, *successful direct* female influence occurs when it is exercised by women with professional or social status. It is their position that gives them the right to expect compliance from those whose status is junior to theirs. Viewed as an equation, the deficit of gender marginalization is cancelled by the authority credit contained in a societal post, particularly that belonging to a recognized profession and organization. This is seemingly at odds with my earlier argument that influence occurs through honor and hard work. It serves as a reminder that there is no one influence strategy that women use in the public sphere. All the mechanisms are available as tactics, to be used as the situation requires.

The equation of gender marginalization and authority credit is closest to the social influence theory of majority influence in that it is the post, not the person, who carries the power to demand compliance. Therefore, as the women explained in their interviews, while a status-based title grants some form of seniority in an organization, it does not necessarily confer an authority its holder can use outside of their work situation. The exception being the status of a powerful family name. The separation of post from person is enhanced by KP's hierarchical societal structure and the existence of pre-existing systems of conformity.

At the same time, low social status *does not* prevent women from successfully exercising direct influence within an organization. Again, viewed as an equation, the debit of low status is offset by the credit of the status and authority implicit in their job. However, once outside the structures of organizational authority, social status *does* determine the effectiveness of female influence. A prestigious family name provides additional weight to female influence, although even then, it is not a

14. Contractor and DeChurch, "Integrating Social Networks."

guarantee of success because of patriarchy and the ever-present belief that influence is male.

Successful indirect influence occurs when women are networked to a group that contains individuals with decision-making power or who have connections to such people. This is the interaction of causative and purposive influence within a relational network or social structure. In KP, networks enable a well-placed woman to use her connections to affect and direct change. Influence also occurs when the network/group speaks as one voice. As a collective, the group carries more weight than a woman trying to influence on her own.

I was able to demonstrate, through the women's stories, that the multiple levels of societal belonging that the women participate in, in KP, are beneficial to their/female influence. They allow women to draw on their social and professional connections to ensure ultimate success. A shared *cause* such as activism can join women together as equals despite differences in socio-religious or societal status. However, within the same networks, as issues of lineage and connection become part of the equation, a marginalization of influence occurs for those who are identified as not belonging to the influential group. They remain in the network but have limited access to those with the power to make decisions.

Unsuccessful influence is caused by marginalization. The absence of a societal proof of a woman's right to influence negates her ability to influence. This lack of proof may be the result of conservative religious or patriarchal attitudes that marginalize the would-be influencer, her lower professional or social status, or an ethno-religious minority identity that could not be surmounted by other means. Yet, lack of success was shown to act as a spur in many cases, as women look for other means by which to gain their goals.

AN UNDERSTANDING OF INFLUENCE

At the start of this research journey, I had set out to understand the ways in which female influence is exercised in its multiplicity of forms in Khyber Pakhtunkhwa's public sphere. A limitation in my research may have been an over-emphasis on influence mechanisms coming from a place of senior leadership, due to the make-up of the sample group. At the same time, I considered the comments and stories coming from every respondent, as they contributed to the understanding of the mechanics of female influence in KP's public sphere. Even with this slight bias, I had expected to find some level of unfamiliarity with influence as a concept among the sample group. However, the degree to which the respondents had never considered influence as something that they were engaged in was unexpected. One reason for this could be the presence of hierarchical patriarchy that ranks men and women into positions of senior-junior. The patriarch exercises power; juniors comply. Therefore, it is possible that the respondents had not considered influence as something they engaged in because power and compliance relationships are the societal norm.

In addition, the respondents may have not considered themselves to be influential because it is not something women do. This is the cultural norm captured in the melon proverb: influence is male, not female. However, as this book has shown, influence is a lived reality for women in KP. Therefore, what I encountered in the interviews may simply have been a lack of engagement with the topic. That is, prior to being interviewed they had never considered the exercise of their or other women's influence, especially in abstract terms.

At the start of my research, I had asked whether women need the help of powerful others if they are to be effective in an environment where influence is traditionally male, or if they are able to influence in their own right, as those who have the necessary power and resources at their disposal. When I asked this question, I had an understanding of societal influence as something that is relational, causative and purposive, seated within the broadest definitions of power and yet distinguishable from it. Influence for women, I had assumed, would be the same as it is for men. I simply needed to identify how it is exercised. My research has affirmed my initial understanding: in the KP context, women view their influence as *an expression of power* in the same way as it is for men. It is exercised by those whose professional or social authority enables them to demand compliance because the right to influence is contained in the post as separate from the person.

However, in the KP context, female influence is understood to be *less effective than that of men*, particularly when used in the area of persuasion or advocacy. This is the result of a patriarchal system that ascribes, within the broadest of terms, moral and intellectual strength to men and moral and intellectual weakness to women. This requires them to draw on the help of powerful others, as required, to attain their goals. In addition, social legitimization is needed if women's influence is to be accepted in the public sphere, and if the entrenched mindset of lesser is to be removed.

Legitimization is achieved by an observable demonstration of women's personal honor. Once personal integrity is recognized, professional capacity can be assessed. It is my observation that this societal legitimization, founded on the women's ability to provide recognized socio-religious proof, is central to their ability to influence in KP's public sphere.

I propose, therefore, that Muslim and non-Muslim female influence in Muslim-majority KP is an expression of power that fits within the normative frame of senior command and junior compliance. This influence is relational, causative, and purposive. However, to be effective in the long term, persuasive female influence requires societal, primarily male, authentication of the influencer's honorable identity, and societal legitimization of the influencer's professional or social status. Religio-cultural norms have already provided men with the right to influence, while women need to earn that right. Carrying less societal weight than male influence, female influence is often used strategically, and somewhat diplomatically, through networked connections that link the influencer to decision-makers, or to those with the power to demand compliance.

RECOMMENDATIONS

The women's movement that began as a response to the Islamization process has been the focus of much of the women's studies literature written about Muslim women in Pakistan, from Mumtaz and Shaheed's inaugural book *Women of Pakistan* to the collection of essays in Rehman's 2021 book *Womansplaining* and Saeed's *Tapestry* accounts of individual Pakistani women active for women's rights. However, feminism, activism, piety, and religio-political Islam were not topics that the women in my sample group chose to speak about in their interviews. The few respondents who talked of their efforts to change entrenched societal practices addressed the obstacles that challenged their influence as women, rather than describing their influence as feminists or activists.

There is a need, therefore, to dig deeper into the influence being exercised by women in women's groups in Pakistan, to identify the specific mechanisms they are using. To address this gap, a purposive sample group of women identified as coming from different expressions of the women's movement is required. This sample group could bring together majority Muslim and ethno-religious minority voices to talk about the influence they are exerting, with a focus on tactics used, not only on results balanced against personal cost. It could also include an exploration of women's ability to (re-)tell their stories in a manner that gives societal and religious legitimacy to their claims for justice and equality.

Further research is also required to explore the steps by which a society moves from private to public patriarchy, and how socio-religious systems like *Pukhto* can change and yet, paradoxically, seem to remain the same. Alongside this, an investigation of the emerging pious middle class across Pakistan, and in comparable Muslim-majority nations, using Maqsood's research as a mirror, would also be an interesting study.[15] Its findings would provide valuable insights for understanding Muslim female influence.

To be included in ongoing research should be an exploration of cognitive dissonance for religiously conservative women, and also an investigation into the changes to male honor and privileging that is occurring in KP. Such research could lead to a deeper understanding of what comprises a tipping-point in the process of the public endorsement of female influence. The 2021 change of government in neighboring Afghanistan has demonstrated how quickly permissions for women's influential presence in the public sphere can be withdrawn when that tipping-point has not been reached. It is, therefore, important to understand what is required for female influence in the public sphere to become an acceptable societal norm. As a norm, women would no longer need to demonstrate personal honor as well as professional ability in order to influence. Currently, only women working in gynesocial settings need not demonstrate their personal respect. Yet, even in these contexts, women from ethno-religious minority communities maybe required to prove that they have similar-to-norm levels of respect, dignity, and honor before their influence can be accepted.

In addition, the social influence frameworks developed in this study sought to provide models by which to explore the power of pre-existing networks to change the authority, and thereby, the influence exercised by women within an organization. These models, made specifically for KP's public sphere, require testing in other comparable situations. This would help determine whether I was simply making explicit that which remains implicit in earlier research, or if my SI models can facilitate the study of (female) influence in contexts where strong pre-existing cultural and religious networks are found.

15. Maqsood, *Pakistani Middle Class*.

Lastly, there is a need for a greater understanding of minority non-Muslim communities outside of the frame of discrimination. Further research could helpfully include the investigation of patriarchy, hierarchy, and other societal structures central to these communities. As a study, it might helpfully include the Muslim ethno-religious minority communities in KP. It should incorporate the investigation of lived honor-shame, and issues of female exclusion from the KP majority public sphere, including the practice of self-exclusion. Further study of how *women* from minority communities view themselves as they relate to the Sunni majority community is also required. This would help balance the studies that talk of community from a male standpoint. While discrimination will be a part of the conversation, the filters of education, professional position, and societal status should assist in uncovering other self-categorization mirrors. Research should also explore the contribution of women from ethno-religious minorities to activism, feminism, religion, politics, and the processes of social change in KP-Pakistan. A limitation of my own study is that it did not look at female influence practiced solely within a non-Muslim minority community.

IN *VOICES OF CHANGE* I have used Khyber Pakhtunkhwa as a case study by which to explore the how, why, and where of female influence in a religiously conservative and highly patriarchal society. I have provided measurable reasons that explain how women are exercising influence in KP's public sphere, even as a popular proverb declares such influence to be inappropriate or impossible. I have brought together Muslim and non-Muslim voices to present proverbially impossible *female* influence as a possible lived reality within the KP context. I have used women's studies literature and social influence theories as lenses by which to identify and analyze specific influence mechanisms within the complexity of KP's public-sphere melon field. I have exposed the challenge that female influence presents to patriarchy and socio-religious codes in KP's conservative Muslim and non-Muslim communities. I have also demonstrated the part that female influence plays in the quiet recasting of these societal norms.

My research has shown that none of the tactics used by women in KP can be graded against an effectiveness scale; why and how certain mechanisms work better than others. The effectiveness of each mechanism is determined by the lived context of the individual influencer, including her societal status—her weight. At the same time, I have demonstrated that the double-sided mechanism of honor and hard work enables women to obtain and maintain their places in KP's public sphere. Other mechanisms are exercised from that space as the means by which ideas and projects are moved forward, and societal goals achieved.

Voices of Change has shown that influence is not impossible nor inappropriate for the women of KP. Influence can be female, too. I therefore conclude this book by returning to the popular proverb for influence. "Male and female melons gain their color by sitting with other melons." Men and women can beneficially influence or be influenced by each other when they are given the opportunity to sit side-by-side in Khyber Pakhtunkhwa's public sphere.

Bibliography

Abu-Lughod, Lila. *Do Muslim Women Need Saving?* Cambridge, MA: Harvard University Press, 2013.

Afary, Janet. "Seeking a Feminist Politics for the Middle East after September 11." *Frontiers: A Journal of Women Studies* 25, no. 1 (2004): 128–37. https://www.jstor.org/stable/3347261.

———. *Sexual Politics in Modern Iran.* Cambridge: Cambridge University Press, 2009.

Afary, Janet, and Kevin Anderson. *Foucault and the Iranian Revolution: Gender and the Seductions of Islamism.* Chicago: University of Chicago Press, 2005.

Aghaie, Kamran Scot. "Gendered Aspects of the Emergence and Historical Development of Shi'i Symbols and Rituals." In *The Women of Karbala: Ritual Performance and Symbolic Discourses in Modern Shi'i Islam,* edited by Kamran Scot Aghaie, 1–21. Austin: University of Texas Press, 2005.

———. "The Gender Dynamics of Moharram Symbols and Rituals in the Latter Years of Qajar Rule." In *The Women of Karbala: Ritual Performance and Symbolic Discourses in Modern Shi'i Islam,* edited by Kamran Scot Aghaie, 45–63. Austin: University of Texas Press, 2005.

Ahmad, Sadaf. "Al-Huda and Women's Religious Authority in Urban Pakistan." *The Muslim World,* Special Issue: Muslim Women and the Challenge of Authority, vol. 103, no. 3 (2013): 363–74. https://doi.org/10.1111/muwo.12019.

———. "Identity Matters, Culture Wars: An Account of Al-Huda (Re)Defining Identity and Reconfiguring Culture in Pakistan." *Culture and Religion* 9, no. 1 (2008): 63–80. https://doi.org/10.1080/14755610801963236.

———. "The Multiple Locations and Competing Narratives of Pakistani Women." In *Pakistani Women: Multiple Locations and Competing Narratives,* edited by Sadaf Ahmad, 1–11. Oxford in Pakistan Reading in Sociology and Social Anthropology, edited by Ali Khan. Karachi: Oxford University Press, 2010.

———. *Transforming Faith: The Story of Al-Huda and Islamic Revivalism among Urban Pakistani Women.* Syracuse: Syracuse University Press, 2009.

Ahmed, Akbar S. *Pukhtun Economy and Society: Traditional Structure and Economic Development in a Tribal Society.* Lahore: Peace Publications, 2017.

Ahmed, Amineh. *Sorrow and Joy among Muslim Women: The Pukhtuns of Northern Pakistan.* Cambridge, UK: Cambridge University Press, 2008.

Ahmed, Leila. *Women and Gender in Islam: Historical Roots of a Modern Debate.* New Haven: Yale University Press, 1992.

Ahmed-Ghosh, Huma, ed. *Contesting Feminisms: Gender and Islam in Asia*. Albany: State University of New York Press, 2015.

———. "Dilemmas of Islamic and Secular Feminists and Feminisms." *Journal of International Women's Studies* 9, no. 3 (2008): 99–116. https://vc.bridgew.edu/jiws/vol9/iss3/7.

Akhtar, Huma, Muhammad Fareed, and Muhammad Sajid Siraj. "Patterns and Processes of Language-Mixing in Pakistani Urdu Newspapers." *Pakistan Business Review* 20 (2018): 235–57. https://pdfs.semanticscholar.org/ef00/3c37560c78272dec6fe747651518c6ebd893.pdf.

Alam, Muhammad Aftab, Adnan Rehmat, and Emilie Lehmann-Jacobsen. *Narratives of Marginalization: Reporting Religious Minorities in Pakistani Media*. Institute for Research, Advocacy and Development, 2018. https://www.facebook.com/IRADAPK/posts/narratives-of-marginalization-reporting-religious-minorities-in-pakistani-media-/2045326558929873/.

Alessandrini, Megan. "Non-Positivist Approaches to Research in the Third Sector: Empowered Policy-Making." *ISTR Working Papers Series Volume VIII* (2012). https://www.istr.org/page/WP_Siena

Asch, Solomon E. "Studies of Independence and Conformity: I. A Minority of One against a Unanimous Majority." *Psychological Monographs: General and Applied* 70, no. 9 (1956): 1–70. https://doi.org/10.1037/h0093718.

Badran, Margot. "Engaging Islamic Feminism." In *Islamic Feminism: Current Perspectives*, edited by Anitta Kynsilehto, 25–36. Tampere: Tampere Peace Research Institute, 2008.

Baig, Nadeem, dir. *Sinf E Aahan*. TV series. Next Level Entertainment and Six Sigma Plus in collaboration with ISPR. ARY Digital, 2021. https://videos.arydigital.tv/search?query=sinf+e+aahan.

Bajwa, Asif, and Munir Ahmad Aslam. *Pakistan Standard Classification of Occupations*. Pakistan Bureau of Statistics, 2015. https://www.pbs.gov.pk/sites/default/files/other/documents/PSCO_2015.pdf.

Banerjee, Mukulika. *The Pathan Unarmed: Opposition & Memory in the North West Frontier*. Karachi: Oxford University Press, 2000.

Banks, Robert, and Bernice M. Ledbetter. *Reviewing Leadership: A Christian Evaluation of Current Approaches*. Engaging Culture. Grand Rapids: Baker Academic, 2004.

Barlas, Asma. *"Believing Women" in Islam: Unreading Patriarchal Interpretations of the Qur'an*. Austin: University of Texas Press, 2002.

———. "Engaging Islamic Feminism: Provincializing Feminism as a Master Narrative." In *Islamic Feminism: Current Perspectives*, edited by Anitta Kynsilehto, 15–23. Tampere: Tampere Peace Research Institute, 2008.

Barth, Fredrik. "Pathan Identity and Its Maintenance." In *Ethnic Groups and Boundaries: The Social Organization of Cultural Difference*, edited by Fredrik Barth, 117–34. Boston: Little, Brown & Co, 1969.

Bartlotti, Leonard N., and Raj Wali Shah Khattak, eds. *Rohi Mataluna: Pashto Proverbs. Revised and Expanded Edition of the Original Work by Mohammad Nawaz Tair & T.C. Edwards*. Peshawar: InterLit Foundation & Pashto Academy, Peshawar University, 2011.

Bartos, Otomar J., and Paul Wehr. *Using Conflict Theory*. Cambridge, NY: Cambridge University Press, 2002.

Bass, Bernard M. *Bass & Stogdill's Handbook of Leadership: Theory, Research, & Managerial Applications*. 3rd ed. New York: The Free, 1990.

Benford, Robert D., and David A. Snow. "Framing Processes and Social Movements: An Overview and Assessment." *Annual Review of Sociology* 26, no. 1 (2000): 611–39. https://doi.org/10.1146/annurev.soc.26.1.611.

Bennett, Clinton. *Muslim Women of Power: Gender, Politics and Culture in Islam*. New York: Continuum, 2010.

Bennoune, Karima. *Your Fatwa Does Not Apply Here: Untold Stories from the Fight against Muslim Fundamentalism*. New York: W. W. Norton & Company, 2013.

Berman, Rachel C., and Vappu Tyyskä. "A Critical Reflection on the Use of Translators/Interpreters in a Qualitative Cross-Language Research Project." *International Journal of Qualitative Methods* 10, no. 2 (2010): 178–90. https://doi.org/10.1177/160940691101000206.

Boulding, Kenneth E. *Three Faces of Power*. CA: Sage, 1989.

Boxberger, Linda. "From Two States to One: Women's Lives in the Transformation of Yemen." In *Women in Muslim Societies: Diversity Within Unity*, edited by Herbert L. Bodman and Nayereh Tohidi, 119–33. Boulder: Lynne Rienner, 1998.

Braun, Virginia, and Victoria Clarke. "Using Thematic Analysis in Psychology." *Qualitative Research in Psychology* 3, no. 2 (2006): 77–101. https://doi.org/10.1191/1478088706qp063oa.

Brohi, Khalida. *I Should Have Honor: A Memoir of Hope and Pride in Pakistan*. New York: Random House, 2018.

Bucar, Elizabeth M. *Pious Fashion: How Muslim Women Dress*. Cambridge, MA: Harvard University Press, 2017.

Burchell, Graham, Colin Gordon, and Peter Miller, eds. *The Foucault Effect: Studies in Governmentality: With Two Lectures by and an Interview with Michel Foucault*. Chicago: University of Chicago Press, 1991.

Chaudhry, Lubna Nazir. "Women and Poverty: Salient Findings from a Gendered Analysis of a Quasi-Anthropological Study in Rural Punjab and Sindh." In *Pakistani Women: Multiple Locations and Competing Narratives*, edited by Sadaf Ahmad and Ali Khan, 47–119. Oxford in Pakistan Reading in Sociology and Social Anthropology, edited by Ali Khan. Karachi: Oxford University Press, 2010.

Cialdini, Robert B. *Influence: The Psychology of Persuasion*. Revised. New York: HarperCollins eBook, 2009.

Clark, Janine. "Social Movement Theory and Patron-Clientelism: Islamic Social Institutions and the Middle Class in Egypt, Jordan, and Yemen." *Comparative Political Studies* 37, no. 8 (2004): 941–68. https://doi.org/10.1177/0010414004267982.

Coleman, Isobel. *Paradise beneath Her Feet: How Women Are Transforming the Middle East*. New York: Random House Trade Paperbacks, 2013.

Constitution of the Islamic Republic of Pakistan (2018). https://na.gov.pk/uploads/documents/1549886415_632.pdf.

Contractor, Noshir S. and Leslie A. DeChurch. "Integrating Social Networks and Human Social Motives to Achieve Social Influence at Scale." *Proceedings of the National Academy of Sciences* 111, no. Supplement_4 (2014): 13650–57. https://doi.org/10.1073/pnas.1401211111.

Dad, Nighat, and Shmyla Khan. "#MeToo: Women's Rights and the Trials of the Digital World." In *Womansplaining: Navigating Activism, Politics and Modernity in Pakistan*, edited by Sherry Rehman, 171–82. Lahore: Folio, 2021.

Dale, Moyra. *Shifting Allegiances: Networks of Kinship and of Faith. The Women's Program in a Syrian Mosque*. Eugene, OR: Wipf and Stock, 2016.

Devji, Faisal. "Changing Places: Religion and Minority in Pakistan." *South Asia: Journal of South Asian Studies*, ahead of print, January 3, 2020. https://doi.org/10.1080/0 0856401.2020.1694466.

D'Souza, Diane. *Partners of Zaynab: A Gendered Perspective of Shia Muslim Faith*. Studies in Comparative Religion. Columbia, SC: University of South Carolina Press, 2014.

Du Boulay, Juliet. "Women—Images of Their Nature and Destiny in Rural Greece." In *Gender & Power in Rural Greece*, edited by Jill Dubisch, 139–68. Princeton: Princeton University Press, 1986.

Dubisch, Jill, ed. *Gender & Power in Rural Greece*. Princeton: Princeton University Press, 1986.

Edwards, David Busby. "Marginality and Migration: Cultural Dimensions of the Afghan Refugee Problem." *The International Migration Review* 20, no. 2 (1986): 313–25. https://doi.org/10.2307/2546038.

Esposito, John L. *Islam: The Straight Path*. 5th ed. New York: Oxford University Press, 2016.

Festinger, Leon. "Informal Social Communication." *Psychological Review* 57, no. 5 (1950): 271–82. https://doi.org/10.1037/h0056932.

Foucault, Michel. *Discipline and Punish: The Birth of the Prison*. 2nd ed. Translated by Alan Sheridan. New York: Vintage, 1995.

———. *Ethics: Subjectivity and Truth*. Edited by Paul Rabinow. Translated by Robert Hurley. Vol. 1. The Essential Works Of Michel Foucault 1954–1984. New York: New, 1997.

———. "Questions of Method." In *The Foucault Effect: Studies in Governmentality: With Two Lectures By and An Interview With Michel Foucault*, edited by Graham Burchell, Colin Gordon, and Peter Miller, 73–86. University of Chicago Press, 1991.

———. *The History of Sexuality: An Introduction*. 1st ed. Translated by Robert Hurley. Vol. 1. New York: Pantheon, 1978.

———. "The Subject and Power." *Critical Inquiry* 8, no. 4 (1982): 777–95.

Fraser, Nancy. "Overcoming Displacement and Reification in Cultural Politics." In *Recognition Struggles and Social Movements: Contested Identities, Agency and Power*, edited by Barbara Hobson, 21–32. Cambridge, UK: Cambridge University Press, 2003.

———. "Rethinking the Public Sphere: A Contribution to the Critique of Actually Existing Democracy." *Social Text*, no. 25/26 (1990): 56–80. https://doi. org/10.2307/466240.

French, John R P, and Bertram Raven. "The Bases of Social Power." In *Studies in Social Power*, edited by D Cartwright, 259–69. Ann Arbor: Institute for Social Research, 1959.

Friedl, Ernestine. "The Position of Women: Appearance and Reality." In *Gender & Power in Rural Greece*, edited by Jill Dubisch, 42–52. Princeton: Princeton University Press, 1986.

Fuchs, Maria-Magdalena, and Simon Wolfgang Fuchs. "Religious Minorities in Pakistan: Identities, Citizenship and Social Belonging." *South Asia: Journal of South Asian Studies*, ahead of print, December 12, 2019. https://doi.org/10.1080/00856401.2020.1695075.

Fuchs, Simon Wolfgang. "Reclaiming the Citizen: Christian and Shi'i Engagements with the Pakistani State." *South Asia: Journal of South Asian Studies*, ahead of print, January 3, 2020. https://doi.org/10.1080/00856401.2020.1689616.

Gabriel, Theodore. *Christian Citizens in an Islamic State: The Pakistan Experience.* Burlington: Ashgate, 2007.

Gill, Aisha K, and Avtar Brah. "Interrogating Cultural Narratives about 'Honour'-Based Violence." *European Journal of Women's Studies* 21, no. 1 (2014): 72–86. https://doi.org/10.1177/1350506813510424.

Glatzer, Bernt. "Being Pashtun - Being Muslim: Concepts of Person and War in Afghanistan." *Essays on South Asian Society: Culture and Politics II (Zentrum Moderner Orient)* 9 (1998): 83–94. http://www.khyber.org/publications/021–025/glatzer1998.pdf.

Gordon, Colin. "Introduction." In *Power: Essential Works of Foucault 1954–1984,* edited by James D. Faubion, xi-xli. Translated by Robert Hurley and others. Vol. 3. UK: Penguin, 2020.

Government of Khyber Pakhtunkhwa. "Languages." 2018. http://kp.gov.pk/page/languages.

Gramsci, Antonio. *Selections from the Prison Notebooks of Antonio Gramsci.* Translated by Quentin Hoare and Geoffrey Nowell Smith. London: ElecBook, 1999.

Greenacre, Luke, Ngo Manh Tung, and Tom Chapman. "Self Confidence and the Ability to Influence." *Academy of Marketing Studies Journal* 18, no. 2 (2014): 1–14. https://www.researchgate.net/publication/286318041_Self_confidence_and_the_ability_to_influence/citation/download.

Grima, Benedicte. *Secrets from the Field: An Ethnographer's Notes from North Western Pakistan.* Bloomington, Ind: AuthorHouse, 2004.

———. *The Performance of Emotion among Paxtun Women: "The Misfortunes Which Have Befallen Me."* Karachi: Oxford University Press, 2004.

Habermas, Jürgen. *The Structural Transformation of the Public Sphere: An Inquiry into a Category of Bourgeois Society.* Translated by Thomas Burger. Cambridge, MA: Massachusetts Institute of Technology, 1991.

Haddad, Yvonne Yazbeck. "Islam and Gender: Dilemmas in the Changing Arab World." In *Islam, Gender and Social Change,* edited by Yvonne Yazbeck Haddad and John L. Esposito, 3–29. New York: Oxford University Press, 1998.

Haddad, Yvonne Yazbeck, and John L. Esposito, eds. *Islam, Gender, and Social Change.* New York: Oxford University Press, 1998.

Haddad, Yvonne Yazbeck, and Barbara Freyer Stowasser, eds. *Islamic Law and the Challenges of Modernity.* Walnut Greek: Altamira, 2004.

Haeri, Shahla. "Fascination with 'Difference': Democratizing Anthropology, Conducting Fieldwork among Equals." In *Pakistani Women: Multiple Locations and Competing Narratives,* edited by Sadaf Ahmad, 278–87. Oxford in Pakistan Reading in Sociology and Social Anthropology, edited by Ali Khan. Oxford: Oxford University Press, 2010.

———. *No Shame for the Sun: Lives of Professional Pakistani Women.* Karachi: Oxford University Press, 2004.

Hall, Shereen. "12 Influential Pakistani Women Leaders You Should Know." Huffpost, December 6, 2017. https://www.huffpost.com/entry/pakistan-female-leaders_b_1501214.

Hallaq, Wael B. "Can the Shari'a Be Restored?" In *Islamic Law and the Challenges of Modernity*, edited by Yvonne Yazbeck Haddad and Barbara Freyer Stowasser, 21–53. Walnut Creek: Altamira, 2004.

Halliday, M.A.K., and Christian M.I.M. Matthiessen. *Halliday's Introduction to Functional Grammar*. 4th ed. New York: Routledge, 2014.

Hanneman, Robert A., and Mark Riddle. "Centrality and Power." In *Introduction to Social Network Methods*, edited by Robert A. Hanneman and Mark Riddle. Riverside: University of California, 2005. https://faculty.ucr.edu/~hanneman/nettext/C10_Centrality.html

Hassan, Syed Rameez ul, and Raja Ahmed Jamil. "Influence of Celebrity Endorsement on Consumer Purchase Intention for Existing Products: A Comparative Study." *Journal Of Management Info* 4, no. 1 (2014): 1–8. https://doi.org/10.31580/jmi.v4i1.18.

Hasso, Frances S. "The Sect-Sex-Police Nexus and Politics in Bahrain's Pearl Revolution." In *Freedom Without Permission: Bodies and Space in the Arab Revolutions*, edited by Frances Susan Hasso and Zakia Salime, 105–137. Durham: Duke University Press, 2016.

Hasso, Frances S, and Zakia Salime. "Introduction." In *Freedom Without Permission: Bodies and Space in the Arab Revolutions*, edited by Frances Susan Hasso and Zakia Salime, 1–24. Durham: Duke University Press, 2016.

Hegland, Mary Elaine. "Marriage Modifications in Aliabad: Social Change Overrides Clerical Directives." In *Global Dynamics of Shi'a Marriages: Religion, Gender, and Belonging*, edited by Yafa Shanneik and Annelies Moors, 21–39. New Brunswick: Rutgers University Press, 2021.

———. "A Mixed Blessing: The *Majales*—Shi'a Women's Rituals of Mourning in Northwest Pakistan." In *Mixed Blessings: Gender and Religious Fundamentalism Cross Culturally*, edited by Judy Brink and Joan Menchers, 179–96. New York: Routledge, 1997.

Herzfeld, Michael. "Honour and Shame: Problems in the Comparative Analysis of Moral Systems." *Man* 15, no. 2 (1980): 339–51. https://doi.org/10.2307/2801675.

Hine, Catherine. "Untying the Hard Knot of Her Subjugation: Women Activists Negotiating Change in Pakistan." Ph.D., Australian National University, 2010. https://openresearch-repository.anu.edu.au/handle/1885/150416.

hooks, bell. "Marginality as Site of Resistance." In *Out There: Marginalization and Contemporary Cultures*, edited by Russell Ferguson, Martha Gever, Trinh T. Minh-ha, and Carnel West, 341–43. Cambridge, MA: Massachusetts Institute of Technology, New Museum of Contemporary Art, 1992.

Hussein, Jeylan W. "The Social and Ethno-Cultural Construction of Masculinity and Femininity in African Proverbs." *African Study Monographs* 26, no. 2 (2005): 59–87. https://doi.org/10.14989/68240.

Hylen, Susan E. *Women in the New Testament World*. Oxford: Oxford University Press, 2019.

Inglehart, Ronald, and Wayne E. Baker. "Modernization, Cultural Change, and the Persistence of Traditional Values." *American Sociological Review* 65, no. 1 (2000): 19–51. https://doi.org/10.2307/2657288.

International Phonetic Association. *Handbook of the International Phonetic Association: A Guide to the Use of the International Phonetic Alphabet*. Illustrated edition. Cambridge: Cambridge University Press, 1999.

Iqtidar, Humeira. *Secularizing Islamists?: Jama'at-e-Islami and Jama'at-ud-Da'wa in Urban Pakistan*. Chicago: University of Chicago Press, 2011.

Ispahani, Farahnaz. *Purifying the Land of the Pure: A History of Pakistan's Religious Minorities*. Revised and Updated. Noida, UP: HarperCollins, 2018.

Isran, Samina, and Manzoor Ali Isran. "Patriarchy and Women in Pakistan: A Critical Analysis." *Interdisciplinary Journal of Contemporary Research in Business* 4, no. 6 (2012): 835–59.

Jamal, Aamir. *The Gatekeepers: Engaging Pashtun Men for Gender Justice and Girls' Education*. Islamabad: Iqbal International Institute for Research and Dialogue, International Islamic University, 2018.

Jamal, Amina. "Gendered Islam and Modernity in the Nation-Space: Women's Modernism in the Jamaat-e-Islami of Pakistan." *Feminist Review* 91, no. 1 (2009): 9–28. https://doi.org/10.1057/fr.2008.43.

———. *Jamaat-e-Islami Women in Pakistan: Vanguard of a New Modernity?* Syracuse: Syracuse University Press, 2013.

———. "Transnational Feminism as Critical Practice: A Reading of Feminist Discourses in Pakistan." *Meridians* 5, no. 2 (2005): 57–82. https://www.jstor.org/stable/40338666.

Jivan, Jennifer Jag, and Peter Jacob. *Life on the Margins: A Study on the Minority Women in Pakistan*. National Commission for Justice and Peace, 2012. http://archive.paxchristi.net/MISC/2014-0250-en-ap-HR.pdf.

Kakar, Palwasha. "Tribal Law of Pashtunwali and Women's Legislative Authority." *Harvard Islamic Legal Studies Program*, 2004, 1–12. https://connections-qj.org/article/tribal-law-pashtunwali-and-womens-legislative-authority.

Kandiyoti, Deniz. "Bargaining with Patriarchy." *Gender and Society* 2, no. 3 (1988): 274–90. https://www.jstor.org/stable/190357.

———. "Reflections on the Politics of Gender in Muslim Societies: From Nairobi to Beijing." In *Faith and Freedom: Women's Human Rights in the Muslim World*, edited by Mahnaz Afkhami, 19–32. Syracuse: Syracuse University Press, 1995.

Karmi, Ghada. "Women, Islam and Patriarchalism." In *Feminism and Islam: Legal and Literary Perspectives*, edited by Mai Yamani, 69–83. New York: New York University Press, 1996.

Keddie, Nikki R. "The Minorities Question in Iran, 1995." 2013. https://web.archive.org/web/20131126160727/http://nikkikeddie.com/n-keddie/writings/the-minorities-question-in-iran-1995-34#_ftn1.

Kendall, Diana Elizabeth. *Sociology in Our Times*. 6th ed. Belmont, CA: Thomson/Wadsworth, 2007.

Khan, Ayesha. "The Politics of Activism: Bridging the Generational Arc." In *Womansplaining: Navigating Activism, Politics and Modernity in Pakistan*, edited by Sherry Rehman, 37–43. Lahore: Folio, 2021.

———. *The Women's Movement in Pakistan: Activism, Islam and Democracy*. London: I. B. Tauris, 2020.

Kirkpatrick, Pamela, and Edwin van Teijlingen. "Lost in Translation: Reflecting on a Model to Reduce Translation and Interpretation Bias." *Open Nursing Journal*, no. 3 (2009): 25–32. https://doi.org/10.2174/1874434600903010025.

Klein, Laura F. *Women and Men in World Cultures*. Boston: McGraw-Hill, 2004.

Koburtay, Tamer, Tala Abuhussein, and Yusuf M. Sidani. "Women Leadership, Culture, and Islam: Female Voices from Jordan." *Journal of Business Ethics*, ahead of print, February 28, 2022. https://doi.org/10.1007/s10551-022-05041-0.

Krackhardt, David. "Assessing the Political Landscape: Structure, Cognition, and Power in Organizations." *Administrative Science Quarterly* 35, no. 2 (1990): 342–69. https://doi.org/10.2307/2393394.

Lindholm, Charles. *Generosity and Jealousy: The Swat Pukhtun of Northern Pakistan*. New York: Columbia University Press, 1982.

Loewen, Arley. *Towards True Honour*. Afghanistan: Rahmat Publications, 2020.

Lukes, Steven. *Power: A Radical View*. 2nd ed. New York: Palgrave Macmillan, 2004.

Lyon, Stephen M. "Power and Patronage in Pakistan." Ph.D., University of Kent, 2002. https://dro.dur.ac.uk/183/.

Mahmood, Saba. *Politics of Piety: The Islamic Revival and the Feminist Subject*. Princeton: Princeton University Press, 2005.

———. *Religious Difference in a Secular Age: A Minority Report*. Princeton: Princeton University Press, 2016.

Malina, Bruce J. *The New Testament World: Insights from Cultural Anthropology*. Rev.ed. Louisville: Westminster/John Knox, 1993.

Mansoor, Nasreen. "Exploring Honour and Shame for South Asian British Muslim Men and Women." Ph.D., Manchester, 2017. https://search.proquest.com/docview/2230803494?pq-origsite=primo.

Maqsood, Ammara. *The New Pakistani Middle Class*. Cambridge, MA: Harvard University Press, 2017.

Maududi, Abul Ala. *Al-Hijab: Purdah and the Status of Woman in Islam*. 18th ed. Translated by Al-Ash'ari. Lahore: Islamic Publications (Pvt.) Limited, 2004.

———. *Towards Understanding Islam*. 24th ed. Translated by Khurshid Ahmad. Lahore: Idara Tarjuman-ul-Quran, 2001.

McLeod, Saul. "Moscovici and Minority Influence." *Simply Psychology*, 2018. https://www.simplypsychology.org/minority-influence.html.

Mernissi, Fatima. "Arab Women's Rights and the Muslim State in the Twenty-First Century: Reflections on Islam as Religion and State." In *Faith and Freedom: Women's Human Rights in the Muslim World*, edited by Mahnaz Afkhami, 33–50. Syracuse: Syracuse University Press, 1995.

———. *Beyond the Veil: Male-Female Dynamics in Modern Muslim Society*. Rev. ed. London: Saqi, 2003.

Middle East Institute. *The Islamization of Pakistan, 1979–2009*. Viewpoints Special Edition. Middle East Institute, 2009. https://www.mei.edu/sites/default/files/publications/2009.07.Islamization%20of%20Pakistan.pdf.

Milgram, Stanley. *Obedience to Authority: An Experimental View*. London: Tavistock, 1974.

Mills, Margaret A. "Between Covered and Covert: Traditions, Stereotypes, and Afghan Women's Agency." In *Land of the Unconquerable: The Lives of Contemporary Afghan Women*, edited by Jennifer Heath and Ashraf Zahedi, 60–73. Berkeley: University of California Press, 2011.

Mirza, Jasmin. "Accommodating Purdah to the Workplace: Gender Relations in the Office Sector in Pakistan." *The Pakistan Development Review* 38, no. 2 (1999): 187–206. https://doi.org/10.30541/v38i2.

———. *Between Chaddor and the Market: Female Office Workers in Lahore.* Oxford: Oxford University Press, 2002.

Moghadam, Valentine M. *Modernizing Women: Gender and Social Change in the Middle East.* Boulder: Lynne Rienner, 2003.

Mohydin, Rimmel. "Field Notes from the Aurat March: The Millennial Megaphone." In *Womansplaining: Navigating Activism, Politics and Modernity in Pakistan*, edited by Sherry Rehman, 241–48. Lahore: Folio, 2021.

———. "Let Me Womansplain the Aurat March to You." Dawn, Prism, March 12, 2019. https://www.dawn.com/news/1469183.

Moscovici, Serge. "Toward a Theory of Conversion Behavior." In *Advances in Experimental Social Psychology*, vol. 13, edited by L. Berkowitz, 209–39. Elsevier, 1980. https://doi.org/10.1016/S0065-2601(08)60133-1.

Moscovici, Serge, and Claude Faucheux. "Social Influence, Conformity Bias, and the Study of Active Minorities." In *Advances in Experimental Social Psychology*, vol. 6, edited by L. Berkowitz, 149–74. Elsevier, 1972. https://doi.org/10.1016/S0065-2601(08)60027-1.

Moscovici, Serge, and Bernard Personnaz. "Studies in Social Influence: V. Minority Influence and Conversion Behavior in a Perceptual Task." *Journal of Experimental Social Psychology* 16, no. 3 (1980): 270–82. https://doi.org/10.1016/0022-1031(80)90070-0.

Moussaïd, Mehdi, Juliane E. Kämmer, Pantelis P. Analytis, and Hansjörg Neth. "Social Influence and the Collective Dynamics of Opinion Formation." *PLOS ONE* 8, no. 11 (2013): e78433. https://doi.org/10.1371/journal.pone.0078433.

Mumtaz, Khawar, and Farida Shaheed. *Women of Pakistan: Two Steps Forward, One Step Back?* London: Zed, 1987.

Nayyar, A H, and Ahmad Salim. *The Subtle Subversion: The State of Curricula and Textbooks in Pakistan.* Sustainable Development Policy Institute, 2005. https://sdpi.org/the-subtle-subversion-the-state-of-curicula-and-textbooks-in-pakistan/publication_detail.

Nemeth, Charlan Jeanne. "Minority Influence Theory." *IRLE Working Paper* 218, no. 10 (2010). https://irle.berkeley.edu/wp-content/uploads/2010/05/Minority-Influence-Theory.pdf

Nouri, Melody. "The Power of Influence: Traditional Celebrity vs Social Media Influencer." *Advanced Writing: Pop Culture Intersections* 32 (2018). https://scholarcommons.scu.edu/engl_176/32.

O'Brien, John. *The Construction of Pakistani Christian Identity.* Research Society Publication; Subaltern Studies Series 96; 1. Lahore: Research Society of Pakistan, 2006.

Overland, Indra. "Introduction: Civil Society, Public Debate and Natural Resource Management." In *Public Brainpower: Civil Society and Natural Resource Management*, edited by Indra Overland. 1–22. Palgrave Macmillan, 2018. https://doi.org/10.1007/978-3-319-60627-9

Pakistan Bureau of Statistics. *Population Census 2023.* Government of Pakistan, 2024. https://www.pbs.gov.pk/content/population-census.

Parray, Tauseef Ahmad. "Islamic Modernist and Reformist Thought: A Study of the Contribution of Sir Sayyid and Muhammad Iqbal." *World Journal of Islamic History and Civilization* 1 (2), (2011): 79–93.

Pavlides, Eleftherios, and Jana Hesser. "Women's Roles and House Form and Decoration in Eressos, Greece." In *Gender & Power in Rural Greece*, edited by Jill Dubisch, 68–96. Princeton: Princeton University Press, 1986.

Pew Research Center. "The World's Muslims: Unity and Diversity." Pew Research Center's Religion & Public Life Project, August 9, 2012. http://www.pewforum. org/2012/08/09/the-worlds-muslims-unity-and-diversity-executive-summary/.

Pizzuto-Pomaco, Julia. *From Shame to Honor: Mediterranean Women in Romans 16.* Lexington, KY: Emeth Press, 2017.

Rabinow, Paul, ed. *The Foucault Reader.* New York: Pantheon, 1984.

Rehman, Sherry. *Womansplaining: Navigating Activism, Politics and Modernity in Pakistan.* Lahore: Folio, 2021.

Rehman, Sumaira. "A Life Course Approach to Understand Work-Life Choices of Women Entrepreneurs: Evidence from Pakistan." Ph.D., Middlesex University, 2015. http://eprints.mdx.ac.uk/id/eprint/18308.

Richards, E. Randolph, and Richard James. *Misreading Scripture with Individualist Eyes: Patronage, Honor, and Shame in the Biblical World.* Downers Grove: IVP Academic, 2020.

Rieck, Andreas. *The Shias of Pakistan: An Assertive and Beleaguered Minority.* Oxford: Oxford University Press, 2015.

Rizvi, Sumaenah. "25 Non-Muslim Pakistanis Who Have Contributed a Lot to Our Society." *Parhlo,* August 13, 2017. https://www.parhlo.com/25-non-muslim-pakistanis-who-have-contributed-a-lot-to-our-society/.

Rouse, Shahnaz. "Gender and Identity in Pakistan." *Against the Current* 97, March/ April (2002). https://againstthecurrent.org/atc097/p1035/.

Ruffle, Karen G. *Gender, Sainthood, & Everyday Practice in South Asian Shi'ism.* Islamic Civilization & Muslim Networks. Chapel Hill: University of North Carolina Press, 2011.

Saeed, Fouzia. *Tapestry: Strands of Women's Struggles Woven into the History of Pakistan.* Karachi: Lightstone, 2022.

Said, Edward W. *Orientalism.* New York: Vintage, 1979.

Saigol, Rubina. "Decades of Disaster: Islamization and the Women of Pakistan." In *The Islamization of Pakistan,* 1979–2009, 71–73. Middle East Institute, 2009. https:// www.mei.edu/sites/default/files/publications/2009.07.Islamization%20of%20 Pakistan.pdf.

———. "Feminism and the Women's Movement in Pakistan: Actors, Debates and Strategies." *Friedrich-Ebert-Stiftung* Country Study (2016): 60. https://library.fes. de/pdf-files/bueros/pakistan/12453.pdf.

———. "The Partitions of Self: Mohajir Women's Sense of Identity and Nationhood." In *Pakistani Women: Multiple Locations and Competing Narratives,* edited by Sadaf Ahmad, 194–232. Karachi: Oxford University Press, 2010.

Salamone, S. D., and J. B. Stanton. "Introducing the *Nikokyra*: Ideality and Reality in the Social Process." In *Gender & Power in Rural Greece,* edited by Jill Dubisch, 97–120. Princeton: Princeton University Press, 1986.

Schaflechner, Jürgen. "Betwixt and between: Hindu Identity in Pakistan and 'Wary and Aware' Public Performances." *South Asia: Journal of South Asian Studies,* (2020): 1–17. https://doi.org/10.1080/00856401.2020.1692277.

Schaller, Mark. "Unintended Influence: Social-Evolutionary Processes in the Construction and Change of Culturally-Shared Beliefs." In *Social Influence: Direct and Indirect Processes*, edited by Joseph P. Forgas and Kipling D. Williams, 77–93. Philadelphia: Psychology, 2001.

Shah, Nafisa. *Honour Unmasked: Gender Violence, Law and Power in Pakistan*. Karachi: Oxford University Press, 2017.

Shaheed, Farida. *Great Ancestors: Women Claiming Rights in Muslim Contexts*. Pakistan: Oxford University Press, 2011.

———. "Networking for Change: The Role of Women's Groups in Initiating Dialogue on Women's Issues." In *Faith and Freedom: Women's Human Rights in the Muslim World*, edited by Mahnaz Afkhami, 78–103. Syracuse: Syracuse University Press, 1995.

———. "The Women's Movement in Pakistan: Anatomy of Resistance." In *Womansplaining: Navigating Activism, Politics and Modernity in Pakistan*, edited by Sherry Rehman, 21–35. Lahore: Folio, 2021.

Shaikh, Farzana. *Making Sense of Pakistan*. Revised and Updated edition. London: Hurst & Company, 2018.

Shanneik, Yafa. "Religion and Diasporic Dwelling: Algerian Muslim Women in Ireland." *Religion and Gender* 2, no. 1 (2012): 80–100. http://dx.doi.org/10.1163/18785417-00201005.

———. *The Art of Resistance in Islam: The Performance of Politics among Shi'i Women in the Middle East*. Cambridge Middle East Studies. Cambridge University Press, 2022. https://doi.org/10.1017/9781009030335.

Shehadeh, Lamia Rustum. *The Idea of Women under Fundamentalist Islam*. Gainesville: University Press of Florida, 2003.

Siddiqi, Dina M. "Taslima Nasreen and Others: The Contest over Gender in Bangladesh." In *Women in Muslim Societies: Diversity Within Unity*, edited by Herbert L. Bodman and Nayereh Tohidi, 205–27. Boulder: Lynne Rienner, 1998.

Siddiqui, Shahid. *Language, Gender, and Power: The Politics of Representation and Hegemony in South Asia*. Karachi: Oxford University Press, 2014.

Simon, Louise. "Muslim Women's Perspectives on Honor." *Missiology: An International Review* 5 (2023) 297–308.

Singha, Sara. "Christians in Pakistan and Afghanistan: Responses to Marginalization from the Peripheries." In *Under Caesar's Sword: How Christians Respond to Persecution*, edited by Daniel Philpott and Timothy Samuel Shah, 229–58. Cambridge University Press, 2018. https://www.cambridge.org/core/books/abs/under-caesars-sword/christians-in-pakistan-and-afghanistan/B7A979E2637948A4C08872D2C726DB07.

Sookhdeo, Patrick. *A People Betrayed: The Impact of Islamization on the Christian Community in Pakistan*. Scotland: Christian Focus and Isaac, 2002.

Spain, Daphne. "Gendered Spaces and Women's Status." *Sociological Theory* 11, no. 2 (1993): 137–51. JSTOR. https://doi.org/10.2307/202139.

Stock, Frederick, and Margaret Stock. *People Movements in the Punjab*. South Pasadena: William Carey, 1975.

Stowasser, Barbara Freyer. *Women in the Qur'an, Traditions, and Interpretation*. New York: Oxford University Press, 1994.

Taj, Sumaira. "Challenges to Female Educational Leaders in Kyber Pakhtunkhwa, Pakistan." Thesis, The University of Iowa, 2016. https://doi.org/10.17077/etd.ze62n263.

Tajfel, Henri, and John Turner. "An Integrative Theory of Intergroup Conflict." In *Organizational Identity: A Reader*, 1st ed., edited by Mary Jo Hatch and Majken Schultz, 56–65. Oxford: Oxford University Press, 2004.

Tarar, Mehr. *Do We Not Bleed? Reflections of a 21st-Century Pakistani.* New Delhi: Aleph, 2018.

Taylor, John R. *Linguistic Categorization: Prototypes in Linguistic Theory.* 2nd ed. Oxford: Clarendon, 1995.

Terry, Gareth. "Doing Thematic Analysis." In *Analysing Qualitative Data in Psychology*, 3rd ed., edited by Evanthia Lyons and Adrian Coyle. London: Sage, 2021.

Thompson, Geoff. *Introducing Functional Grammar.* 3rd ed. New York: Routledge, 2014.

Turner, John C. *Social Influence.* Mapping Social Psychology Series. Pacific GroveBrooks/Cole, 1991.

Turner, John C., Penelope J. Oakes, S. Alexander Haslam, and Craig McGarty. "Self and Collective: Cognition and Social Context." *Personality and Social Psychology Bulletin* 20, no. 5 (1994): 454–63. https://doi.org/10.1177/0146167294205002.

United Nations Development Programme. *National Human Development Report: Unleashing the Potential of a Young Pakistan.* United Nations Development Programme, Pakistan, 2017. https://hdr.undp.org/content/national-human-development-report-2017-pakistan.

Vatanka, Alex. "The Guardian of Pakistan's Shia." *Current Trends in Islamist Ideology* 13 (2012). https://link-galegroup-com.libproxy.murdoch.edu.au/apps/doc/A34765 6566/AONE?sid=lms.

Wadud, Amina. *Qur'an and Woman: Rereading the Sacred Text from a Woman's Perspective.* New York: Oxford University Press, 1999.

Walby, Sylvia. *Theorizing Patriarchy.* Oxford: Basil Blackwell, 1991.

Weber, Max. "Domination by Economic Power and by Authority." In *Power*, 2nd ed., edited by Steven Lukes, 28–36. New York: New York University Press, 1986.

Weiss, Anita M. *Interpreting Islam, Modernity, and Women's Rights in Pakistan.* New Delhi. Orient Blackswan, 2015.

———. "Within the Walls: Home-Based Work in Lahore." In *Pakistani Women: Multiple Locations and Competing Narratives*, edited by Sadaf Ahmad, 12–24. Karachi: Oxford University Press, 2010.

Willemse, Karin, and Sylvia I. Bergh. "Struggles over Access to the Muslim Public Sphere: Multiple Publics and Discourses on Agency, Belonging and Citizenship (Introduction to the Themed Section)." *Contemporary Islam* 10, no. 3 (2016): 297–309. http://dx.doi.org/10.1007/s11562-016-0367-1.

Wren, Kevin. *Social Influences.* Routledge Modular Psychology. London: Routledge, 1999.

Yousafzai, Malala, and Christina Lamb. *I Am Malala: The Girl Who Stood up for Education and Was Shot by the Taliban.* London: Phoenix, 2014.

Yukl, Gary A. *Leadership in Organizations.* 8th ed. Boston: Pearson, 2013.

Zaidi, S. Akbar. "The Ulema, Deoband and the (Many) Talibans." *Economic and Political Weekly* 44, no. 19 (2009): 10–11.

Zia, Afiya Shehrbano. "Contesting the Class Question: Moving beyond Piety and Patriarchy." In *Womansplaining: Navigating Activism, Politics and Modernity in Pakistan*, edited by Sherry Rehman, 75–87. Folio, 2021.

Index